## Praise for *Starting Up Silicon Valley: How ROLM Became a Cultural Icon and Fortune 500 Company*

"*Starting Up Silicon Valley* provides an insider's view of what made ROLM, one of Silicon Valley's most important companies, succeed. While immersed in its pages, you experience the agonies, successes, challenges, doubts, and the convictions of inspired leadership that turn big ideas into results that transform industries. Everyone thinking about going to work for a start-up, investing in one, or thinking about starting a great company should read this book."

—**BILL DAVIDOW**, TECHNOLOGY COLUMNIST FOR *THE ATLANTIC*, VENTURE CAPITALIST, AND FORMER SENIOR VICE PRESIDENT OF MARKETING AND SALES AT INTEL

"ROLM was one of the first great Silicon Valley ventures that reflected the unique culture of entrepreneurialism, innovation, and company building. This book tells ROLM's story in a straightforward way and reveals the unique culture, style, and creativity that were essential to the company's success and that set an example for other ventures to follow."

—**LARRY SONSINI**, CHAIRMAN, WILSON SONSINI GOODRICH & ROSATI

"Only after reading this book did I understand how exciting it must have been to face the challenges presented to my father and everyone else who worked at ROLM. For young people who hope to start companies of their own, this book provides a tangible example of how they can make those companies stimulating and rewarding great places to work."

—**DAVID OSHMAN**, SON OF ROLM CEO KEN OSHMAN

"This is a fascinating story of ROLM, started by four Rice University graduates in Silicon Valley in the early 1960s who were recruited by Sylvania and IBM to work. They ended up creating one of the all-time great places to work that defined a style that remains a hallmark of Silicon Valley today. This is a well-told story packed with personal insights on the dreams, fears, and sacrifices of a group of pioneers. A great history of corporate strategy."

—**BILL GLICK**, DEAN OF JONES GRADUATE SCHOOL OF BUSINESS, RICE UNIVERSITY

KATHERINE MAXFIELD

............

# STARTING UP SILICON VALLEY

............

HOW **ROLM** BECAME A CULTURAL ICON
AND FORTUNE 500 COMPANY

EMERALD
BOOK CO.

Published by Emerald Book Company
Austin, TX
www.emeraldbookcompany.com

Distributed by Emerald Book Company

For ordering information or special discounts for bulk purchases, please contact Emerald Book Company at PO Box 91869, Austin, TX 78709, 512.891.6100.

Design and composition by Greenleaf Book Group LLC
Cover design by Greenleaf Book Group LLC
Cover Photo by Jose Morales, Xinia Productions

Cataloging-in-Publication data
Maxfield, Katherine.

   Starting up Silicon Valley : how ROLM became a cultural icon and Fortune 500 company / Katherine Maxfield.—1st ed.

   p. : ill. ; cm.
   Issued also as an ebook.
   Includes bibliographical references and index.

   ISBN: 978-1-937110-62-8

   1. ROLM Corporation—History. 2. Computer industry—California—Santa Clara County—History. 3. Santa Clara Valley (Santa Clara County, Calif.)--History. 4. Success in business—California—Santa Clara County. 5. Corporate culture—California—Santa Clara County. 6. Technological innovations—California—Santa Clara County—History. I. Title.

HD9696.2.U64 R65 2014

338.7/61004/0979473                                        2013955281

Part of the Tree Neutral® program, which offsets the number of trees consumed in the production and printing of this book by taking proactive steps, such as planting trees in direct proportion to the number of trees used: www.treeneutral.com

TreeNeutral®

Printed in The United States of America on acid-free paper

14 15 16 17 18   10 9 8 7 6 5 4 3 2 1

First Edition

*This book is dedicated to the thousands
of ROLMans who made ROLM a huge success . . .
and a Great Place to Work.*

# CONTENTS

......................

# PREFACE

.....................

Beneath the enduring success of familiar technology companies—Apple, eBay, Facebook, Google, Intel—lies the bedrock of a pioneering company whose name is seldom heard around Silicon Valley these days. Thanks to its technological breakthroughs, stellar financial performance, and unique corporate lifestyle, ROLM regularly made headlines in the *New York Times*, the *Wall Street Journal*, and *BusinessWeek*. Known as a Great Place to Work, ROLM blurred the line between work and play, etching a cultural heritage that continues to distinguish Silicon Valley today. I embarked on this journey—writing the story of ROLM Corporation—because the company played such a vital role in the creation of Silicon Valley that its history deserved to be recorded.

Four young Texans, all engineering graduates from Rice University— whose last names began with *R, O, L,* and *M*—founded the company in 1969 in an abandoned prune shed in Cupertino, California. ROLM's meteoric rise began in the mid-1970s, at the same time the phrase *Silicon Valley* displaced Santa Clara County's previous nickname: the "Valley of Heart's Delight." Facilities for technology companies uprooted thousands of acres of fruit orchards. When ROLM started out, only a few individuals would invest in bright, new technology ideas. Ten years later, dozens of venture capital firms bankrolled innovation, to the tune of nearly $500 million in 1979 alone.[1]

"ROLM pioneered so many things," said Larry Sonsini, Silicon Valley's premier legal counsel, who has advised hundreds of start-ups and mature companies for over four decades now. ROLM was the first to develop and market a rugged mini-computer for the military, one capable of being roughly handled in helicopters, jeeps, tanks, and jet fighters. It was the first to show the defense industry that computers could be bought inexpensively—"off the shelf"—with thirty days' notice, instead of through the standard, yearlong proprietary process of designing new computers from scratch for each new application.

When ROLM entered the telecommunications market in 1975, the tiny $10 million company went head-to-head with the world's largest corporation, AT&T, a communications monopoly with more than $3 billion in revenue. ROLM's broad-application, computer-based digital telephone system transformed the stodgy business communications industry, which had seen very little innovation for forty years. Punch-cord switchboards were still in general use. In today's jargon, ROLM introduced disruptive technology into a market that had been in stasis for decades.

With the digital smarts of the ROLM CBX (Computerized Branch Exchange), corporate telecom managers had their introduction to information technology. For the first time, they could manage their telephone expenses, which could account for as much as 10 percent of total corporate expenses at the time. And the company's phones were no longer hardwired to a specific location. With the CBX, phones could be moved, added, or deleted with a simple software command. ROLM quickly became one of the top two competitors behind AT&T in the PBX market.

ROLMLink was a global technology first—the first time that voice, high-speed data, and power were transmitted over one pair of wires to the desktop. It was deployed in ROLMphones and in the Cypress, Cedar, and Juniper terminals, demonstrating the CBX's capability as a hub for the integration of voice and data communications.

From the mid-1970s to the mid-1980s, ROLM was *the* place to work in Silicon Valley. Its groundbreaking personnel policies and perks rewarded hard, smart work with stock options, profit sharing, and a state-of-the-art campus—including a gym, tennis courts, two pools, a Jacuzzi, a gourmet cafeteria that offered breakfast through early dinner, and outdoor dining facilities. All this was offered in a pastoral setting, with winding paths lined with ginkgoes and decorative fruit trees, and a brook babbling over small waterfalls and under wooden footbridges.

The company's philosophy became known as GPW—a Great Place to Work. ROLM was the cultural icon of Silicon Valley. It forged the path that companies like Google, eBay, and Facebook later followed to entice good people to come work for them and to hold on to those people by keeping them healthy, happy, motivated, and striving to do their best. ROLM's documented ROLM Philosophy, Attributes of Success for ROLM Managers, and Attributes of Success for All ROLM People provide guidelines that are an intrinsic part of today's most progressive businesses and yet are timeless and universal. Any organization today that wishes to improve or change its culture would find them helpful.

By 1983, ROLM was a public Fortune 500 company. IBM bought 15 percent for $225 million, and the two companies entered into a strategic partnership. A little more than a year later, IBM bought the rest of the company for $1.25 billion. Shareholders who purchased stock at the initial public offering (IPO) in 1976 made a forty-fold return on their money in eight years. Most employees were shareholders and reaped rich rewards for their hard work. The merger resulted in the largest return on investment of almost 2,000 U.S. IPOs launched between 1975 and 1985.[2] It was the largest, most profitable, most dramatic merger Silicon Valley had ever seen. It set the benchmark for a "good deal" for many years to come.

ROLM did all this before 1990. Why write about it now?

Ken Oshman, the *O* in ROLM, died in 2011 at age seventy-one. A month later, the *M*—my husband, Bob Maxfield—turned seventy. These were wake-up calls. The information about and inside perspectives of a company that had played a key role in the cultural and technological development of Silicon Valley were at risk of slipping away. Silicon Valley historians would be able to retrieve the front-page articles of the *New York*

*Times*, the *Wall Street Journal*, and *BusinessWeek*, but they would not have access to the tales and insights of the insiders—the people at ROLM who had made things happen. Companies are people, in effect, and people have personalities. This story reflects those personalities.

This book is divided into broad segments that move somewhat but not exactly along chronological lines. The introduction of new CBX products escalated after 1979, as did the business and strategic issues facing the company. To keep the focus on a parade of telecommunications products and on mil-spec products in the early 1980s, I separated these topics from the company's business challenges, even though they overlapped in time. Likewise, the ROLM culture permeated all of ROLM's years but deserves to be highlighted by its own chapter. All these pieces come together in the ROLM merger with IBM. This book presents a rare inside view of an IBM merger—in this case, that of a nimble, entrepreneurial company with a century-old, traditional company that nonetheless tried hard to blend disparate cultures, technologies, and businesses.

Worried that my shared last name would make the book less credible, I almost did not embark on the journey of writing it. But in fact, that unique accessibility to Bob Maxfield and my acquaintance and friendship with many ROLM people and industry leaders made the book doable. The task felt important to achieving a richer understanding of the nature and course of Silicon Valley.

This corporate history illuminates decision processes every step of the way. It illustrates how disorganized a start-up can be and yet still coalesce; how decisions were made midstride as obstacles appeared; how the company scrambled to accommodate its enormous growth and rapidly changing competitive environment; and the bedrock shock of its attempt to blend with IBM. The book can be a useful resource for anyone considering the glories and perils of becoming an entrepreneur.

ROLM developed products through teams—through the collaboration of representatives from all aspects of a product's life cycle: engineering, marketing, manufacturing, and service. To illustrate the team process, the book presents a case study of the development of ROLMphones, including a look at how the product decisions evolved . . . what the issues were . . . what was done . . . what wasn't done. I was deeply involved with this team. I joined ROLM in 1979, doing market research. In 1980, when ROLM decided to make digital phones, I became phones product marketing manager, a member of the team that took the concept all the way through to a thriving product line. At first, I hesitated to insert myself into the book, but it seemed illogical to delve into another product when I knew this one well and had the contacts to round out the picture. My name when I worked at ROLM was Kathie Hullmann, and that is the name used in the book.

The perspective of former IBM executive Ellen Hancock balances what is otherwise a rather ROLM-centric book. Balance is also achieved by the many smart people I interviewed who have the wisdom, mature perspective, and openness to say, "It seemed to be the right decision at the time, but . . ."

Otherwise, the defense and telecommunications industries are presented primarily from ROLM's point of view. I am not privy to the ins and outs of, for example, AT&T's decision to divest itself of its telecom subsidiaries in order to gain entrance to the computer industry in the mid-1980s. Hundreds of articles have been written about it. I reviewed many of them, but I did not seek interviews with AT&T executives from that time or get access to AT&T's corporate archives. Nor did I attempt to search IBM's or Siemens's archives. I do not present myself as an expert on these major industry earthquakes. I leave that to professional corporate historians, who may provide a different perspective.

I present this book as an intimate look at a company that had a significant impact on each industry it entered, a company that accomplished many "firsts'" and "near firsts," including being on the forefront of the information technology revolution—a company that shaped Silicon Valley. I hope this book will be welcomed by many former ROLMans and their family and friends; by Silicon Valley historians; and by anyone who seeks to understand how a start-up becomes a Fortune 500 company, wants to experience the vicarious thrill of being in a start-up, or wants to learn what makes a company or organization a great place to work.

To readers who were ROLM employees or who provided invaluable support from outside the company, I encourage you to record your own personal involvement with the company. Then tuck those pages inside this book to keep as a family memento, so your progeny will understand your own contribution to starting up Silicon Valley.

**Katherine Maxfield**

# ACKNOWLEDGMENTS

....................

Writing this book often felt like the team effort characteristic of product development at ROLM. Dozens of people contributed to the endeavor, and I am deeply grateful to all of them.

Bob Maxfield's mind and memories are treasure troves. So are his files—nine boxes full of his own notes in tiny handwriting on narrow-lined yellow pads, quarterly and annual reports, corporate brochures, newspaper clippings, magazine articles, press releases, internal memos, and memorabilia. These materials will eventually be donated to the Silicon Valley Archives at Stanford University. Bob also answered hundreds of questions over the past two years—at meals, in airplanes, in the car. Thank you for your patience and thoroughness. (Now what will we talk about over dinner?!)

I am also grateful to Gene Richeson, Barbara Oshman, and Walter Loewenstern for granting in-person interviews, taking part in phone conversations, indulging innumerable email exchanges, and sifting through old files and photo albums.

Ken Oshman's words were retrieved from people's memories, press articles, and audio and video interviews recorded by the two nonprofits that are preserving the history of Silicon Valley. The Silicon Valley Historical Association (www.siliconvalleyhistorical.org) granted access to its 1995 audiotaped interview with Ken. The Computer History Museum in Mountain View (www.computerhistory.org) made available a video recording of its 2004 event "Competing with Giants," which featured the four founders on a panel moderated by Leo Chamberlain. CHM also provided a one-on-one audio interview with Bob Maxfield made in 2004. I am very grateful for access to these invaluable resources.

I am grateful, too, to former IBM executive Ellen Hancock for talking with me freely and responding unreservedly to provide the IBM side of the story.

Thank you, Don Armstrong, Leo Chamberlain, Bob Dolin, Bob Finocchio, Jim Kasson, Bob Maxfield, Ron Raffensperger, and Solomon Wu for the sidebars. And thank you also, Jim Kasson, Ken Lavezzo, Walter Loewenstern, Barbara Oshman, and Ron Raffensperger, for being diligent readers and resources.

I am hugely grateful to Jim Kasson for working with the photographs so they could be published at their best. And many thanks to Bette Daoust for designing Excel charts.

I give my thanks to many others who invariably handled my requests promptly and with a wholehearted willingness to help move the book forward, including digging through garages and files for photos and notes: Bobby Alvarez, Fawn Alvarez, Gibson Anderson, Don Armstrong, Paul Baszucki, Jeff Blohm, Alex Bochannek, Jim Buchholz, Tony Carollo, Leo Chamberlain, Joao Chaves, Evelyn Cozakis, Ric Cozakis, Mark Daley, Michael Davis, Bob Dolin, Mercedes Lee Epp, Bob Finocchio, Larry Gary, Tony Gerber, Alex Gil, Mike Gilbert, Val Gillen, Nadine Grant, Janet Gregory, Pat Groves, Joey Harris, Joanne Kanow, Jim Kasson, Johnnie LaJolla, Ken Lavezzo, Wilson Lee, John Litland, Duncan MacMillan, Mo Maxfield, Dean McCully, Burt McMurtry, Kevin Meyer, Dick Moley, Laura Kolbe Nelson, Mark S. Nichols, Bob Nugent, Ken Peterman, Steve Plant, Keith Raffel, Wes Raffel, Ron Raffensperger, Don Saunders, Heidi Schoolcraft, Tony Seidel, Bruce Skillings, Larry Sonsini, Stan Tenold, Laura Watkins, Steve Whittaker, Carol Wingard, Solomon Wu, Ben Yamada, and Charles Yates. Many thanks also to the members of the active Facebook ROLM Alumni site who posted photos and stories, and who responded enthusiastically, and often humorously, to queries I posted.

Thanks to Dr. Leslie Berlin, historian of the Silicon Valley Archives at Stanford University, for her early encouragement to move from a corporate scrapbook to a professional book that would be valuable to Silicon Valley historians. Leslie authored *The Man Behind the Microchip: Bob Noyce and the Invention of Silicon Valley* and is currently working on a book of Silicon Valley history, to be published by Simon and Schuster in 2014.

Thanks for help with editing and book production, Glenn Bugos, Alice LaPlante, Mavis Lehmann, Amy Dorta McIlwaine, Diana Russell, and the team at Greenleaf Book Group. And for your unflagging encouragement, thank you, Alix Christie, Jan Ellison, Elizabeth Fergason, Veronica Kornberg, Vonnie Madigan, and Amy Payne. To anyone else who helped with this effort whose name is not mentioned, I apologize for the omission and am grateful for your contribution.

# INTRODUCTION

.....................

When I heard that Kathie Maxfield was writing a history of ROLM—a real history based on primary sources and interviews—I was thrilled. ROLM is an essential company in the history of Silicon Valley that has not received the attention it deserves. This book takes a strong first step toward correcting the oversight.

Gene Richeson, Ken Oshman, Walter Loewenstern, and Bob Maxfield—ROLM's founders—chose a pivotal time to come to the narrow stretch of northern California peninsula that would one day be called Silicon Valley. When they arrived in the early 1960s (drawn by the pied-piping of Burt McMurtry), the region's population was exploding: It would nearly triple between 1950 and 1970. Many of the newcomers, like the ROLM founders, were young, educated, and eager to try something new. These were the people who helped transform a place best known for its plum and apricot orchards into the tech capital of the world.

By 1969, when ROLM formed, the transformation had picked up steam. Hewlett-Packard, headquartered in the Palo Alto industrial park built by Stanford University specifically to attract tech companies to the area, employed some 16,000 people. Not too far south, also in Santa Clara County, was the headquarters of Fairchild Semiconductor, birthplace of the microchip, with roughly 10,000 employees. The bold Ampex sign in Redwood City marked a company with 12,000 employees, whose products would soon transmit images from humans' first visit to the moon. Up and down the recently completed Highway 101, tiny start-ups dotted the landscape—Intel, AMD, and National Semiconductor were all less than a year old. Lockheed, Sylvania, and IBM also had significant presences in the Valley. The groundwork was being laid upon which amazing technological innovations would fuel whole new industries or alter existing ones.

One of my favorite things about ROLM is how neatly its story encapsulates much of the history of the Valley from 1969 forward. Permit me to offer four examples. First: ROLM began life as four guys in an abandoned prune shed. Fewer than sixteen years later, the company was worth more than $1 billion and comprised nearly 10,000 employees who together developed sophisticated electronic systems. No better symbol of the Valley's transition exists. Second: ROLM's initial products targeted a military market; later, the company expanded into systems for commercial customers. So it was with Silicon Valley writ large. Nearly every important Silicon Valley company founded before 1970 met payroll thanks to military contracts, subcontracts, or purchases—but today the Valley's best-known companies serve commercial or consumer markets. Third: ROLM's Great Place to Work—its emphasis on a vibrant and satisfying work culture—both reflected and inspired similar efforts throughout the Valley. Surely the beautifully landscaped campuses and facilities available to so many employees today owe something to ROLM's pioneering in this area.

And finally: ROLM's success was not the product of a single mind but the result of productive collaboration that could be traced to the founding team and extended beyond it. This tendency toward collective, multifaceted innovation is also a Silicon Valley hallmark. We like to lionize individual entrepreneurs, but anyone who knows the Valley knows that innovation is a team sport—as this history so amply illustrates.

**Leslie Berlin**
*Historian, Silicon Valley Archives at Stanford University*

# CHAPTER 1

# THE ROADS TO ROLM

....................

On a drizzly California day on the San Francisco peninsula, a Navy Thunderjet on approach to Moffett Field exploded just blocks away from where Burt McMurtry, age twenty-two, was interviewing over lunch for a job with defense contractor Sylvania. The scattered debris destroyed homes and narrowly missed an elementary school. The cause was not disclosed.[3] The Cold War was at its chilliest that spring of 1957. Almost all technology work in the Bay Area supported the American military. Government grants funded most university research, and government purchases drove the revenues of the area's major firms: Sylvania, Lockheed, Philco, Varian, Hiller, Ampex.

McMurtry's interview proceeded undisturbed by the plane crash. In fact, he was surprised to read about it in the newspaper the next morning. In any case, McMurtry was not the sort of young man to be thrown off course. He was about to graduate near the top of his electrical engineering class from Rice University in Houston, Texas, his hometown. He had grown up working summers as an oil field laborer and had worked in electronics only once, during his last summer in college, for General Electric. But the opportunity to work in early microwave research—with Sylvania's new Microwave Tube Division, focused on radar applications—was quite appealing to him.

The real clincher, though, was Sylvania's work–study arrangement with Stanford University. Rice University's engineering degree was a five-year program, granting a BA in four years and a BS the fifth year. Having achieved his bachelor's degrees, McMurtry was well prepared for further study at Stanford. He would be allowed time off from work to attend classes alongside regular Stanford students working toward a master's degree and then a doctorate—with fully paid tuition while bringing in a full salary. Stanford charged companies double tuition for the privilege. The school's annual tuition then was $1,000 (equivalent to $8,300 in 2013). The surcharge was worth it, enabling companies to attract vital engineering talent like Burt McMurtry, who accepted Sylvania's offer. He and his wife (Deedee Brown, Rice '56) packed up and moved to Mountain View. McMurtry, of course, had no idea that his personal job choice would have ramifications far beyond his own career . . . that within his first decade in California, he would have helped build the foundation for Silicon Valley . . . and that he would spend decades afterward nourishing the Valley in multiple ways. And it all began with a lunch during which a jet crash wreaked such destruction.

## Setting Roots in the Future Silicon Valley

Burt McMurtry returned to Rice each fall to recruit engineers for Sylvania. In the fall of 1958, McMurtry talked with Walter Loewenstern (Rice '59 BSEE), another Houstonian. Loewenstern had been accepted to both Rice and MIT for his undergraduate schooling, but only Rice was tuition-free. Going to MIT would have placed a financial burden on his family, and he wasn't the kind of guy who would put them through that. Instead Loewenstern lived at home during college and joined Rice's ROTC (Reserved Officer Training Corps) to cover books and expenses. In exchange, he explained to McMurtry during the interview, he owed the U.S. Navy two years of active duty following graduation. McMurtry told him to call when he was clear of his obligation.

In 1961, after two pleasant years with the Navy in Japan, Loewenstern stepped off the ship in San Diego and dropped coins into a pay phone. McMurtry immediately set him up with interviews in Sunnyvale.

Loewenstern drove north, accepted an offer, and then went home to visit his folks for a few days before moving to Sunnyvale to work in Sylvania's Electronic Defense Lab.

In the fall of 1962, at the end of a recruiting day at Rice, McMurtry cross-checked his impressions with Professor Paul Pfeiffer, who asked, "Did you talk to Ken Oshman?"

No, McMurtry replied, he hadn't.

"Too bad," the professor said. "We've never been able to challenge him sufficiently." Oshman, who was top in his class, happened by at that moment. Pfeiffer stopped the slight young man, who wore black-rimmed glasses that seemed to cover half his face. The student seemed reluctant to stop for a chat, but he forced a smile and gave a quick handshake.

McMurtry asked Oshman, "What will you do when you graduate?"

"Get an MBA at Harvard" came the answer. Oshman had already applied and apparently felt confident of acceptance.

"What will you do then?"

Oshman inched away. "Start a company."

"What kind?"

"I don't know. Might be a shoe factory," Oshman said, making something up as he backed off, trying to make his getaway.

McMurtry called after him, "Give some thought to coming to California and Stanford."

........................................ ⏻ ........................................

### *"What kind of company will you start?" asked Burt McMurtry. "I don't know. Might be a shoe factory," replied Ken Oshman.*

........................................

Even after a few months of phone conversations, Oshman was still set on heading to Harvard. On a flight home from Europe in March 1963,

McMurtry penned a six-page letter to him on onionskin paper. He emphasized the young man's interest in both management and engineering, a combination seldom encountered. He cited some of the exciting things going on in Sylvania's laser research and development laboratory and spelled out the Stanford work–study program. The opportunity to earn a salary and get a Stanford degree at the same time sold Oshman at last. He accepted Sylvania's offer to work in laser R&D. He and his wife (Barbara Daily, University of Texas '62), both from small towns near Houston, moved to Sunnyvale.

Gene Richeson, who came from a small oil town in northeast Texas, was in the same graduating class as Oshman. He too went to work for Sylvania, in the same military defense division as Walter Loewenstern. Richeson and Oshman were among the one-third of Rice's thirty-two electrical engineering graduates of 1963 who went to Sylvania. Thanks to McMurtry's annual fall pilgrimages, those were "pretty typical results" from 1958 to 1968. The legacy is a lasting one: Rice engineering graduates, continually rated among the best in the nation, remain naturally attracted to the Stanford Graduate School of Business and to the spirit of entrepreneurship and technical excellence that thrives in Silicon Valley. The so-called Rice Mafia in Silicon Valley now numbers about 2,000 graduates, the largest collection of Rice alums outside of Texas.

Bob Maxfield, another Texan, was the top engineering graduate of 1964. Maxfield was being heavily recruited to work for IBM in Kentucky and remained noncommittal when he talked with McMurtry about Sylvania during McMurtry's fall 1963 pilgrimage to Rice. So McMurtry put Ken Oshman on the task of recruiting him. When Maxfield visited the Bay Area for a job interview with Sylvania, Oshman and his wife wined and dined him in San Francisco. "It was the first time I drank wine that didn't have a screw-top," Maxfield recalled decades later. The dinner seeded a lifelong friendship.

Maxfield wanted to be on the front lines of computer technology, and IBM promised he could "play with computers" in Lexington. But he found Stanford's work–study opportunity appealing and told IBM he would rather do computer work in San Jose. IBM agreed. Maxfield married Melinda "Mo" Harrison (Texas Tech '62) a few days after graduation, and they headed for San Jose. McMurtry called it his biggest recruiting loss ever but later said, "It turned out to be a good thing. He was going to need that computer experience."

Maxfield's class of electrical engineers, among the last to enjoy a tuition-free education at Rice, were still studying electrical generators, transformers, and vacuum tubes. The slide rule was the engineer's most important tool—always near at hand, offering quick answers to multiplication, division, square roots, logarithms, and trigonometry, though the answers could be reliably discerned to no more than two decimal points. All this would soon change. The new world of computers and semiconductors had sprung up in the late 1950s, largely because of work done by IBM, Texas Instruments, and Fairchild Semiconductor. The impact of this nascent technological revolution was being felt in all facets of industry and was trickling into education. Rice had two digital computers, each occupying its own large room: the IBM 1620 scientific computer and a research computer built by Professor Martin Graham for graduate students to run calculations. Walter Loewenstern had helped build a small part of that computer—his first experience in making a piece of electronic equipment.

The Stanford work–study program enabled all these young men to earn a master's degree in electrical engineering: McMurtry in 1959, Loewenstern in 1963, Richeson and Oshman in 1965, and Maxfield in 1966. All but Richeson went on to get PhDs, finishing in three years instead of the typical six. McMurtry completed his in 1962. Loewenstern's PhD, earned in 1966, was from the Engineering Economic Systems department. His dissertation was on the economics of using microwaves for the transmission of large amounts of power. Oshman's doctorate, in 1968, was in laser physics, with a dissertation titled "Studies of Optical Frequency Parametric Oscillation" that is still cited in the field today—eleven times in 2011, forty years after its publication. Maxfield earned his PhD in 1969;

his dissertation, "Computing Optimal Controls for Linear Systems with Inequality Constraints," could be applied to such problems as how to get a space rover to Saturn on minimal fuel.

Stanford's work–study program was a key factor in the foundation of Silicon Valley and part of the answer to the question pondered by many: What makes the Valley so persistently different from other industrial areas? Why there? Why then? Four of these men who took advantage of the program would go on to found one of the first start-up tech companies in that region—and one of the greatest contributors to that persistently different work culture.

## It's in the Cards

Even as a teenager, Walter Loewenstern knew he wanted to start a company. His father had a business and was "always my inspiration," said Walter. Loewenstern Senior had left Germany in 1929 because Jews weren't allowed to work as engineers. He had settled in Houston and opened his own company in electrical work, though it "wasn't particularly success-

Walter Loewenstern in about 1970.
Photo courtesy of Walter Loewenstern.

ful." Walter had always kept his eye out for the right business opportunity.

He spotted it in mid-1968 when he was working in a small Sylvania group chartered to come up with product proposals that used military technology in civilian applications. Loewenstern had thoroughly researched and proposed a police vehicle tracking system that he thought had great potential, but Sylvania (by then acquired by GTE) declined to consider it. He privately pursued the idea on weekends until he decided he'd better let his boss know what he was up to. He was told, "We don't want to do the project, and we don't want you to do it. Either you quit pursuing this, or you quit Sylvania."

Loewenstern wasn't about to stop pursuing the idea. "I quit," he replied.

"You're fired" came forth his boss's simultaneous reaction.

Loewenstern's boss then sent him a letter that said, basically, *You may not compete with any product GTE makes. If you form a company, GTE will buy it—and fire you.* At the time, GTE made "just about every electronic product known to man." Still, Loewenstern said later, "The threat didn't frighten me—I had no assets to lose, and there were abundant job openings for engineers." He took a consulting job and continued pursuing the idea.

Loewenstern was part of a Monday night poker game that brought the Texans and a few Californians to the table, with penny antes and maximum pots of $5 because no one had any money to speak of. The after-game conversation invariably swung toward one topic: "What are you going to do when you grow up?" The summer of 1968 was winding down when Loewenstern rocked the table one night by reporting that he'd just quit Sylvania to work on a business project.

Ken Oshman wasted no time in calling him after that night's game. Oshman was working for McMurtry at Sylvania, developing nonlinear optical techniques involving how light behaves in high-intensity laser situations. "So you're thinking of starting a company," he said to Loewenstern. "How about we do something together?" Looking back, Loewenstern said, "That was the best phone call I ever got."

Kenneth Oshman had been raised by adoptive parents in a tight-knit Jewish community in Rosenberg, Texas. His father was a dentist, but the rest of the family ran small businesses. His mother had a dress shop; cousins had dry goods stores. Other family members were ranchers, cattlemen, and cotton traders. His cousin Milton was all three, "a larger-than-life genuine Texan Jewish cowboy," who was like a second father to him. Oshman worked on his cousin's ranch from the time he was twelve years old, doing anything he was asked—chopping down huisache trees and rounding up and branding cattle. When he was fifteen and sweeping floors in the ranch office, Milton gave him a checkbook and told him to go buy cotton—

Ken Oshman in about 1970. Photo courtesy of Barbara Oshman.

a very technical skill. Decades later, Oshman marveled at his cousin's "audacity to say, 'Here, go try it.'"[4]

Oshman turned out to be better than many of the old-timers at judging the quality of the fibers by examining a plug cut from a bale, and then making a profit selling the bale at the Houston Cotton Exchange. That experience surely played a key role in building the confidence that Oshman carried with him always. In the future, he would often repeat the scenario—saying, "Here, go do this," when that person had no idea he or she could. That casual confidence expressed in handing over even major responsibilities made Oshman's cohorts and employees want to live up to his expectations.

Oshman and Loewenstern mulled over a number of ideas besides vehicle location—some involving defense systems. Oshman suggested they bring in Gene Richeson, saying, "Gene's full of ideas. And he's dealt with the military."

Eugene Richeson, born in Paris, Texas, had grown up in the tiny town of Talco, a couple of hours east of Dallas. His mother taught school, and his father worked for an oil company. His business experience began at age eleven, when he bought a hundred baby chicks. He raised them, sold fifty, and kept fifty hens to sell eggs door to door. He grew the business to 600 hens and "signed up half the town for egg delivery in the morning before school started." He bought a motor scooter with the profit. That trend continued into adulthood, with Richeson "buying bigger and bigger motorized vehicles" with his earnings.

When Oshman called Richeson in 1968, he was working at ESL—Electromagnetic Systems Laboratory, the military contracts spin-out from Sylvania run by Bill Perry, later secretary of the U.S. Department of Defense.

Before that Richeson had been assigned to classified military projects at Sylvania for five years. He'd authored several classified papers on electronic reconnaissance and countermeasures. His career was going great. But Richeson held Oshman's intelligence and confidence in high regard, and he jumped at the chance to work with him.

Loewenstern, Oshman, and Richeson continued to toss around ideas, most of them involving using computers in electronic systems. But there was a catch: They knew nothing about computers. Finally Oshman suggested calling Bob Maxfield.

Robert Maxfield grew up in Wichita Falls, Texas, where his father was an orthopedic surgeon. A career in medicine never interested him, and he saw no examples of entrepreneurship in his family. But he was by nature very competitive, in the sense of being "the best I could be" when something grabbed his interest. He progressed from Cub Scout to Eagle Scout. He swam compet-

Gene Richeson with his new son in 1970. Photo courtesy of Gene Richeson.

itively from an early age and joined the high school swim team despite being smaller than everyone else. By his senior year, he was setting records. He was a "nervous wreck" before swim meets—the result of "a significant fear of failure," which was never anything his family instilled in him. "It was just part of my constitution."

Maxfield began to acquire leadership skills while working summers in high school and college as a counselor at Camp Longhorn, teaching water sports. His models

New dad Bob Maxfield prepares a baby bottle in 1968. Photo courtesy of Mo Maxfield.

were the founder, Tex Robertson, a legendary swim coach and officer in the original Navy SEALS during World War II, and the director, Bill Johnson, who'd fought at Iwo Jima. Math, science, and engineering were key interests for him from a young age, and in middle school as a science project he created a two-bit adding computer made of discarded aircraft relays. During his last summer of college, he worked at Texas Instruments testing the parameters of new semiconductor devices and knew from that that he wanted a career in technology.

At IBM in San Jose, Maxfield had worked with the 1600 process control computer group, but on the periphery of computers without getting to play with them nearly as much as he had hoped. He had devised a custom input-output interface, designing and testing the circuit board, overseeing production, even writing the maintenance manual, not a part of the job he relished. He left IBM in 1967 when he received a fellowship from Stanford to work on his doctorate, though by then he was fairly sure he didn't want an academic career. He still wanted to be involved with developing products, but to Maxfield a PhD seemed like "the ultimate academic challenge." He wanted to see if he was up to it.

Oshman called Maxfield in early fall 1968 and asked about his plans after his degree program wrapped up in January. Maxfield replied that he was looking at research and engineering jobs with IBM and other computer companies. Oshman said, "Gene Richeson and Walter Loewenstern and I are thinking of forming a company. Want to join us?"

Although he and his wife had no savings and an infant daughter, Maxfield thought about it "for about thirty seconds" before saying yes. Years later, his rationale remains crystal clear:

Ken's commitment was all the assurance I needed. I was thrilled at the prospect of working with him and, frankly, surprised that I was asked. Among my peers, he was the smartest guy I'd ever met. And not just in technology or book learning. He knew something about a lot of things. He knew about wine and had opinions about art; I knew Ripple and barely noticed art. He was outgoing but not brash, and he had charisma, something I always admire in others. I'm fundamentally too shy to have charisma. But I knew I could contribute technically. It seemed like it could be a good balance. We had become good friends as couples, and our wry Texas humor provided plenty of laughs. I thought it could be fun. I was willing to give it a go.

Ultimately, it came down to the winning combination of unwavering determination and unshakable faith. According to Maxfield, Ken Oshman always knew what he wanted to do: start a company, run a company. Oshman was "a natural business genius, and he sensed that even early on. It was hard not to sign up with that kind of guy."

Loewenstern was the oldest at thirty-three. Richeson and Oshman were twenty-eight, though Oshman looked older, with his black hair and signature black-rim glasses. Maxfield was twenty-seven but looked like a kid in his midteens. Richeson was the only one of the four taller than five foot seven. All four of them were trim, athletic, smart, and eager to get started.

## But Doing What?

Loewenstern, Oshman, Richeson, and Maxfield set a ground rule that first time they got together in the fall of 1968: Whatever they did, it would not directly compete with anything that they had worked on at Sylvania or IBM. They christened their new company Datel.

Oshman typed a thirty-three-page "Plan for the Formation of Datel Corporation," dated January 1969. The plan stated, "Datel is a totally new concept in the electronics business. It will be the first corporation whose central objective is to apply electronic systems techniques . . . to urban problems." At the time, the federal government was funding programs for Lyndon Johnson's Great Society, programs such as transportation improvements, public health and safety, and federal support for education. The plan discussed multiple divisions that would make multiple products in the fields of law enforcement (police vehicle tracking), public safety (electronic control of street lights), transportation (devices to control entry to major highways electronically, charge bridge tolls automatically, and identify stranded motorists), and speech privacy (products to block civilian monitoring of police communications). The document could have been the overview of a large, mature corporation. In the plan, Oshman named himself president and general manager, with Richeson as vice president and manager of systems, Loewenstern as vice president and manager of products, and Maxfield as vice president and director of research. Surprised to read that Oshman had named himself CEO, Loewenstern confronted him: "Wait a minute, Ken. I started this ball rolling. Who made you president?"

"I did," replied Oshman, "because that's what I can do best."

In hindsight, Loewenstern commented, "I'm a conflict avoider. Within three minutes I'd given in. Thank goodness."

They figured they needed $175,000 to get started, equivalent to about $1.17 million in 2013, for salaries, rent, office supplies, and development and test equipment. At the time, only a few small venture capitalists (VCs)—among them Arthur Rock, Tommy Davis, Sheldon Roberts, and Gene Kleiner—were investing in start-ups with innovative ideas. Oshman met with all of them. None expressed interest in the business plan.

Oshman next showed the plan to Jack Melchor, who was getting his new VC firm under way. Melchor loved to call himself "just a farm boy from North Carolina," but that farm boy had earned a PhD in physics from Notre Dame. He ran Sylvania's Electronic Defense Laboratory from 1953 until 1956; then he founded Melabs, which he sold to Hewlett-Packard in 1958. He started a second company, HP Associates, an investing joint venture with HP. In 1967, he took over HP's floundering computer division and quickly turned it around. After leaving HP, Melchor had raised a small venture capital fund, Triad Ventures, and he had begun seed investing in start-up companies when Oshman visited him at his office above a pizza parlor in Los Altos. After looking over the Datel plan, he told Oshman in his usual blunt style, "You've got four markets and five products. No one can succeed trying to do all this junk. Narrow it down."

⏻

## "No one can succeed trying to do all this junk. Narrow it down."— Jack Melchor

## Honing In

In early 1969, Maxfield received his PhD and began teaching a semester course in electronics circuits at Stanford and took on a consulting gig at Hewlett-Packard, thanks to his friend and former Rice lab partner Gibson Anderson, who had also gotten a master's degree on the IBM/Stanford co-op program and had since moved to HP. Maxfield's pay was meager in comparison to what he would have been earning if he'd pursued a corporate research job, but his primary focus was helping to get this start-up under way.

One Saturday in February 1969, just a few days after Melchor told Oshman to "narrow it down," the four young men met at Richeson's house. They wracked their brains, with beer and pretzels for inspiration. They crossed off Loewenstern's original vehicle tracking system or anything else that targeted police departments, which notoriously had little money or interest in investing in new technology. All the ideas that were nonmilitary, commercial applications were tossed out. Hours into the session, in midafternoon, Richeson said, "What the world really needs is a militarized version of a commercial mini-computer."

Computers built to military specifications (mil-spec)—built to withstand the temperatures and hazards of use in the field—were not new. At Sylvania, Richeson had designed systems using digital, militarized computers. Sperry Univac, IBM, RCA, and others were all soliciting military contracts to build digital computers. Each system took more than a year to develop, was funded by the military at a cost well over $200,000 per unit ($1.3 million in 2013), and was uniquely built to meet the specifications of a particular program, including the programming language instructions used to tell the computer what to do. When the system was complete, the buyer—ultimately, the U.S. military—and not the contractor company, owned the design. That way, if the computer was needed in volume, the government could put the design out for competitive bids to get the lowest price. The long process started all over again with the next military program.

Maxfield and Richeson had prowled through the 1968 Fall Joint Computer Conference (FJCC), the premier trade show of the computer industry, conveniently held in nearby San Francisco. That show had revealed the burgeoning world of mini-computers.

Until then, the computer market had been dominated by mainframes built by IBM and "the BUNCH"—Burroughs, UNIVAC, NCR, Control Data Corporation, and Honeywell. Mainframes were temperamental, almost delicate; had the computational power of today's simple calculator; and were the size of a large living room. Power requirements and expelled heat increased as more disk and tape storage units were connected to expand data storage capacity. Linked in multiples, these units required a specially built room with raised floors so massive cables could run between the machines. The room had to be chilled to control failure rate, because the computer components failed twice as often at 83 degrees F (28 degrees C) as they did at 65 degrees F (18 degrees C). Priced at hundreds of thousands or even many millions of dollars, mainframes were used primarily by the government, banks and finance companies, and insurance firms for processing large amounts of data, such as the information handled by the Census Bureau.

The 1968 FJCC opened up the whole new world of abundant, affordable mini-computers. A few had already trickled into the market, starting in 1960 with the PDP-1, the precursor mini from DEC (Digital Equipment Corp.). IBM had later come up with the 1800. Both were the size of a chunky undercounter refrigerator. At the 1968 FJCC, more than a dozen companies announced remarkably small computers—about the size of a toaster oven—that could fit atop a desk. These were typically aimed at corporate finance departments and manufacturing process control, and they cost a few tens of thousands of dollars—"about the price of a house in Sunnyvale then," according to Richeson. The leaders were DEC, Hewlett-Packard, and a slew of start-ups.

## "Mini-computers cost about the same as a house in Sunnyvale then."—Gene Richeson

As that Saturday afternoon at Richeson's house wore on, the idea of a mini-computer that met mil specs gained traction. The market for military products was driving much of technological development. The Vietnam War was escalating. (Loewenstern had fulfilled his military obligation. The other three had draft deferments because they worked in industries critical to national defense.) The Cold War had both the East and the West armed to the teeth. The four guys honed in on the idea of making a computer that could bounce around in jeeps and withstand the vibration of helicopters and aircraft carriers, in the freezing tundra and the wilting, humid jungle.

They brainstormed about a computer product that would be in continuous production, with off-the-shelf availability, that could run commercially available software programs. They would tell their customers, "None of this 'one year' nonsense. Datel can get it to you in a month." Rather than design the computer from scratch, which would be an expensive investment and take a long time to accomplish, they would license an existing commercial mini-computer design and adapt it for ruggedness. Customers could build a prototype using the original supplier's commercial version; then they could buy Datel's more expensive "rugged" version of that computer for deployment in the field. Further, the computer would run all the software programs available on the commercial computer and would directly connect to standard input-output devices such as disk drives, tape readers, and keyboards. The market would be military intelligence for radars, missile firing systems, data acquisition in the field, and some encrypted applications. Maxfield, the one computer-savvy guy among them, was asked what such a device might sell for at a reasonable profit. He took a stab at it: "Somewhere around $30K."

Whose computer should they license? Large, bureaucratic DEC and HP were obvious choices, but negotiating with them could take months. Even approaching them carried a big risk—it could pique their interest in the market. They might listen carefully, decline to offer Datel a license, and pursue their own mil-spec project. Datel would have difficulty competing against such deep-pocketed competitors; they could be shut down before they had barely gotten started. Instead, their interest turned to Data General, the darling of the '68 FJCC.

Data General (DG) was a start-up—a serious negative for Datel's purposes. One start-up basing its product on that of another amplified the risk. But DG seemed to be doing things in a smart way. Its marketing materials were slick and contemporary. Its Nova mini-computer was powerful and cheap, touted as "the first computer with 4,000 16-bit words of core memory for under $10,000," according to its brochure. The price was right for Datel to ruggedize and sell for $30,000. The Nova had a housing that was streamlined, glossy, and white, a real standout in the gray computer world. According to Maxfield, it looked a lot like the Apple II did when it came out eight years later.

At the show, Data General had displayed the Nova running Spacewar, one of the earliest computer games. People crowded around, excited to see two rocket ships battling in outer space instead of the ubiquitous static rows of eerie-green words and dots slowly marching across the screen, the standard display of other computers. The Nova used a new generation of semiconductor chips from Fairchild called *medium-scaled integration (MSI)*, which meant that its central processing unit (CPU) had fewer than 200 chips rather than the typical 1,000 chips. Thus the processor would be relatively small, use less power, and be more reliable. Maxfield called it "very sexy compared to everything else."

By late that February afternoon, the young men were energized, feeling as though they'd hit on a workable, unique idea. They agreed that Oshman would contact DG to begin the conversation, with the others assuming that he'd call first thing Monday. Oshman asked if anyone knew the president's name. Maxfield did. In his typical no-time-like-the-present style, Oshman picked up the phone, dialed Information, and asked for the home phone number of Edson de Castro in Boston.

Richeson sat stunned as Oshman made the call right then and there. He wanted to yell, "Stop! Put the phone down now. Let's think about this till we figure out the fatal flaw." If it had been up to Richeson, they would've still been talking about the idea a week later.

De Castro had left Digital Equipment Corporation just a year prior, to cofound Data General. The man himself answered, at home on a Saturday evening. Oshman gave him a quick pitch and then asked, "Can we come talk to you about a license?"

De Castro answered, "Sure, why not? But not during the week." All thirteen DG employees were working feverishly to ship their first computer. De Castro agreed to meet the following Saturday. The pitch was polished, and Oshman and Richeson, whose wife was due to give birth at any moment, grabbed a red-eye the following Friday. On Saturday they met de Castro and his team at Data General's office in a vacated beauty parlor in Hudson, Massachusetts. "They didn't even have furniture yet," Richeson later recalled.

He and Oshman returned home with a memo of understanding. Datel would license DG's Nova mini-computer under certain conditions:

- Datel was barred from competing in the general, commercial mini-computer market;
- Datel's mil-spec computer would have to be developed without much technical support from DG, which was busy implementing its own business plan; and
- DG would receive 5 percent equity in Datel and would be paid a royalty on each rugged computer shipped.

Oshman rewrote the Datel business plan to focus on a single rugged, mil-spec computer. He estimated the total military market for mini-computers at $100 million. With the new plan and the DG memo of understanding in hand, Oshman hit the streets again, looking to bowl over the venture capitalists who had previously rejected him. The four young Datel founders could get going on as little as $175,000—but they hoped to raise $500,000.

## A $75,000 Start-up

Just a few weeks later, in mid-February 1969, venture capitalist Gene Kleiner shook hands on a deal. "We were off and running," Richeson said in an interview, "so I quit my job." Loewenstern had already quit his, though Oshman and Maxfield were still employed. Kleiner backed out the next week. Richeson felt panicky and was on the verge of telling ESL that he didn't want to leave after all. Oshman reassured him, "No problem—we have a backup plan." Richeson recalled that "it took a lot of faith to just sit tight."

Arthur Rock had expressed interest in the Datel plan, but he wanted Max Palevsky's opinion before making a decision. Rock had backed Palevsky's Scientific Data Systems (SDS) in 1961; Xerox had recently bought SDS for the record price of $1 billion. Rock had also fared well investing in Fairchild Semiconductor when the "traitorous eight" walked out of Shockley Labs in 1957 to seek the freedom to invent and manufacture silicon-based semiconductors. Only months prior, in summer 1968, Rock had invested in start-up chip manufacturer Intel (cofounded by two of the "traitors," Robert Noyce and Gordon Moore) and in *Rolling Stone* magazine, of Santa Clara and San Francisco, respectively. His investment would be a big boost to Datel's credibility.

In *The Money Game* by Adam Smith, the nonfiction bestseller of 1967, Palevsky was asked what difference his $50 million share of the SDS sale had made in his life. He responded that there was no difference, that he had the same house and the same friends. Richeson, Oshman, and Maxfield looked forward to meeting this down-to-earth millionaire. Along with Arthur Rock's assistant, Dick Kramlich, they flew to Los Angeles and drove to Bel Air, where they were shocked to enter a grand circular driveway that led to a brand-new, enormous château—to Maxfield, it looked like Versailles. A butler answered the door, in full livery: a white starched shirt, a black long-tailed coat, and black pants with satin leg-stripes. They were shown into a mammoth living room, where they perched for some time on the edge of a deep, velvet sofa and were served "little dried-up bear claws," said Richeson.

Palevsky finally entered, wearing a baby-blue jumpsuit. In the midst of the conversation, Palevsky's attractive new wife drifted through in a negligee.

Perhaps that took the young men off their game. Palevsky wasn't impressed with them or their plan. Rock declined to invest, as did all other venture capitalists whom the Datel execs had approached. Oshman later recalled Rock's reasoning:

> I was going to run the company, and I'd never managed but one technician. Bob was going to be head of engineering, designing computers, and he'd never worked in computer design. Gene was going to be VP marketing and sales, and he'd never been in

21

marketing and sales. Walter was going to head research efforts, and he'd never done anything in the computer world.[5]

Like the other VCs, Rock just couldn't invest in the founders' "miserable track record."

One potential investor remained on the list. Jack Melchor had turned them down once, but maybe he'd be interested in the new, improved plan. The four execs pondered how to sweeten the deal so Melchor would not turn them away again. They decided to offer him one-fifth of the company. He would be an equal owner with each of them.

Oshman, Maxfield, and Loewenstern called on Jack Melchor. Gene Richeson missed the meeting due to an emergency appendectomy. Melchor recalled that Maxfield looked like he was in high school. When asked what his goals were, Maxfield replied, "I just want to help build a successful company." Melchor indicated that he was interested in the investment and would think about it.

After the meeting, Oshman sought advice from his boss, Burt McMurtry, at Sylvania, where he and Loewenstern still worked. Many months prior, Oshman had warned McMurtry that he might be leaving to start a company, but the subject had not arisen since then. Now Oshman walked into McMurtry's office and said that a man named Jack Melchor, who had worked at Sylvania in the mid-1950s, was interested in investing in this new company he and some others were forming. They didn't know much about Jack. Could McMurtry tell them anything?

The situation presented a complicated dilemma for McMurtry, who was in the midst of discussions with Melchor about going to work for him to form Palo Alto Investment Company, a new venture capital firm. He couldn't reveal that to Oshman, and his sense of ethics barred him from discussing the plan that would cause Oshman to leave the company for which they both worked. All McMurtry could say at the moment was that he couldn't talk about it. Oshman made another stab, got the same reaction, and left, puzzled and unhappy.

McMurtry resigned from Sylvania within a few weeks and went to work with Melchor. Once the situation became clear to Oshman, their friendship was restored. They remained close personal friends and later sat on several boards together.

In the end, Melchor committed to purchase his 20 percent share with his personal money, unwilling to risk impugning the early reputation of his venture fund with this high-risk proposition. He also committed to helping Datel secure a bank line of credit. Plus, he promised to help raise a round of venture capital if two milestones were met. First, Datel had to show a working prototype at the 1969 Fall Joint Computer Conference, a mere eight months away. The second milestone was an even more formidable task: Orders had to come in soon after the show.

Years later Melchor laughed as he recalled his reasons for investing: "They said they'd rather I join on an equal basis than as a VC. And besides, they were cheap."[6]

In March 1969, the four founders and Melchor anted up $15,000 each, equivalent to $95,000 today. Maxfield's paternal grandmother loaned him the money. Richeson borrowed from his dad. For years afterward, he put a small repayment into an envelope in his desk drawer once a week.

The $75,000 would quickly run out. A $100,000 line of credit, for use as needed, was secured with Bank of America. Decades later, Oshman claimed that Melchor had cosigned for the loan when the bank had required the signature of a "responsible adult," but to this Melchor replied, "Not true." Oshman bet him $1,000, and old records were dug out. Melchor won; he had not signed the note. The bank had believed in the company's future—though probably due to the confidence Melchor had expressed behind the scenes. Oshman paid up—with a $1,000 check embedded in a Lucite brick that Melchor could display on his desk but never cash.

Upon filing incorporation papers with the state of California, however, the founders discovered that a company working on keyboard technology had locked up the name Datel. A new, unique name was needed—and fast. The brainstorming session took place in the Oshmans' living room, with the four founders sitting around on the floor, on a chair, on the sofa. After rejecting numerous ideas, they toyed with a combination of the first letter of each last name. *Molr* sounded like a dental office. They settled on ROLM, in all capital letters. Ken Oshman often joked that the only reason he was allowed in the group was because they needed a vowel.

Their lawyer, John Wilson (of what is now Wilson Sonsini Goodrich & Rosati), seemed unimpressed by the name. "Oh well," he said, "you can always change it later." ROLM incorporated in California in May 1969, with Oshman, Melchor, and Wilson as the board of directors.

## *"Oh well, you can always change the name later." —Attorney John Wilson*

The four founders and Melchor each received 15,000 shares at $1 per share, and 4,500 shares went to Data General. ROLM was a reality—on paper. Now it needed a phone number and an address.

## From Prune Shed to Storefront

Office space was needed, ideally in an industrial complex. The most appealing was Stanford Industrial Park in Palo Alto. In 1951, Stanford University had dedicated a 700-acre portion of its 9,000-acre campus for use in attracting businesses to the region. But space there was very expensive and available only to companies prepared to build their own facilities. ROLM was certainly not ready for that.

About twelve miles down the peninsula from Palo Alto, the development of Vallco Park in Cupertino was just getting under way. That moniker was an acronym of the last names of the primary developers: Varian Associates, Lester, Leonard, Craft, and Orlando. Hundreds of acres of plums, peaches, apricots, and cherries were being bulldozed at the corner of Interstate 280 and Wolfe Road to make way for technology research, sales, and manufacturing facilities. The same thing would happen on many thousands of acres throughout Santa Clara Valley over the next twenty-five years as the Valley of Heart's Delight—a phrase coined in the mid-1940s to promote the area's agricultural bounty—gave way to technology, the new bounty.

Rental rates at Vallco Park were far cheaper than at Stanford, but the multitenant building would not be ready for about nine months. The developer had a small retail and business strip mall, adjacent to Vallco, that was near completion. Storefronts would be available there in six weeks, and ROLM could set up shop there. To tide them over, he offered space in an abandoned prune-drying shed at the edge of the orchard he was leveling. Plums for prunes had once been the area's most extensive crop, with more than 200 million pounds exported from Santa Clara County annually.[7]

On June 1, 1969, ROLM began operations in the prune shed, surrounded by the noise and dust of demolition. R, L, and M received annual salaries of $20,000 (equivalent to $127,000 in 2013), with $500 more for O. Without air-conditioning, they sweated freely over their four desks and one phone. They had all the cherries, plums, and apricots they could eat.

Vendors who visited the prune shed seemed dubious of the start-up's prospects. Many required advance cash payment. Electronic Memories and Magnetics, the only company that made the mil-spec core memory arrays that ROLM needed, was one of the few that agreed to normal purchase terms. "They did very well by us for many years," Maxfield later acknowledged, "until core memories became obsolete."

While the tiny company was gestating

ROLM's first office the summer of 1969 was upstairs in this shed where plums had been dried into prunes for years. The rent was $85 per month, equivalent to $540 in 2013. Photo courtesy of Bob Maxfield.

in the prune shed, the rest of the United States was experiencing broad social and political upheaval, with the New Left, counterculture, women's liberation, and the sexual revolution. The 1967 Summer of Love had left San Francisco teeming with hippies. UC Berkeley and many U.S. campuses reeled with frequent and sometimes violent anti–Vietnam War protests. Weekend parties, even for those with regular day jobs, offered the traditional range of alcohol, with reefers passed from hand to hand and lines of cocaine laid out on a table in a side room. Thanks to Timothy Leary of Harvard and author Ken Kesey and his Merry Pranksters in the Bay Area, however, LSD, with its "enlightening" capacity, was the drug of choice for those who could get their hands on it. Loewenstern has said he "may have participated in the drug culture a bit." Richeson, Oshman, and Maxfield were oblivious to it.

Neil Armstrong and Buzz Aldrin walked on the moon that July 20. In August, with considerable relief, ROLM moved into air-conditioned space in a storefront, next to The Cookie Jar and across from Meyberg's Delicatessen. A poster-board nameplate was tacked to the door of 10925 North Wolfe Road.

In 1982, *Technology* magazine ran an article about companies that began in strange locations, saying, "To reach stardom in technology requires many things—brains, ideas, luck—but Spartanism is mandatory. You must rise from nothing to prove you're something." HP's garage, ROLM's prune shed, and Data General's hair salon were among the highlights. The article quotes Oshman on how forced frugality can benefit the company work ethic:

> We did a lot of very intensive, very cost-effective work in those first six months. Having a very limited budget greatly focuses your mind on getting things running in a heck of a hurry. The money was absolutely going to run out in six months, and if we didn't have some major milestones to our credit by then, there was no way we were going to get any more.[8]

ROLM now had a real office and the equipment needed to turn its first product concept into reality—but it was July already, and that real product had to be working and demonstrated within four months for the company to survive.

# CHAPTER 2

# TARGETING THE MILITARY

.....................

Roles clarified as work intensified: Oshman was CEO; Richeson, VP marketing; Maxfield, VP engineering and operations; and Loewenstern, VP research, working with Maxfield in engineering. Talking about his engineering responsibilities, Maxfield told Rice University's alumni magazine *Sallyport* in spring 2005, "It was sheer terror, because once we decided on this idea, it was all on my shoulders, and I knew how little I knew."[9]

ROLM's first development project required far more mechanical design than electronic design—and not one of the four founders was a mechanical engineer. Bob Maxfield became one very quickly. As the lone project manager on that first system, he kicked into workaholic mode, a lifelong characteristic. According to Gibson Anderson, his friend and lab partner from college, "It didn't start with ROLM. He was like that at Rice." Years later, *Saratoga News* ran a front-page article about its famous resident, the *M* in ROLM, in which Maxfield admitted, "I think about work all the time. It takes four days away before I stop. Weekends just don't do it."[10] That type-A tendency was showing up a lot around Santa Clara County, as the type Bs of agriculture receded to the edges—south toward Hollister, north to Napa, and east to the Central Valley.

## Ingenuity and Long Hours

The Data General Nova enclosure—the case—and the circuit boards inside it were about twice the size ROLM would need in order to meet military specifications. The ROLM box would have to fit into a compact opening the size of an air transport rack (ATR), a rectangular space about 7 × 10 inches. The large Nova boards had to be redesigned so all the components fit within that compact layout, and they had to be able to withstand rugged use. No delicate, temperamental connections—typical of early computers—could be tolerated.

ROLM needed to design memory, power supply, and a very sturdy box. The whole package had to withstand severe shock, heat, cold, vibration, and humidity. ROLM's first hire, Merle Wetherell, an experienced engineer whom Richeson had known at ESL, helped modify Data General's CPU design for extreme-temperature operation. The memory design was outsourced to a subcontractor, managed by Maxfield. Walter Loewenstern designed the power supply. Maxfield and Al Foster, a newly hired mechanical designer, developed the ruggedized housing.

Keeping the case interior cool enough so components did not malfunction presented a significant challenge, especially with no vents and no fan. Considerable heat would be generated by the fifty to sixty components on each of the fourteen integrated circuit boards, stacked together with barely a quarter of an inch between them. Maxfield hit upon a solution: having the boards straddle a copper bar that conducted the heat away from the electronics, out of the interior, and to the case, where it could dissipate externally.

The circuit boards had to be stabilized. Otherwise, they would warp as a jeep with one on board bounced over rocky terrain, popping off the dozens of components soldered onto them, or fracturing the connections between the components. An aluminum bracket was added to each board to provide stiffening. Special heavy-duty connectors ran between each

ROLM's first product, the RuggedNova 1601 computer, with its separate control panel sitting on top. Photo from ROLM *Severe Environment Minicomputers* brochure, 1961.

circuit board and the motherboard. The fit was so snug that there was no space on the boards for finger holds. A special leveraging tool was designed, manufactured, and provided with each computer so the boards could be removed for service or upgrade. The result was a practically indestructible, ATR-size computer precisely packed into a case made of machined aluminum.

Everyone worked six and a half days a week, trying to ready a system for the computer show in just a few months. This meant adding a few more employees: engineer Bud Thiel, technician Ron Diehl, and an assembler, Vineta Alvarez, who came over from Sylvania. Alvarez recruited her two teenage daughters, Bobby and Fawn, to stuff envelopes, run errands, and even solder circuit boards. They were paid from petty cash because they were too young for payroll. For ROLM's tenth anniversary employee newsletter in 1979, Diehl recalled the first time Maxfield loaded something into the Nova that caused it to type out his name: "Everyone thought he was a genius for sure."

ROLM launched the RuggedNova 1601 at the '69 Fall Joint Computer Conference in Las Vegas. The idea of demonstrating the computer at work in a vat of boiling water was jettisoned as just a bit too risky. So two systems were displayed: one static, nonworking to display parts, and one functioning. A Lucite top on the nonworking static display unit allowed visitors to peer inside at the 1601's remarkably compact boards. You could tell by looking at it, with the thick walls and all the bracing, that it was—according to Maxfield—a "very rugged bugger." The functioning unit, mounted on a shelf above a monitor, was running the Spacewar game. That unit was missing its integral memory module, however, because the vendor had not completed it in time. Instead, a hidden cable connected the computer to a DG memory board behind the scenes.

Months of eighteen-hour days had taken a toll on Maxfield. As soon as the booth was set up and the functioning system was humming along, he headed for the hospital—down and out with pneumonia.

Data General was once again the star of the FJCC. DG's mini-computers were selling well. The company had catapulted in one year to about $30 million in revenue and had just gone public. DG's four founders were each worth about $6 million, and, as Maxfield described it, "walked around with stars in their eyes."

Two things happened in Las Vegas that convinced Richeson this venture would fly. First, a woman in uniform came by the booth. "At first, I thought she was with the Salvation Army, with all her ribbons and stars," he later confessed. "But I could tell from her questions that she clearly knew a lot." The woman turned out to be U.S. Navy Commander Grace Hopper, who was highly significant in the development of early computers and, later, the military computer language Ada. Second, two "suits" came to the booth, shoved Richeson aside, and took over the product demo. One of the men had previously canvassed the show. "I'd given him a demo, and he'd gotten it down pat," explained Richeson. The man was giving his IBM senior VP a quick tour of the show's high points—and ROLM was one of them.

The RuggedNova 1601 product brochure teased of more to come from ROLM: "We value innovation highly . . . We're betting that our innovations will open up new and economical ways to use small computers. The RuggedNova severe environment mini-computer is just the first step." It was an audacious statement, wordsmithed to

"Take the world's toughest mini-computer anywhere. Name the place. Air, land, or sea." ROLM's first ad, in *Electronics*, fall 1969 Fall Joint Computer Conference. Photo courtesy of Bob Maxfield.

say, basically, *You just watch—you're going to be amazed at what this little start-up will do.*

Once the team was back in Santa Clara, the success of meeting the first Melchor milestone was celebrated with ROLM's first Friday beer bust, establishing a weekly tradition that held while the company was small. Oshman would lean against the counter in the tiny lunchroom, smoking a cigar while the others enjoyed their cans of beer. It wasn't long before the beer was rolled in in kegs, and bags of chips gave way to Meyberg's catering.

In the early days, most employees had just a beer or two, then headed home to young families. Ken and Barbara Oshman had two small boys, Peter and David, by the early 1970s. Bob and Mo Maxfield had baby daughters, Melinda and Mary Jane. Gene and Donna Richeson had two young sons, Stephen and Paul. But Loewenstern, who was single during those first years of ROLM, said the Friday night parties often got pretty good, continuing on to a private home, and ending with breakfast at Denny's in the wee hours.

Some employees were also up in the predawn hours and arriving at ROLM—but not for official business. The Spacewar game was so popular that engineers would come to the office to play before starting work—early gamers. ROLM published a technical bulletin on how to play the game on the 1601 so customers could enjoy it too. Already, ROLM was exhibiting signs of being a fun place to work.

## The World's Toughest Computer

The product had to be tested by an independent lab to prove its severe-environment claims. They had tested it pretty well at ROLM for temperature, but vibration, shock, and humidity tests take a long time—time that ROLM didn't have. Maxfield "sweat blood" over that testing. "It was a huge relief when it passed." The 1601 met specs for airborne, shipboard, and ground electronic equipment. The system could operate under

temperature extremes of –67 degrees
F to 203 degrees F (–55 degrees C to
95 degrees C), could resist radio frequency interference, could withstand
up to 15 Gs of shock and 10 Gs of
vibration, and could endure 95 percent humidity for thirty days. Plus, it
met the specification for high-impact
shock: the Navy's 400-pound ham-
mer test. The RuggedNova was indeed
rugged.

Drawings in ads portrayed action that static photos
could not, such as this vibrating helicopter. Photo
from ROLM *Severe Environment Minicomputers*
brochure, 1961.

In addition, it was one of the most
functional computers available in
1970, because its architecture was identical to DG's Nova. The basic unit
had a maximum capacity of 32,000 16-bit words (64 kilobytes, compared
to 4,000,000 kilobytes in today's basic laptops). According to the product data sheet, the basic device included "the Central Processor Unit with
four hardware accumulators, 4K memory, 16 level programmed priority
interrupts, I/O (input/output) capability for up to 62 devices, Direct Memory Access, Power Failure Protect and Auto Restart, Teletype interface and
power supply." It was priced off-the shelf at just under $20,000 (equiva-
lent to $123,000 in 2013). Still, it had far less power than a child's hand-
held electronic game does today.

The first production (non-prototype) RuggedNova was shipped to Syl-
vania in March 1970, thirteen months after Oshman had telephoned de
Castro. Richeson leveraged his contacts to make the first sale, to Sylvania.
The product performed as advertised, and a good reference was estab-
lished. Several more computers went out the door during the next quarter,
April to June, just in time for the end of the first fiscal year. ROLM had met
Jack Melchor's second benchmark.

The $75,000 seed money plus the line of credit had held the company
for the nine months since incorporation. But a lot of equipment would

be needed to design, build, and test the next computer. Melchor held to his word and, in spring 1970, helped raise the first round of venture capital: $600,000 (equivalent to $3.6 million in 2013) for 75,000 shares of stock, representing about 50 percent ownership. The investors were Triad Ventures (Melchor's venture fund), Continental Capital, and Wells Fargo Small Business Investment Company. The Wells Fargo decision was shepherded by Dan Tompkins, a Rice engineering classmate of Maxfield's who had gone on to get an MBA at Stanford. Each of these new investors received one-third of 50 percent of the company. The cofounders' and Melchor's original investments were diluted to a bit less than 10 percent ownership each.

The company turned a profit that spring quarter of 1970 and every quarter thereafter. Revenue that first fiscal year ending June 1970 was $240,000, with a net loss of $350,000 due to the start-up investment. In early summer 1970, ROLM moved into 5,000 square feet of space in Vallco Park, at 10300 North Tantau Avenue, Cupertino. Not one remnant of the orchards or the old prune shed remained in the new office park nearby. The Libby's and Del Monte fruit canning operations in Sunnyvale, once among the largest in the world, would close in another few years. Cupertino's 120-foot water tower, painted to look like a giant can of Libby's fruit cocktail, is one of the last remaining vestiges marking the Valley's rich agricultural heritage. The lush orchards and aromatic canneries—residents could sometimes identify by smell what was being processed that day—gave way to parking lots and featureless facilities for semiconductor manufacturers and makers of the equipment and services that those manufacturers needed.

## Seeking Equilibrium

As ROLM began to prosper and activities became more complex and diverse, Oshman's and Maxfield's roles became increasingly well defined.

Ken Oshman seemed to have business sense in his DNA—an MBA would have been redundant. Walter Loewenstern made no bones about calling him "one of the brightest business guys I ever met." As president and CEO, he was the company's very capable visionary and public persona.

Bob Maxfield, vice president of engineering, was committed to keeping ROLM on the forefront of technology. That first year and a half, he never had reason to call DG with a technical issue. "We made the right choice, going with them," he later said. "They had a clean product." Maxfield was already developing good business and strategic sense, which he said came from reading and experience, not background. Oshman thought big and had the broad vision, while Maxfield worked on how to technically accomplish the vision, often pushing back with more realistic expectations.

Richeson's and Loewenstern's roles in the company were less clear. According to Gene Richeson, VP marketing and sales, "Frankly, marketing wasn't going well. Sales either. I'd rather die than make a cold call." He hired an effective salesman, Tony Gerber, a Brit with a PhD in electrical engineering who had engineered aircraft simulators before heading up sales and marketing for a database start-up. Gerber had chutzpah. Coming home from a business trip, he and Richeson arrived too late at the gate to board the plane. Gerber demanded that the attendants let them through. "I'm a doctor," he claimed, "and this is my patient. We have to get back to Stanford Hospital. *Now*." The plane doors were reopened, without anyone even asking to see his credentials.

The first customer-training session was held in the fall of 1970 at Vail, Colorado, organized by Richeson and taught by Maxfield. Richeson didn't know what to do in marketing, so he just copied DG: DG provided a week of training for its computer customers—so ROLM did too. Whatever materials DG had, ROLM adopted something comparable. "We didn't even know the difference between sales and marketing," Richeson confessed decades later. ROLM soon hired its first real marketer, Jim Willenborg. Richeson seemed more comfortable falling back on what he'd done at Sylvania: selling contracts to develop unique systems for a contractor, talking to the same customers he'd had in his previous job. He would bring in custom opportunities rather than seek new customers for the product ROLM was developing—an off-the-shelf computer, which is what the business plan specified. Selling what ROLM had to offer meant that Richeson would have to find customers he didn't know. That was a serious problem for a marketing and sales executive reluctant to make cold calls.

When it came time to set targets for ROLM's second year, Oshman felt strongly that they had to hit $1.5 million revenue to support investment and growth. Richeson balked. He couldn't see how more than half of that could be achieved in off-the-shelf products. He felt ROLM would have to become a custom-design house to hit that number.

In early fall 1971, Oshman, Richeson, and Gerber met to discuss the sales forecast. Out of the blue, Oshman declared that he was taking over sales and marketing and that Gerber would report directly to him. Richeson, who had not been forewarned privately, sat stunned and embarrassed. He was dismayed—and also a bit relieved. But the meeting just moved on from there. "Nothing was said about where I should go, what I should do," Richeson later recalled. "I was simply supposed to figure out on my own where I fit in." He didn't go talk to Oshman about it one on one. "I really didn't want to hear it," he said.

So Richeson bounced around doing odd jobs. He ended with a stint in engineering—and by then, Maxfield noted, he was "not a happy camper." The stress of the early ROLM days was horrific for Richeson. "Business was so shaky," he said. "Donna and I had a baby, a house, a mortgage. And my dad was dying." His hair turned white that year, at age thirty-one. He left the company in the fall of 1972, with his founder shares intact. He skied through the winter and then returned to ESL, where he'd worked before becoming the R in ROLM.

Once development was under way, it became clear that Maxfield was in charge of engineering. Walter Loewenstern "sort of felt like the odd man out." He began handling administrative duties: facilities, human resources, and security clearances. One day Gerber said he thought Loewenstern might make a good salesman and asked him to come along on a sales call. It seemed to Loewenstern that "a whole new world opened up." He soon went to a three-day intensive course with Max Sacks Sales Training in Los Angeles. He learned that sales is all about handling "FUD"—the customer's *fear*, *uncertainty*, and *doubt*. The course broke sales into a process that gave him all the hooks and handles he needed to transition into a sales role.

## "In those days, anyone could just walk in and wander around the Pentagon." —Walter Loewenstern

After Loewenstern had a few months' experience in sales, Oshman approached him and said the company needed a presence at the Pentagon—how would he like to move to Washington, D.C.? Loewenstern headed east. The title *Vice President and Cofounder* on his business card provided entrée to high-level military contacts. When he first arrived, the Pentagon had open access. "Anyone could just walk in and wander around," he said—until May 1972, when the Weather Underground planted and detonated a bomb in a second-floor women's restroom to protest the Vietnam War. After that, badges were required. Loewenstern's Pentagon ID of 1977 shows him with bushy mustache and hair, wearing a bold, plaid sport coat—a rather distinctive visage in that uniformed, close-shaved culture. "Would you buy a computer from that guy?" Loewenstern would later laugh.

Walter Loewenstern's appearance seemed consistent with his temperament—laid-back, stress-free, and unworried—though he considered it the most stressful time of his life. He was between marriages, had no mortgage to fret about, and was confident he could get a fine engineering job elsewhere if ROLM didn't work out. On the job, he was willing to do whatever was needed at the moment.

Gene Richeson was in the opposite situation. The risk of a start-up combined with personal obligations weighed heavily on him. Plus, a job for which he was not well suited took a huge toll. He could be explosive at times. The stress he felt lay barely below the surface.

Bob Maxfield responded to stress by working constantly to solve known problems and to anticipate and prevent future problems. Quiet by nature, he was often silent and distant around family and friends as his mind obsessively pondered issues. When he spoke up in meetings, everyone listened because they knew he always thought things well through before weighing in. ROLM benefited from the considerable intelligence Maxfield applied to serious issues during most of his waking hours—but his home and personal life were often neglected.

Ken Oshman seemed to have a balanced approach. He was dedicated and focused at work, but he had the ability to leave issues at the office so he could enjoy his family and golf games. He was low-key, soft-spoken, and articulate. His natural confidence and optimism carried him—and ROLM's employees—through difficult times.

A 1970 conversation with a subcontractor, himself a company founder, remained etched in Maxfield's mind. The man reacted strongly when he learned that ROLM had four founders—"two too many," he said. The man predicted that within a year there would be only two. And by late 1972, Loewenstern was on the East Coast, uninvolved in day-to-day operations, and Richeson was gone—for the time being, anyway. Oshman was running ROLM, with Maxfield as his quiet, strong right arm.

## A ROLM-Designed Computer

Shortly after Tony Gerber took over the top sales role, Jack Melchor popped into his office and promised a case of champagne if the 1971 sales target of $1.5 million was hit. Gerber's primary focus was to develop and implement a cohesive strategy and to quantify the sales opportunities—geographically, by application, by available funding.

The Vietnam War was at its peak. All weapons and electronics being deployed, however, had been developed years prior. A large portion of the U.S. military budget was going toward personnel and logistics—moving and feeding troops. ROLM wanted its products to be embedded in new R&D projects for systems that wouldn't be ready for several years. "The Vietnam War was pulling funds away from R&D at the moment," explained Gerber. "Between that and a recession, it was a tough marketplace." But the military clearly had a need for a general-purpose mil-spec processor, supported by a high-level language, and available off the shelf. The traditional suppliers such as IBM or UNIVAC were not offering these as standard price-list products. ROLM had found its niche.

The marketing and sales strategy evolved into a top-down/bottom-up approach. ROLM had to establish key contacts at the Pentagon—top down, Loewenstern's job. ROLM also had to establish contacts with military contractors that were implementing the systems projects, to sell the ROLM computer as the central processing unit for those projects—bottom up. *Aviation Week* magazine—"We called it *Aviation Leak*," said Gerber—was a primary source of information on military contracts, both rumored and real. ROLM's sales force of two or three people had top-security clearances and could go to both the Pentagon and the contractors to get more solid information and find out where the opportunities lay.

Dalmo Victor, a company located near ROLM, secured a large defense contract to build a sophisticated electronic warfare system called the Wild Weasel project. Wild Weasel's mission was to locate enemy radars and then blind or attack them using jet fighters. The need was urgent due to the sophistication of Russian surface-to-air missile (SAM) systems in use in the Vietnam War. It was such a high-priority, quick-production program that normal bureaucratic procurement rules were set aside.

# "Some meetings to discuss the use of ROLM computers were so top secret, they were held inside a metal-lined vault."— Tony Gerber

Dalmo Victor asked ROLM to sell it the 1601's CPU, the heart and soul of the RuggedNova—just the five electronic boards, without the chassis, memory, or power supply—to embed in its own system. It seemed a perfect fit for a massive project that needed a speedy solution. Oshman stuck to the business plan, however, and refused the sale, insisting that ROLM was not a components supplier. So Dalmo Victor bought a few 1601s, reverse engineered them, and proceeded to develop its own equivalent CPU. When ROLM and Data General got wind of this, together they warned Dalmo Victor that it would promptly face a lawsuit. Through Tony Gerber's efforts, Maxfield remembered, Oshman relented and agreed to sell Dalmo Victor the CPUs.

Gerber recalled on the phone, "Some meetings to discuss the use of ROLM computers were so top secret, they were held inside a metal-lined vault." The vault was soundproof and prevented RFI (radio-frequency interference) detection. Over the next several years, Dalmo Victor bought many thousands of 1601 CPUs for use in F-4s and F-111s, creating important revenue for ROLM during those tough economic years.

ROLM hit the 1971 sales target of $1.5 million by a hair, with a net profit of $150,000. Melchor promptly delivered the bubbly.

"We were very focused in getting the company off the ground," said Oshman in a 1995 interview. "I attribute that in great part to the stern and valuable advice of Jack Melchor."[11] McMurtry too observed that Melchor was a "phenomenal resource," citing his "uncommon common sense and extreme smarts." He noted that Oshman and Melchor got together frequently: "Jack would state his candid opinion about everything, and yet he never wanted to run the company or have undue influence. They had enormous respect for each other. Ken deferred to Jack more than to anyone else, to the extent that Ken ever deferred to anyone."

Even with Melchor on their side and everything moving in the right direction, it took Oshman three or four years to be convinced that ROLM would survive. His concern was well justified. The economy was rough by late fall 1971, with both inflation and unemployment approaching 6 percent.[12] Social and political unrest continued as the Vietnam War escalated. Budgets were tight everywhere in the Valley. Two ROLM employees were let go—the only layoffs ROLM ever experienced. Oshman called an "all hands" meeting and took to the podium—he stood on a table in the lunchroom. He explained what a tough spot the company was in and promised, "We'll come through this." He then asked if the employees were willing to take a 10 percent cut in pay. They agreed. The long workdays, however, remained uncut.

The 1601 sold well enough to increase revenue by 50 percent, to $2.3 million by 1972's fiscal year end (June). Profit was up 12 percent, to $338,000. There were fifty-eight employees.

As soon as the 1601 was shipping without glitches, Maxfield trained his laser-like focus on the next product, the 1602. The hardware would be designed by ROLM, with only the software and operating system coming from Data General. A separate royalty license was negotiated with DG. The 1602 was to be a very powerful, new-generation 16-bit computer, designed for higher-performance military jobs than the 1601 had been.

Bob Maxfield and engineer Merle Wetherell, the company's first hire and the only employee with extensive digital design experience, were the prime architects of the 1602. There was no "computer design" labor pool to draw from. HP and IBM were the only companies in the Bay Area making mini-computers, and little start-up ROLM was not yet appealing enough to lure away their top engineers. Most ROLM employees came from Sylvania and knew a lot about electronics, but not a lot about digital computers. ROLM was breaking new ground in the future Silicon Valley, the first mini-computer start-up in the midst of all the semiconductor action. Amdahl, which started up a few months after ROLM to compete with IBM in mainframes, was in the same boat, scrambling to hire computer designers. Everything had to be learned each step of the way.

Debugging the prototype was a case in point. It went painfully slowly as a new technician learned on the job. To speed things up, Maxfield would start testing after the tech left at 5:00 p.m., working until 10:00 p.m. He'd leave a note on Wetherell's desk, spelling out the problems to be addressed first thing in the morning. Wetherell would redesign on paper by noon, the tech would change the breadboard (test board) layout accordingly by 5:00 p.m., and the cycle would start again, with Maxfield testing at night. Months later, they had a working prototype. By the time the 1602 was done, ROLM's employees had gained considerable digital computer expertise, the hard way.

The 1602 presented the first serious need for top-notch software engineering. ROLM's first software engineer, Steve Plant, was happy to finally dig in. Despite his master's degree in computer science from Purdue, most of his first year at the company had been spent providing technical support to the sales department and doing occasional minor hardware engineering for the 1601. The friend who had told him about ROLM was DG's West Coast sales rep, who had warned him that the head of engineering looked as if he was about sixteen years old, implying, *So how much could he possibly know?* Plant had called ROLM anyway to ask for an interview. He was an early example of ROLM's penchant for hiring inherent talent even if it was not apparent at the moment how that talent would be utilized.

Back then, software engineering involved using punch cards and paper tapes. The 1602 had its own instruction set—its basic operations as seen by application programmers—implemented in microcode, presenting Plant with his first really challenging programming task at ROLM.

Growing and in need of more space, ROLM moved its headquarters in the midst of the 1602 design effort, in September 1972, to a larger facility at 18922 Forge Drive, also in Vallco Park in Cupertino. ROLM occupied half the building, about 30,000 square feet. It rented a phone system from AT&T and erected a respectable corporate sign.

The RuggedNova 1602, introduced in 1972, was intended for more demanding, more precise jobs than the 1601 could handle, such as power management of electronic warheads that required vast amounts of high-speed calculations. This mil-spec, rugged computer, according to the bro-

ROLM's unique letter font, shown here on the first corporate sign (1972) at 18922 Forge Drive in Cupertino, remained unchanged throughout the company's existence. Photo from ROLM corporate brochure 1973.

chure, "goes substantially beyond its predecessor . . . six times faster and significantly more powerful than the 1601." It offered greatly enhanced "interrupt processing" speed—the capability to respond to external events requiring it to process new data and make appropriate control decisions.

The 1602 was priced at $12,500 off-the-shelf ($70,000 in 2013), with an 8K memory add-on for $6,000 more. There were three different operating temperature range options. The extreme range allowed for operation from –67 degrees F to 203 degrees F (–55 degrees C to 95 degrees C) for an additional $7,500.

The 1602 was targeted for direct use in rugged environments or to be embedded in contractors' products. ROLM placed an ad in *Spectrum* magazine in March 1973 that read, "Attention Program Managers: How to win a $10 million government contract with the new $20,250 ROLM RuggedNova." ROLM offered a full set of development tools to support this approach.

The first 1602 shipped that month. Seventy units sold the first year, and many hundreds annually after that. It was placed on board Boeing

This RuggedNova 1602, bought on eBay for $2000 in 2012, was donated to the Computer History Museum, where it was displayed in the lobby. Photo by Alex Bochannek, courtesy of the Computer History Museum.

test flights. *Aviation Week* said, "engineers use this capability to analyze test results while a flight is in progress, verifying that all test conditions have been met and valid data obtained . . . Without this capability, they would have to await post-flight data analysis and a subsequent flight."[13]

The RuggedNova 1602 was also sold to nonmilitary customers for applications that needed reliability and confidence of operation, such as for data buoys in the ocean, geophysical exploration for oil and gas, pumping or substation control in utilities, and monitoring and control of nuclear-power installations. A Canadian physicist put RuggedNovas on snowcats to facilitate research near the Arctic.

In an interview, Ken Oshman commented how unique ROLM was in its methods of selling to the military, which he called "a sort of club, a difficult place to sell into." Before ROLM, selling computers to the military typically was a very expensive and time-consuming process. But ROLM had a new, different philosophy: promising that whenever the military needed a new computer, ROLM would produce and deliver it in thirty days. "We were trying to break [the military] in to this new way of buying," he explained. "It was a very challenging process."[14] Before ROLM, the military had been unable to get its hands on a computer in less than a year, because each was specially designed for its purpose. ROLM was the first to offer off-the-shelf availability, and the company held to that philosophy throughout the expansion of its military product line.

Fiscal year 1973 again saw a 50 percent increase in revenue, to $3.6 million. Net income, however, declined slightly to $321,000, the only time that happened in ROLM's fifteen-year history. Oshman wrote his first letter to shareholders, stating, "This was the year in which ROLM established a new record in sales"—not knowing, of course, that every year would bring a new record. It was also the first year that ROLM had a chief financial officer, Tony Carollo. Up to this point, a bookkeeper and accountant had kept the books. Bill Friedman also came in, as the company's first general counsel.

Bursting at the seams, ROLM leased the rest of the Forge Drive building, increasing its space to 47,000 square feet. As with most high-tech companies, about 12 percent of annual net revenue was invested in research and development. The number of employees had doubled in the past year, to 114 employees. Twenty-seven of them were engineers and engineering support people, and one-third of those had master's degrees or PhDs—a very sophisticated engineering team.

As the company continued to grow, Oshman worked hard behind the scenes to more fully develop his early vision of running a large company that manufactured multiple product lines. In the fall of 1972, after a management off-site meeting, he wrote an all-employees memo that provided the first glimpse of what ROLM might become. Oshman stated that ROLM's "bedrock" objectives were "to grow to be a large, profitable company in an atmosphere where everyone contributing to that growth learns, grows, and is financially rewarded"—the foundation of the future Great Place to Work philosophy. Specific objectives included achieving an annual growth rate greater than 15 percent, building relevant skills in all employees, responding to changes in the marketplace, and avoiding wild fluctuations in levels of business, which could create a chaotic, negative working atmosphere.

Oshman also mentioned in that memo the possibility of expanding into a new arena: business telephones. The idea gained little traction. As exciting as the changes of the past several years had been, the mission was still focused on the stability of the organization. As Maxfield pointed out, "We had no capacity to do anything but nourish the 1601 and 1602."

## Serious Threats to Survival

About the time Oshman was beginning to feel that ROLM would in fact succeed, in 1973, each of the three branches of the U.S. military decided to standardize on a single computer for all of its applications. Until then, every plane, ship, and jeep had a different type of computer. "The Navy issued a spec for a uniform computer that looked a lot like a Sperry Univac system," Oshman told the Silicon Valley Historical Association. "Lo and behold, Sperry won the contract and our Navy business went to zero." This wiped out about one-third of ROLM's business overnight. It was not a matter of whether ROLM had quality goods and services or a cost-effective solution. "This is not a fun kind of market," Oshman remarked.[15]

About that same time, ROLM smacked up against a government regulation called "rights in data" that required certain military vendors to provide the government with complete cost information and design documents. The policy was intended to give the government the rights to equipment designs for which it had paid the development costs—a reasonable concept. The policy also policed price gouging by forcing disclosure of costs. However, the government had not paid for the development of ROLM computers and therefore had no moral right to own the designs. ROLM considered its designs proprietary and was not in the least bit inclined to share them with anyone. The policy also had the possible outcome of forcing arbitrary price reductions on ROLM's already low-priced system just because ROLM was able to achieve a good profit on the product.

*When a general from Macon, Georgia, called and said, "Son, you have to hand over that data," Oshman replied, "No, sir, we won't do that."*

Military purchasing contractors were not used to doing business with companies that had developed products using their own money rather than the government's. ROLM got a big contract from Dalmo Victor, and that put it in the regulators' sights. But Oshman refused to comply with the rights-in-data requirement. When a general from Macon, Georgia, called and said, "Son, you have to hand over that data," he replied, "No, sir, we won't do that. We've been slogging a long time, taking a lot of risks. If we're a very competitive product that provides your solution, that should be all that counts." Oshman hung up and made lots of calls. Eventually ROLM received a waiver from the secretary of the Air Force. But it was a "serious warning bell." They weren't going to escape the government's notice for long.

Those two incidents got Oshman quite concerned. The market was not totally rational, and ROLM's product niche was not very big. He wanted to figure out something else—to enter a different, large market with a new ROLM product line. "I thought at $10 million we'd have saturated the market," he later recalled. "Thankfully I was wrong about that, but it was another key motivator to diversify."

The forecasted $10 million cap was another major alarm. Management thought that the company, at $3.6 million in revenues for fiscal 1973, was well on the way toward maximizing its market share. And there was a catch-22 with continuing growth: As the company became more visible in the market, the bureaucrats became aware of it. If ROLM were deemed too profitable, regardless of the up-front risks it took to get to profitability, the government could demand that its designs be made basically public so other companies could bid on them without having to go through the manpower and dollar investment it took to achieve those designs. Plus, other regulations could pop up that forced the military to standardize on a non-ROLM product, which would lock ROLM out of the bidding.

Oshman wasn't interested in building a $10 million or even a $20 million company. Maxfield reasoned that if the rest of management had entrenched and said, "No, we've got enough on our plate as it is—let's just keep doing what we're doing," Oshman would've said, "Well, I wish you luck," and departed. Fortunately, most of them fell in line behind Oshman. It was time to look for a second market in which ROLM could grow.

# CHAPTER 3

# SEEKING A BIGGER MARKET

....................

A second market was needed, one in which increasingly powerful mini-computers could make a significant impact—and one that would play into ROLM's technology strengths and its reputation for product reliability and quality. Oshman, Maxfield, and the marketing team (Gerber, Willenborg, and now Dave Pidwell) brainstormed on applications utilizing a mini-computer that would fall within the bounds of the contract with Data General, which barred ROLM from entering the commercial computer market. The closest link would be industrial use of a rugged computer for, perhaps, factory floors and transportation, where mainframes and minis were just beginning to appear. The form factor would be different for an industrial rugged computer than for a military one, and cost would have to be reduced. But after investigating possibilities, each application seemed to have a different specification for how rugged such a computer would need to be. Plus, there was considerable skepticism about whether such a device was needed at all.

Into the center of the collective radar screen popped the business tele-phone industry, which had had a glancing mention in Oshman's memo the year prior. Digital electronics and computing, combined with ROLM's emphasis on reliability and performance, had the potential to wildly alter products and service in the telecommunications industry. This vital Amer-ican "utility" had seen very little improvement in decades.

In the 1970s, as it had been for forty years prior and would be for thirty years after, all businesses with more than fifty employees used a PBX (private branch exchange) so workers could easily call each other internally or be connected to the outside world. PBXs had hardly changed in forty years. As Oshman pointed out, no one was using computers in this field. Instead, they were using fragile electromechanical equipment.[17] ROLM had recently rented an AT&T phone system, "an atrocious monstrosity that weighed about 1,000 pounds," said Maxfield—and that was for fewer than one hundred employees. To even have such a thing on the premises was "embarrassing." The telecommunications industry seemed ripe for an overhaul—a digital revolution—and ROLM once again honed in on disrupting an industry's status quo.

## Unraveling a Monopoly

Telephone service for both homes and businesses was provided by only one telephone company (telco) monopoly within each region of the United States. AT&T, known as Ma Bell, was the telephone company for 90 percent of the country in 1973. Its customers were served by AT&T's regional subsidiaries, like Pacific Bell and Bell Atlantic. GTE (General Telephone Equipment) served about 5 percent of the U.S., and the remaining 5 percent was splintered among 1,800 small telcos, independent of Ma Bell and scattered around generally rural parts of the country. AT&T customers used only telephone equipment manufactured by its manufacturing subsidiary Western Electric, while GTE's Automatic Electric supplied equipment to its customers and most of the many small telcos.

The phone companies had a full-circle monopoly: They made the phone equipment, rented it to customers, and provided those customers with dial tone to make local and long-distance calls. This was true of homes with one or two phones and huge companies with thousands of phones connected to switchboards. Monthly phone bills showed a few gross categories and typically had no information about the actual cost of individual calls—because no computer power had yet been applied to providing it. The rental of a PBX, telephones, trunks on which calls could go in and out, and the fees for local and long-distance calls could comprise 5 to 10 percent of a company's total expenses. Companies paid their AT&T or GTE bills begrudgingly, having no other option.

In fact, providing a business user with the ability to gain control of its telephone costs was counter to the telephone company's interest. The phone bills from one dominant, large corporation in a medium-size city— for example, State Farm in Bloomington, Illinois—might represent 50 percent of the telephone company's local revenues. Naturally, the phone companies wanted that revenue to increase, not decrease.

The first thread of the telephone companies' monopoly came unraveled with the 1968 *Carterfone vs. AT&T* decision by the Federal Communications Commission (FCC). Before *Carterfone*, no individual or company could legally own telephones or telephone equipment such as switchboards or PBXs. All equipment had to be rented from the local phone company. "It was like having to rent lamps and lightbulbs from the electric company," said Maxfield in an interview. "With no competitive motive, the electric company would invest very little in innovation. And lamps and lightbulbs would be ridiculously expensive."

After the *Carterfone* decision, customers could buy any manufacturer's equipment that met specifications to hook up to the phone company's service lines. This opened a new business dubbed the "interconnect" industry, made up of non-phone-company manufacturers of telephone equipment and service companies that installed it.

Yet the practice of renting phones largely continued due to inertia and—as Loewenstern learned in his sales training course—FUD. AT&T stoked FUD by claiming that interconnect equipment could damage the network and deteriorate service. Many companies and individuals continued to rent telephones and PBXs from the phone company. Ironically, Bob Maxfield discovered in 2006, when his father died at age ninety-three, he was still renting his home phones from AT&T, amounting to tens

Attendants at the San Jose City Hall in the early 1960s used a plug-in cable to "switch" an incoming call to the desired extension. The rotary dial was used to make outside calls. Photo by Arnold Del Carlo, Sourisseau Academy for State and Local History, San Jose State University.

of thousands of dollars wasted on monthly rental fees over almost forty years.

Telecom giants AT&T and GTE had no motivation to innovate before *Carterfone*, and little in the early years afterward, as no serious competitors challenged them. When ROLM began looking at telecommunications for a possible second product line, business calls came into a company's central phone number rather than directly to the intended individual. Attendants then transferred each call to the appropriate extension. Many companies still used switchboards—plug-in boards where the attendants physically moved plug-in cables to "switch" a phone call from one extension to another. When the caller wished to speak to another individual, the call had to be sent back to the operator rather than transferred directly to another extension. There was no voice messaging. Secretaries took messages by hand on pink pads. Message slips piled up when someone was away from the office.

AT&T's research arm, Bell Labs in New Jersey, had new-generation technology under development. But AT&T figured that technology didn't have to be adapted to a real product for the marketplace for five to seven years. Yet technological developments were sweeping through other sectors of industry as many corporate tasks such as inventory management and finance moved from electromechanical or manual operations to mainframe or mini-computer-based solutions. A simple example was calculators. Big, plug-in adding machines that used special narrow paper tape were still the norm in the early 1970s. Engineers used slide rules for more complex functions like square roots and logarithms. HP introduced high-end desktop calculators in 1970 and brought out a handheld in 1972, literally the size of a hand. The HP-35, with 35 keys, had more functions than a slide rule. Enthusiasm for the product was so great, even at $395 (about $2,000 in 2013), that sales far exceeded forecast.

A few of AT&T's central offices (COs), through which all U.S. calls were routed before reaching the end point, were already using computer-based switching equipment. But AT&T had no notion of applying that new technology to a PBX anytime soon.

More than 125,000 PBXs existed in the United States in 1973, worth some $3 billion. Ninety-nine percent of them were electromechanical, with only the most basic capability. They offered almost no flexibility to change as the company changed, as employees were added, moved, or let go. Plus, AT&T seemed oblivious of customers' desires to track, account for, and control their huge telephone expenses.

A Houston friend of Oshman's, Tom Fatjo, knew of a Dallas company called Danray that was using a computer to make a very specialized phone system. Oshman and Maxfield visited Danray and came away with the impression that the basic idea was right—applying computers to telecommunications—but the implementation was wrong. Danray's application was "limited, expensive, and cumbersome," said Maxfield. ROLM saw a window of opportunity for a small, nimble, technologically advanced company to change that situation. Explained Maxfield, "We figured we could do it right."

## Is It Feasible?

In January 1973, Oshman asked Maxfield to look into the technical feasibility of developing a PBX. Maxfield was personally debugging the 1602 and managing the early specifications of the next mil-spec family member, the 1603. With no resources in his department to look into the issue, he sought outside help. He thought of Jim Kasson, HP's highly capable young engineering manager for process control and data acquisition, with whom he'd become acquainted socially. Maxfield had already made a run at Kasson to come work on mil-spec computers. But Kasson wasn't interested in just computers—he was a systems guy.

Gibson Anderson had left HP to join ROLM the prior year. "I wanted to join a start-up," he said later, "and Ken and Bob were simply the best guys I knew." Anderson, a friend of Kasson's, invited Kasson to bring his sack lunch over to ROLM one day in February.

When he passed by the lab, Kasson saw Maxfield "literally up to his elbows inside the computer box." Maxfield looked up and asked if he'd like to take on a feasibility study in his spare time. "We chatted about the telecommunications concept," said Kasson. Maxfield stressed that this telecom product would be a system. As Kasson listened, he "saw an opportunity to do some actual engineering again instead of just managing." He jumped at the chance.

Over the next four months, Kasson moonlighted for ROLM while overseeing the tail end of his HP project. Oshman provided business and market research, and Maxfield gave what little time he could spare to discuss technology. Kasson developed the broad outlines of the design for a digital, computer-controlled PBX that could be cost-competitive for between 80 and 400 telephones. He and Maxfield partially disassembled a TeleResources PBX on a customer's site. Kasson was dismayed to see the low-quality design and construction inside the box and hoped that cost pressures would not force ROLM to cut as many corners.

A real product development plan was the next step, but Kasson could spare only ten to twenty hours a week, not enough for the time frame ROLM needed to satisfy. In June, Oshman asked Kasson to his house for a drink and applied his low-key charm. Oshman agreed that Kasson could give HP a month's notice to assure that his project was handed over smoothly. ROLM could hold off only that long. Kasson realized there was no real downside: If ROLM didn't make it and HP didn't want him back, the Valley was teeming with great jobs. During the month, he convinced one of his engineers, Ken Lavezzo, a gifted HP analog/digital designer, to move to ROLM with him. Lavezzo was less sanguine about other job opportunities if ROLM didn't make it. He asked Kasson to be sure to check the box on his HP exit papers that said "eligible for rehire." They had a common going-away lunch.

Kasson and Lavezzo were joined by mil-spec software engineer Steve Plant, and in July 1973 the three began work on a preliminary design and development schedule for a computer-controlled PBX.

Shortly after Kasson came on board, he confided to Anderson that he was baffled by Bob Maxfield's quiet management style. So little feedback was offered that he couldn't tell if his boss thought he was doing a good job. Anderson replied, "Oh no, that's good news. If he leaves you alone, all is going well. He'll let you know if there's a problem."

Kasson gained great respect for Maxfield, who "focused like a laser on a problem," said Kasson in an interview:

> Bob considered himself part of any technology team in the company. Whatever time and attention it took to work through a problem, he was right there in the lab working on it, as a technician, an engineer, a designer—whatever was needed. But he never looked over your shoulder. As long as you had good answers to tough questions, he gave you the room to do the job.

Now Oshman needed a marketing manager for the PBX. Several months prior, Jack Melchor had set up a lunch so he and Maxfield could get acquainted with a guy named Dick Moley, who was in charge of commercial marketing for the HP 3000 mini-computer. He called Moley now. "I didn't know what the hell a PBX was—and it was just a gleam in ROLM's eye," Moley remembered later. "But I had that Silicon Valley fever to take the leap."

# *"I didn't know what the hell a PBX was, but I had that Silicon Valley fever to take the leap."— Dick Moley*

Moley had gotten his master's degree in computer science through Stanford's work–study program. As soon as he got to ROLM, he did the obvious thing: He talked to big companies about what they liked and didn't like about their phone systems. "I've been on a lot of boards since then," he said recently, "and it's amazing how often the 'obvious' things are not done." In his discussions with companies, Moley uncovered the three things telecom managers of the era were most concerned about:

1. The inability to manage the cost of long-distance calls, which typically made up about 40 percent of their phone bills.
2. The high cost of adding, moving, or deleting phones as corporate needs changed. (When Ken Oshman moved from one corner office to another the very summer the plan was written, AT&T needed three days to move enormous bundles of cables.)
3. The lack of accountability—who made the call, for how long, at what cost—so departments could be charged for their own calls.

These three factors were especially important for large companies with enormous telecommunications expenses. Of course, Moley pointed out, the phone company wasn't exactly in a hurry to help them reduce long-distance fees or fees for moves and changes. And the interconnect companies had nothing that could address these major issues—they were busy trying to sell trivial features such as music on hold. So it's no surprise that interconnects were able to sell only to small companies.

Moley knew that these three major customer issues could be addressed by a computer-controlled digital system, through the flexibility of software configurations (rather than hardwired configurations) and with the tracking and management capability of computer intelligence. Such a system would not only address the mutual problems of corporate telecom managers but also give corporate telephone users far more capabilities that would enhance worker productivity through such features as *hold*, *forward*, and *do not disturb*. Plus, organizations would see customer satisfaction improve by virtue of simple features such as transfer—the ability to directly transfer a call without having to go back through the attendant.

As the essential system features of the new PBX were being defined, Kasson designed the product architecture and Lavezzo worked on feasibility studies for the critical analog-to-digital conversion circuits and other hardware. Steve Plant began a software design with the aim of estimating development cost and finding out whether the newly introduced mil-spec 1603 central processor would offer sufficient performance for use in telecom. If not, designing a new central processor would be a major development expense and possible manufacturing cost hit.

Plant had picked up some knowledge of switching system software during his time at Bell Labs, but Kasson and Lavezzo lacked any telephony experience. Not knowing anything about how a PBX was supposed to be designed, Kasson designed one that looked a lot like a huge data acquisition/process control system, about which he knew quite a bit. "I figured if you stood back from the problem a mile or so, it looked almost the same," he has explained. "The only difference was that the data would go in one line and out another, instead of going to and from the computer." In this case, the data would be the voices of conversations occurring on the digital PBX. As soon as the analog voice hit the box, it was transformed ("digitized") into data (1s and 0s), and it remained data as it flowed through the system. Just before the outgoing data was released, it was transformed back into analog voice. The AT&T long-distance network was using this "digital switching" of voice communications, but it had never been introduced in systems for businesses. The conventional wisdom was that it was not cost-effective, although everyone agreed that the cost of digital technology would drop rapidly compared to that of analog technology.

A further advantage of using digital switching for voice conversations was that the PBX could also be used for nonvoice data switching. The PBX could provide a means by which mini-computers or mainframes could communicate with a large number of desktop terminals. Therefore, rather than being hardwired by bulky cable to a single computer, terminals could "call up" (access) any of several computers or even an outside database. This conceptual breakthrough could create a major competitive advantage and even alter market perception of what a PBX was. But of course, developing the voice applications of a PBX was the first priority.

By the end of August, after less than two months of fiddling with the project, Kasson had a first cut at the spec for the backplane—the central nervous system that would route signals appropriately—and a list of which hardware cards the system would need. Up to this point, all the effort had been expended on proving the feasibility of adding a new telecom product line. Now management would have to prepare to seek board approval to diversify.

## Telecom Is a Go

In late 1973, Dick Moley presented the Business Plan for the Computerized Automatic Branch Exchange (CABX) to the ROLM board of directors. The technical portion of the plan mentioned that the digital nature of the switch had several advantages, including that "data can easily be transmitted at very high rates (to 64K baud) without the use of modems." It also stated that because the mini-computer controlling the system was a general-purpose computer, a wide range of peripherals could be attached to it for applications such as Data Switching, Data Collection, Contact Monitoring, Inventory Status, and Voice Response.

Key elements of the CABX marketing and distribution plan flew in the face of conventional practices in the telecommunications marketplace. First, ROLM, an unknown company, would sell, through its distributors, to large companies in major U.S. cities—companies that were dedicated customers of telecom giant AT&T. Second, to solve these companies' problems, ROLM would sell large systems. The few other manufacturers of non-AT&T PBX systems were thrashing around in small regional markets, mostly selling small, so-called key systems of fewer than thirty lines. Third, ROLM distributors would have regional exclusivity, unheard of in the industry. Price wars were standard among non-AT&T products, since multiple distributors carried the same products wholesaled from GTE's Automatic Electric or from foreign manufacturers such as Hitachi and Eriksson, which had adapted their products for the U.S. market. Fourth, to avoid price competition, ROLM would offer

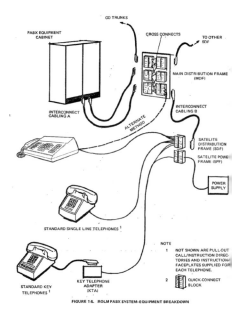

FIGURE 1-6. ROLM PABX SYSTEM-EQUIPMENT BREAKDOWN

The schematic in the 1973 ROLM PBX Business Plan showed the links between the system elements—the attendant's console, the wiring, "punch-down blocks," cabinets, and phones. Photo courtesy of Bob Maxfield.

applications and benefits such as long-distance cost control—capabilities that competitors lacked. It was a daring plan. Oshman loved it.

Much of the early revenue was forecast to come from companies that would opt to buy digital systems for new facilities. They hoped revenue also would come eventually from companies that would be enticed to toss out their antiquated equipment in favor of the new technology. Moley's business plan identified three key risks:

1. "That the problem is not fully understood, and the solution is therefore flawed and major redesign will be necessary."
2. "That the development time, development cost, or manufacturing cost has been seriously underestimated."
3. "That the chosen approach is inherently more expensive and/or has lower performance than some other approach which may become available from one of our competitors."

The business plan showed that the CABX development and initial marketing could be funded entirely out of profits from the mil-spec computer business; no additional cash would need to be raised until the product had proved itself and was into production.

The board approved the plan, setting ROLM on the path of having two diverse product areas that nonetheless had a common goal: using computer technology to solve an industry's problems and to bring new capabilities to that industry by virtue of technology and reliability.

Continental Capital and Wells Fargo SBIC, the two outside venture capital investors, were horrified by the board's decision. Why put ROLM's nice, small, profitable mil-spec business at risk to go up against massive AT&T? But these two VCs had only board visitation rights, not voting board seats. Both would likely have sold their shares immediately—if there had been a buyer. ROLM stock was not publicly held, however, and according to Maxfield, "None of us had the money to buy them out."

Ken Oshman called Walter Loewenstern in D.C. to tell him ROLM was going into the PBX business. "We can't do that!" Loewenstern exclaimed. "AT&T owns that business!"

"We'll do it better," Oshman replied. "We're smarter and faster."

Loewenstern thought it was crazy, but he wished them well and kept his nose in mil-spec sales. He wasn't the only one who objected. Two recent hires, VP of manufacturing Dennis Paboojian and CFO Tony Carollo, had both worked in the interconnect industry and knew how little product differentiation there was—sales were based on price wars. Both men advised against entering telecommunications. Burt McMurtry too recalled being quite skeptical of the plan, although he admitted, "Ken [Oshman] later claimed I was really enthusiastic."

Oshman was an independent thinker. In Maxfield's opinion, the more people told Oshman, "You're crazy," and backed it up with what he considered to be insufficient reasons, the more he became convinced *he* was right. Maxfield praised Oshman's tremendous confidence in his own ability to analyze and understand a situation: "He'd play devil's advocate on any opinion you expressed on any topic. It was his way of shaping his own thoughts." Oshman's confidence was exactly what the company needed to move forward. "Only with a high-risk venture like this did we stand a chance of hitting the ball out of the park," Maxfield said, "which is what made it all worthwhile for Ken."

## Engineering a CABX

Management did not want to risk spreading resources so thin that the thriving mil-spec business would be adversely impacted, so a mostly new team was recruited to prepare ROLM for the telecommunications arena. Jim Kasson headed the PBX engineering team, reporting to Maxfield. Steve Plant and Dave Ladd, a recent hire who had some Bell Labs experience, did software. Ken Lavezzo was in hardware, soon joined by John Edwards. Telephony engineer Sam Woods also joined the group.

The newest mil-spec central processor from the 1603 was repackaged for use as the brains of the PBX. The memory was based on brand-new semiconductor 4K (4,000-bit) memory chips from Intel and others, rather than on the magnetic core memory that mil-spec was using. Many other printed circuit boards (often called "cards") had to be designed. *Line cards* provided connection between the customer's telephones and the PBX, servicing eight phones per card. *Trunk cards* transmitted calls between the PBX and the central office, servicing four trunks each. These boards plugged into the CABX's digital backplane, along with associated digital converter cards, which passed the digitized voice through the system and also passed command and status signals between the CPU—the brain of the system—and the appropriate line, trunk, or application card, such as the tone generator and conference bridge. The CPU responded to commands transmitted up to it through the backplane, such as *Put this call on hold* or *Forward this call to extension 241*, and relayed the implementation of those commands down the backplane to the appropriate cards.

Assuring reliability was a major factor in designing a PBX, which was

Circuit boards (cards) slid into slots on the CBX cabinet shelves. One twisted pair of copper wire per phone went out the back of the cabinet and snaked through the walls to connect the phones. These five cabinets, part of a VLCBX, were in System Test prior to being shipped. The original CBX had up to three cabinets. Photo from ROLM 1980 Annual Report.

expected never to go down for more than a few minutes—because during those potentially crucial minutes, the business would have no telephone service at all. And the system was expected to have a useful life of twenty-five to forty years. On the other hand, mainframe computers, which businesses had the most experience with up to this point, were notoriously unreliable and might take a day or two to repair. The lifetime of a mainframe was perhaps five years. ROLM would have to overcome that generally negative perception of computers in order to succeed in telecommunications.

To assure telecom buyers of reliability, ROLM built redundancy into every corner of the system, including "hot standby" through redundant processors—one would instantly take over in case the other failed; a watch-dog timer to do cross-checks and automatically recover from minor system errors without human interface; self-diagnostics throughout so the system could detect and report the problems that required service; and a cassette tape containing the system program, so in case of a catastrophic failure, the program could be automatically reloaded to bring the system readily back to life. Full redundancy—two of everything—was a customer option that depended on the criticality of having phone service 24/7. Also, remote polling provided the ability to check the health of the system from a remote terminal every night, so the service company could be on the customer's doorstep first thing in the morning to swap out a board before the customer even noticed a problem. "All this sounds mundane now," Maxfield said much later, "but this was 1974. No company had ever attempted to provide this level of reliability in commercial digital systems."

Plant and Ladd designed and wrote the system's software, using assembly code, in just fifteen months. "I now realize that the task was near-impossible, but I didn't then," Kasson said in an email. "And more important, neither did they."

A telephone call was handled by the digital system in the following manner: An incoming call was transmitted as analog voice over a single pair of wires—the same pair of wires that transmitted electrical power to the phone—to the CABX. At the CABX interface, the signal was converted into digital form (data). In the CABX, that data moved through the digital backplane to the line card of the destination telephone, where it was converted back to analog form and transmitted to the appropriate extension telephone. The CPU executed the software programs that implemented commands, such as *Put this phone into do not disturb*. To prevent distortion in what the user heard, the engineering group decided that the voice would be sampled 12,000 times per second (12 kHz) and that each sample would be coded into 12 bits linearly, for 144 kilobits per second (kbps).

When that decision was made in 1974, components for 12-bit linear coding were far cheaper than components for 8 bits companded (simultaneously compressed and expanded data). The AT&T long-distance network was using 64 kbps (8 kHz x 8 bits companded, referred to as "8 by 8"), but there were few other applications. Using 12-bit coding, ROLM could claim that its transmission rate was faster than that of AT&T Long Lines, the subsidiary that handled long-distance calls. That sounded good—although, according to Kasson, it was actually "irrelevant." In ROLM's case, the data was just bouncing around short distances on the backplane, not miles across the nation. The 144-bit decision for the sake of cost control would later become the origin of intense cost and engineering issues.

The target market for the product was originally set at companies that needed between 80 and 400 lines. More in-depth market research, however, found that no company would install a 400-line telephone system

## Cost Impacts of the
## Telco Decision—Jim Kasson

Thanks to the help of a specialized telephony consultant, it became apparent that telcos had a specification that would require a technical change be made to the process of switching analog (continuous) signals to digital form (1s and 0s) and then reversing the process on the other end. The CBX used 12-bit resolution, allowing it to resolve small voltage differences to one part in 4,096 parts. The specs used by the operating companies for PBXs seemed to require that very small signals be quantized to one part in 8,192, implying a 13-bit converter. It seemed a technical impossibility to extend the analog-to-digital conversion precision by one bit.

After considerable effort, I devised a plan to inject a small, noisy signal of narrow spectrum into the analog-to-digital converter that would, on average, allow it to act as if it had

without expansion capability. When investing in a new system, most companies wanted twice the capacity of what was currently needed, pushing the desired product range to 800 lines.

ROLM's engineers soon discovered that increasing the system to 800 lines had significant cost ramifications. Handling more calls simultaneously required another cabinet, more memory on the control card, a faster clock, and—"much to the team's chagrin," admitted Kasson—a different cabling arrangement to go from shelf to shelf and cabinet to cabinet. Three cabinets were needed for 800 lines, rather than one or two for 100 to 500 greater resolution. This is now a common technique in audio recording, but at the time it was a major technological breakthrough. By the time the fix was invented and tested, and the patents were applied for, we'd lost a month on the PBX project.

The decision to distribute through telcos had another cost implication. I had hoped to have an elegant, all-solid-state design, using electronic components only and no transformers. Considerable time had been spent working on a transformerless telephone interface. Transformers were expensive and bulky, and their weight would impact the whole PBX design. However, solid-state devices were more electrically delicate, sensitive to power surges or reductions. The telcos required the flexibility of being able to install PBXs in locations that had power fluctuations and transmitted over outside lines, which meant transformers had to be used. A fully solid-state design was abandoned.

lines. The additional cabinet increased the distance over which the switching bus had to run, which meant the previously planned cable wouldn't allow telephone conversation signals to get from one end of the bus to the other in the necessary time. After a long search, an expensive ribbon cable was found, manufactured by W. L. Gore & Associates (the Gore-Tex company), that had a low enough dielectric constant to allow the signals to flow quickly.

Further cost impacts came from the marketing department's decision that ROLM's PBX would sell not only through interconnect distributors but also through non-AT&T telcos. Telcos had their own requirements of various sorts, which increased the cost of the baseline system.

The second risk identified at the onset of the project soon raised its head: Manufacturing cost estimates jumped 20 percent over original estimates. However, the costs of digital technology were decreasing dramatically. New technology companies were popping up at a fast pace, offering computers, components, and fabrication, and supporting all facets of the burgeoning electronics industry. Numerous venture capitalists competed to provide financial backing for these many high-risk start-ups and to participate in whatever financial success might result. Orchards were rapidly being bulldozed in favor of manufacturing, marketing, and headquarters facilities. "Silicon Valley" had arrived. The phrase, which referred to the silicon used in the manufacture of semiconductor chips, was first used in print in January 1971, when Don Hoeffler introduced a series of articles titled "Silicon Valley U.S.A." in the weekly publication *Electronic News*.[18] By the mid-1970s, the phrase was ubiquitous.

Being located right in the midst of all this action gave ROLM management the confidence that future component costs would rapidly decline, even as computing power increased. With management approval, ROLM went forward with the PBX product despite the higher cost, with the proviso that cost reduction over time was a top priority.

Once the development group got the dial tone connected, the "Time Lady" became an important member of the team. At the time, anyone could dial POPCORN (767-2676) within their own area code to get the exact time, day or night—a free service provided by the phone company. A female voice would answer: "The time is now ten thirty-six and forty seconds," with ten-second updates as long as you stayed on the line. Kasson and his team would call the service and put the call on hold, forward it to another phone in the lab, conference with their spouses at home. "The Time Lady tested all the features," Kasson confessed. "She worked hard, hours on end, and never complained. We couldn't have done it without her." Soon afterward, the phone company must have detected that some

# Impact of Cost-Cutting Decisions—Jim Kasson

The intense pressure to reduce manufacturing costs led to decisions that ROLM's engineering team would later regret. The RuggedNova machine, on which the CBX computer was based, used magnetic core random access memory (RAM). Core memory was reliable and had the great advantage of nonvolatility—you could power down a computer and when power came back, it could continue running without reloading the program. However, core memory was expensive, and it was clear that solid-state memory was the wave of the future. There were 1,024-bit chips available as the CBX design started, but 4,096-bit chips were expected to be shipping shortly before the CBX would need them. The larger chips cost less and used less power. Unfortunately, they also turned out to be unreliable. In retrospect, we should have made the initial shipments with core memory and switched over to semiconductor memory when its reliability was proven.

The other key cost-driven, questionable decision was the selection of the vendor for the power supplies. The team decided to go with the company that submitted the (by far) lowest bid. The power supplies proved to be sensitive to imperfections in the quality of power received from the main supply, which caused early system unreliability. After the problem was understood, most installations used external isolation transformers, at a cost greater than what we saved by going with that vendor. Within a few years, Gibson Anderson headed up a project to replace the power supplies with ones from Lorain, a well-known telephone industry vendor.

calls to the time line were taking far too long, and technology was used to automatically disconnect calls after a few seconds.

"Infant mortality" was a common problem with integrated circuits in those days—electronic components were likely to fail early or last long. Because of this, all systems were submitted to a "hot room" test, about 110 degrees F (43 degrees C) for ninety-six hours, both to test the design under conditions that might be encountered at the customer's site and to weed out weak parts. As component reliability improved, the test was reduced to twenty-four hours. "The hot room was a good way to encourage the ICs that were just days away from failure to fail on our site rather than the customers'," Kasson said.

## Preparing the Sales Side

While the engineering department was developing the product, and the manufacturing and testing folks were laying out plans, Dick Moley was preparing to sell and market the PBX. Launch was targeted for the ICA (International Communication Association) show in January 1975, mere months away.

Distributors were needed. ROLM would not sell direct through its own salespeople, as it did for the mil-spec products, but through established distribution channels. There was only one problem: There were no channels selling medium-to-large PBX systems to medium-to-large companies. Even the telephone companies, AT&T and GTE, weren't selling systems—they were leasing them to customers. Virtually all corporate phone systems were on lease contracts.

Moley had to figure out how to establish and train a distribution channel stocked with salespeople who had the gumption to tell the Sears headquarters telecommunications manager that there were very good reasons this new computer-controlled PBX from a little company in California warranted tossing out the archaic AT&T system—and doing that with an up-front purchase rather than a monthly rental.

Two or three large, national interconnect distributors and forty to fifty regional interconnects sold small systems (typically "key systems") to small companies. Moley thought ROLM would have more control of its business if it could sign up regional interconnect companies, rather than large national distributors, and help them be successful in their regions, selling to small, medium, and large organizations. He scrutinized the regional distributors, trying to discern which were financially solid and might be open to innovation. He selected seven that he felt had the potential to develop a sales force that could sell a fully digital system to a large customer and service it well. Each was invited to visit ROLM following the annual interconnect convention in November 1974 in San Francisco.

After signing a nondisclosure agreement, these interconnects got a preview of the new computer-based PBX with its sophisticated capabilities. Then they were told that they alone would be able to sell ROLM's PBX in their regions—a first in the industry. The interconnects generally sold systems based on price (a few tens of thousands of dollars) because the same brand could be acquired from another distributor in the region. Exclusivity meant improved profitability for the distributors.

They were told of the support they would receive from ROLM and the commitment they would have to make in return. Considerable emphasis was placed on sales training, a major key to success. Selling a ROLM system would require a more sophisticated approach—and ROLM would provide that training. The interconnects' existing sales force would be taught how to sell a system priced at hundreds of thousands, perhaps even a million, dollars. They would also learn how to justify that price based on the significant savings to be gained from solving the customer's major problems. "For large companies," said Moley, "long-distance charges were typically bigger than the monthly rental fee they paid AT&T for their system. We could prove they could save 30 to 40 percent on long-distance calls alone. The savings were huge."

ROLM had a spares program to offer the interconnects. Inventory for spares was an expensive investment for them, so instead inventory would be held at ROLM. Maxfield created a stocking algorithm that promised twenty-four-hour turnaround replacing failed cards.

Still, these small interconnect distributors would have to be brave to sign on as a ROLM distributor—they were going to meet AT&T head-on. To give them confidence when a large customer balked at dealing with them instead of giant AT&T, ROLM promised that in case the distributor went out of business, ROLM itself would step in to service the customer's system. In other words, the service would be handled by a tiny company in California that was new to the telecom industry and not much larger than the interconnect distributor itself. But the promise sounded powerful.

Moley designed a computer-based pricing program called Autoquote. Computer time-sharing was in use, so the interconnects all had access to the program. It was the first pricing program they'd ever seen. "They were blown away," Moley said. "Never had pricing been so easy."

And the result? All seven interconnects signed on as ROLM distributors. They were located in California; St. Louis; Richmond, Virginia; Columbus, Ohio; Manhattan and upstate New York; Boston; and Philadelphia. "They were dedicated to us right off the bat," said Moley. "We had their minds and their hearts." He hired Dave Sant as sales manager to take care of these first interconnect distributors and to sign up more interconnects and independent telcos. Sales training began immediately.

ROLM staffed to get the product out the door. Peter Welch headed documentation (installation, service, and user manuals). Frank Williams set up service, and Duncan MacMillan came in as the first product manager to work out future features and capabilities.

A lot of details had to be determined, including what color to paint the CBX cabinet exterior. The color schemes for computers and other electronics tended toward the boring. Some people at ROLM liked the touch of orange that Siemens had put on its calculator. So a ripe pumpkin color called Burnt Orange was selected for the doors and River Bottom Brown for the frame. "We were the new kid on the block," said MacMillan looking

## Autoquote—Ron Raffensperger

Autoquote was an important sales innovation. Using a program running on Tymshare, ROLM distributors could get a price to quote a customer configuration by using a terminal hooked up to a dial-up modem. This compared quite favorably with competitors' methods: very complicated configuration and pricing books. The first Autoquote was written in Basic by Dick Moley; then a student from Stanford's Earthquake Lab rewrote it into Fortran. I took it on in 1976. It grew into a large program that could price new sales, upgrades, and reconfigurations, using in-house computers. It kept going until 1995, when it was replaced by a suite of PC-based tools.

back, "and we wanted to be noticed." The orange was startling at a time when everything else was black or beige. "It really set us apart," said Bob Nugent, ROLM's first national accounts manager.

Next the product had to be named. ROLM had traditionally given insect code names to its development projects; the 1603 was Gnat. So the PBX became Spider, although the moniker was universally ignored. In practice, the project was simply called the CBX, for "computerized branch exchange." But CBX as a product name could not be trademarked. It was an abbreviation of a generic description, like saying "computerized automobile." Both Philco and Danray used the term *CBX* for their specialized analog computer-controlled PBXs, though neither product was more than a blip on the sales radar screen. ROLM's system was the first time-division multiplexed, pulse-code modulation PBX, but TDM-PCM-PBX did not roll trippingly off the tongue. It would only prompt the question "What the hell is that?"

The distinctive orange doors of the CBX—this one on the shipping dock in 1978—became a ROLM trademark amid the gray and black of other electronic equipment. Photo courtesy of Evelyn Cosakos.

Dick Moley was unperturbed that the term *CBX* could not be trademarked. He figured it wouldn't be long before the marketplace associated CBX capability exclusively with ROLM anyway. And slapping the word *computer* right up front capitalized on the fact that ROLM was already a credible computer company. The product was christened the CBX, untrademarked.

Now it was time to consider how best to introduce the CBX to potential customers. Many companies, small and large—including metal fabricators, plastic molders, general contractors, specialists capable of building semiconductor manufacturing "clean rooms," travel agents, and legal firms—had been established to support the growth of Silicon Valley and its products. In the fall of 1974, Moley selected advertising agency Standbro Drummond, which had sprung up specifically to help tech companies spread their messages. ROLM was the first account for Standbro Drummond's Bruce Skillings, recently out of college. When he presented a draft of the first CBX brochure, it looked nothing like the typical dry columns of text and industrial-looking black-and-white product shots of traditional telecommunications materials. This brochure had a dreamy, romantic quality; the color photographs had soft edges and overlapped. The text was slick, Madison Avenue style. Sentence fragments everywhere.

There were single-sentence paragraphs.

And, heaven forbid, one of them started with a conjunction.

ROLM management was appalled. The prose was punchy and effective, but it made ROLM look "unschooled." Bob Maxfield took the draft home to his wife, who had taught high school English before their daughters were born. She blue-penciled it into a semblance of grammatical rectitude. The ad agency was not amused, but a compromise was reached. And ROLM became accepting of sentences starting with conjunctions. Even sentence fragments.

Skillings caught a red-eye to Chicago—the first business trip of his career—for an early-morning meeting to convince *Telephony* to make the ROLM CBX the cover story of its ICA issue. The magazine was days away from deadline.

## Inflict It on Ourselves First

The CBX was ready for live test by late 1974, but phone systems were a company's life support, and a lot could go wrong. "We didn't dare risk having a customer out there who could tell the press how miserable they were," confessed Maxfield. So they tested it in-house. AT&T was told to come remove its system from ROLM, which took them days to do. The CBX was installed in a few hours.

> *"We didn't dare risk having a customer out there who could tell the press how miserable they were."*— Bob Maxfield

Chaos reigned as the infant CBX failed, dropped calls, and hissed on the line. Leo Chamberlain, ROLM's new VP of marketing, attended a meeting in Ken Oshman's office during which he alone seemed to hear continuous, muted ringing. He wondered if he was going crazy. When he asked if anyone else heard it, Oshman opened a bottom desk drawer and pulled out his phone, smothered in a towel. "I had to stick it in there," he said. "The damn thing won't stop ringing." If nothing else, Moley pointed

# The Leap to ROLM—Leo Chamberlain

I had been sales manager of General Radio Company and was president of its Time/Data subsidiary when I interviewed with Ken Oshman for the role of VP of marketing. He had not yet mentioned stock options, so I used the standard two-question, "take a pick" technique: "Since the *R* in ROLM is no longer here, how would you feel about changing the name to CHOLM?"

Ken sat flabbergasted, of course.

"Well, OK," I said, "then how about stock options?"

He was happy to comply.

At forty-four, I was about ten years older than anyone else at ROLM. I figured I was hired because the company needed a seasoned manager, someone with gray hair. I was so grateful to have such a fun, interesting job compared to the previous drudgery that I sent Ken a humorous thank-you note every week for the first two months.

out, inflicting it first on themselves certainly motivated the engineers to solve problems.

Service and manufacturing plans for the CBX continued apace with marketing and development. Dennis Paboojian, VP manufacturing, laid plans for a new manufacturing line that was very different from the manufacturing process for Mil-Spec's computers. He hired Larry Schmeir from Time/Data (a General Radio Company subsidiary) to head up systems testing. Schmeir spent long hours in the development lab, helping the engineers check out their designs and learning the system so his test group would be able to hit the ground running once manufacturing got under way. Roger Hillsman was responsible for circuit board testing. He gained management approval to build a tester to avoid buying HP's $100,000 device. The tool, which became known as "Roger's tester," was balky and late, but effective. Dave Sederquist, who ran production engineering, often suggested design changes to make the product easier or less expensive to build.

Just as the engineering and marketing kinks of ROLM's new product line were smoothing out, and just prior to introduction, the company received a legislative signal that reinforced its decision to enter the telecommunications market. In late 1974 the U.S. Justice Department filed an antitrust suit, *United States vs. AT&T*, posing the astonishing possibility that the world's largest company would have to divest itself of at least some of its dozens of subsidiaries. A 1974 ROLM business plan summarized the PBX market situation:

> We believe that the structural changes in the Telecommunications Industry brought about by the Carterfone Decision are likely to be accelerated by the recent court action . . . At the same time . . . advances in solid-state technology have made it possible to design and manufacture a computer-controlled TDM (time-division multiplex) PABX at a cost which is competitive with traditional electromechanical systems. This has the effect of changing the nature of PABX manufacture from a capital- and labor-intensive operation to a technology-intensive electronic assembly operation, and of requiring the manufacturer to have mini-computer, software, and solid-state switching expertise— technologies in which ROLM has demonstrated significant strength . . . We are convinced that the tremendous flexibility of

a computer-controlled PABX will change the economics of business communication systems' installation, maintenance, and operation, besides providing exceptional convenience of use.

The new product line was disclosed in a letter Oshman wrote to ROLM's few shareholders, many of whom were employees: "In an effort to diversify and expand our product and marketplace, the last fiscal year saw additional investment in a new product for the telecommunications marketplace. This product will be announced in 1975." The press was not monitoring privately held little ROLM Corporation, and the CBX development proceeded quietly.

## Mil-Spec Holds Steady

Meanwhile, ROLM revenue for fiscal 1974 was $6 million, all from mil-spec computers—up 67 percent over 1973—with net income of $481,000. ROLM had almost 200 employees. This growth had occurred despite the shock of OPEC's oil embargo from October 1973 to March 1974, which posed a major threat to the U.S. economy. The stock market was a disaster: From a Dow peak of 1,051 in 1972, half the value was lost at the bottom of 577 in December 1974 (compared to 15,000 in 2013). In his shareholder letter, Oshman commented, "The Company ended the year in an extremely strong financial position." A bank line of credit for $1.5 million provided backup funds if needed.

Not all of ROLM's corporate investment was being directed toward the new product line. Substantial investment also went into Mil-Spec's computer business during the fiscal year. The 1602 had been further enhanced, and spring 1974 saw the release of the RuggedNova 1603, engineered by digital designer Stan Tenold, who had joined ROLM in 1972 straight out of Stanford's Master of Science in Electrical Engineering program. The 1603 was a lower-cost, souped-up, higher-speed version of the 1601, with new-generation compact hardware that permitted a reduction from five to four cards for the CPU. It was the first mil-spec mini-computer in the industry priced under $10,000, at $9,950 (over $55,000 in 2013), and was designed for navigation, radar homing and warning, and fly-by-wire computations.

ROLM was heartened to see the first article featuring the company appear in a major industry magazine: in *Aviation Week* in August 1974, following the introduction of the 1603: "ROLM develops standard products with its own funds and sells them from published price lists—at prices significantly below those of competing militarized computers." The article pointed out that the new 1603 offered three times the speed of the 1601—at half the cost. "ROLM provides what it believes to be the most extensive library of software routines available for mil-spec."[19]

The 1603 was forecast to sell quite well. Pat Groves, a Rice graduate and computer product manager who reported to Tony Gerber, attended an operations meeting where Dennis Paboojian told Oshman, "You know, Ken, the problem with this forecast is that if it comes true, Ray Thompson [a top salesman] is going to make more money than you next year."

Oshman replied, "That's just the way I'd like to see it."

ROLM's mil-spec computers were being purchased in large and small quantities. Typically they were bought by governments or governments' prime contractors to become part of a much larger defense system. Individual units or small quantities were used as programming stations or prototypes during the R&D phase. A small percentage of R&D projects would progress into actual production, when larger quantities were needed. The lead time from R&D to production could be three to four years.

The Army Security Agency had already standardized on the 1602, declaring the product was the solution for all its computer needs—which assuaged Oshman's fear that non-ROLM products would become the standard. The 1602 eventually was used in electronic warfare suites for most ships of the U.S. Navy as well, in spite of the Navy's earlier standardization on the Sperry Univac computer.

ROLM mil-spec products were also in use in a number of U.S. Army electronic warfare programs: helicopter-borne radar jamming, ground-based radar locating/identifying, ground-based communication transmitter locating, ground-based communications jamming, and airborne communications intelligence collection. ROLM's mil-spec products had gained a solid reputation for reliability, cost-effectiveness, and leading-edge technology. ROLM's first overseas office was opened in Germany, a critical location for the West during the Cold War.

Mil-Spec's operating profits had funded the company's entry into telecommunications. In fiscal 1975, all but 1 percent of ROLM's $10 million of revenue came from mil-spec sales. Revenue grew 70 percent over 1974, with earnings up 16 percent, to $575,000. Mil-Spec had already hit the $10 million threshold that Oshman figured was its cap. When the Vietnam War ended in April 1975, it became clear that the total defense budget would decline. Still, the prospects for ROLM were good: A higher percentage of the budget would be directed at development of sophisticated weapons for use in the Cold War.

ROLM's stock, still privately held, split three-for-one in October 1974. Maxfield recalled that the purpose of the split was psychological. "Stock options were a major hiring carrot," he explained. "Offering three hundred shares seems like a lot more than one hundred, even though the percentage of company ownership is the same. We had to hire a lot of good people to ramp up the CBX." ROLM would need every last hand on deck if it was going to make an impact in that huge telecommunications market.

# CHAPTER 4

# BATTLING A GIANT

..................

Alexander Graham Bell invented the telephone in 1876, and in 1878 he set up the first telephone service, in New Haven, Connecticut. By 1884, long-distance connections existed between Boston and New York and would soon spread worldwide. The ramifications were beyond imagination at the time. Nearly a century later, ROLM Corporation launched a revolution of its own, in corporate telecommunications, when it unveiled the ROLM CBX at the International Communication Association conference in January 1975.

## A New World of Capability

*Telephony* magazine understood the impact—its ICA issue featured the orange cabinet on the cover, with a lengthy article inside. "The CBX had personality," said adman Bruce Skillings. "It was so much more photogenic than anything else out there—all those other grey and black boxes." And it opened a whole new world of cost control and capability that U.S. businesses had never imagined possible. The CBX introduced what would later be called "disruptive technology," overturning a market that for many years had been in stasis.

Danray threatened to sue, furious that ROLM had "stolen" the name CBX. ROLM's response was, "Go ahead. You won't get far. You can't trademark it any more than we can." Danray soon disappeared from the telecommunications marketplace, and ROLM "owned" the CBX name.

Half of all U.S. companies at the time had between 100 and 800 employees, each with a telephone served by a PBX—exactly the target market of the CBX. Many of these companies were on the Fortune 500 list—the 500 largest U.S. corporations by revenue. These sophisticated customers would readily understand the benefits of the new computer technology. The CBX features and speed of operation would improve employee productivity and customer satisfaction. Companies would welcome the ability to easily and inexpensively change the system as employees were transferred to another department or as new hires or layoffs were implemented. Using the cheapest option for long-distance calls and printing reports that showed line and trunk usage would facilitate cost control.

Since many of these large corporations had multiple locations, ROLM could sell the top decision-maker at headquarters and subsequently install systems at the company's facilities throughout the United States. The CBX was priced higher than the industry standard—AT&T's old electromechanical switch—but the seven interconnect distributors had been trained to sell the system's lifetime benefits, which more than offset the initial investment.

The CBX's sleek, sophisticated attendant's console (ATC) replaced many archaic switchboards. Its ergonomic design facilitated learning and use. Calls were processed quickly, thanks to the CBX's computer control. Ken Lavezzo designed the ATC hardware, and Dave Ladd did the software. They used common sense to work through the logic of all the possible demands that callers would place on a switchboard attendant.

But they hadn't thought through possible interference that could come from other nearby equipment. A Sears store in southern California sent several consoles back to the factory with inexplicably blown circuits. Larry Gary, a field service engineer in Santa Clara at the time, flew to Los Angeles to visit the site. He saw that when the attendant sat down to work, she pulled out a huge old mechanical adding machine and plugged it into the same wall socket from which the console received its AC power. The console's lights flickered and went out—dead. An external RFI protector was immediately added to all consoles and later incorporated internally.

An early problem developed with the console's lights. The console used a backlit display with multiple segments to indicate the status of a call, such as *on hold* or *ringing at an extension.* Each segment was lit by an incandescent light that was positioned beneath the display panel. An egg-crate-like device was glued in place beneath the display so each segment's light did not diffuse to other segments. But after the console had been in use for many hours

For many companies, the CBX attendant's console replaced a switchboard. Most attendants used plug-in headsets rather than the handset. Photo from ROLM Corp. SEC S-1 Registration Statement, August 9, 1976.

and had heated up, the glue loosened and the egg crate dropped, so it appeared that too many segments were lit simultaneously. Consoles had to return to ROLM Service for application of new, improved glue.

The ATC keyboard's many unique audible clicks and key layout turned out to facilitate use by people who were blind. Many CBX customers began hiring the handicapped, an unexpected social and public relations benefit. ROLM's own blind attendant recognized most callers' voices after the first phone call and greeted them by name for the many years she worked at headquarters.

After a CBX was installed, employees' telephones typically remained unchanged, except for one simple thing that brought a world of capability to their fingertips—a paper overlay faceplate. The push-button phone with its 12-button key pad had had a startling introduction at the 1963 Seattle World's Fair and within ten years had replaced almost all rotary dial phones, though the phrase *dial a number* still remains in use. Each phone on a CBX system received a template overlay that gave users easy access to features, such as dialing * and then 7 to transfer a call. At last, the baffling star and pound keys had a function. Other key combinations would assign a distinct ringtone to distinguish which phone was ringing, provide

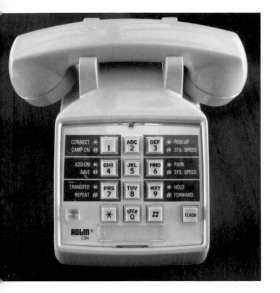

Phones on a CBX system had a faceplate that made features easy to use, such as *7 to transfer a call. This Flashphone, introduced in 1979, had a "flash" button on the bottom right that enabled the user to automatically put the call on hold to answer an in-coming call. Photo courtesy of Bob Maxfield.

speed dial of frequently called numbers, or put the phone into *do not disturb* mode so ringing would not interrupt the user's work. Twelve features were made apparent by the faceplate; many more were spelled out in the CBX user's manual.

Moving an employee's extension number from one location to another, or adding or eliminating a phone or extension, was merely a matter of typing a software command into the CBX control terminal; this made moves and changes within a company easy and inexpensive. AT&T and other electromechanical systems had phones hardwired in place, often linked to the system with huge, heavy cables consisting of sixty-four pairs of wires strung all over the building. The ROLM CBX required only one pair of wires per telephone, resulting in enormous savings in wiring and labor.

Each phone's extension number was its identifier in CBX software. Each extension could be configured to permit or block capabilities. This was particularly significant in saving on long-distance call charges. Phones located in lobbies were vulnerable to unauthorized use, as visitors waiting for appointments sometimes made long-distance calls at the peak billing hours, 8:00 a.m. to 5:00 p.m. on weekdays. Phones there or, say, in the open manufacturing area could be configured to block long-distance calls. Or phones could be configured to permit only calls within the company—no outside calls at all.

Thanks to faster processing of calls and to various features, such as the transfer of a call directly to another person within the company (without having to go back to the operator), companies saw their customer satisfaction increase. Telephone users' productivity increased as the phone became a tool to help get the job done, especially with such features as *do not disturb* and *call forward*, which allowed employees to forward calls to another extension when they worked temporarily in another office.

Another CBX capability, called Least Cost Routing, slashed companies' phone bills. Approximately 75 percent of a typical company's telephone costs went toward local and long-distance calls. When an employee using an AT&T system dialed a long-distance phone number, the call would be routed through AT&T Long Lines—which had higher rates than alternatives such as FX (foreign exchange lines), tie lines, or WATS (wide-area telephone service)—and later through MCI, Sprint, or one of many other providers. Companies that used alternatives to AT&T Long Lines, in an attempt to save money, provided employees with long routing codes to dial before dialing the desired phone number. Different cities required different routing codes. Employees found the process irritating. Without any record of who called where and when, there were no ramifications of ignoring management's instructions and just dialing the phone number, thus putting the call out over the most expensive provider, AT&T Long Lines. But the CBX's computer would automatically select the cheapest route depending on the location dialed and the time of day. All the employee had to do was dial 9 and the long-distance phone number.

*"If I'd known at the beginning everything the CBX was going to have to do, I would have called the project impossible. But every time a new requirement came along, we swallowed hard and figured out a way to make it happen."—Jim Kasson*

A function known as call detail recording provided reports on which extensions made which calls, when, and for how long. For the first time, telecommunications managers could find out exactly where their phone usage costs were going. Departments could be charged for their own expenses. Law offices could allocate phone bills to customers, with recorded proof of when each call was made and how long it lasted.

Each phone in the company could be configured for a specific level of service. Long-distance calls dialed on phones designated as "executive" would go out immediately, even if that meant routing the call through the most expensive alternative. Phone users assigned a lower class of service might find that long-distance calls would sometimes receive a "fast busy" signal, indicating that the cheapest long-distance trunks were filled to capacity at the moment. The system would ring the user back as soon as capacity opened up and would then automatically redial the long-distance number.

The CBX's management features shook up telecommunications managers' notions of their realm of responsibility. Companies gained the revolutionary capability of managing a major system investment—staying informed of how that system was being used and where the dollars were being spent. The system could be configured to produce the most productive, cost-effective result. In effect, the ROLM CBX participated in corporate America's first steps into information management and information technology (IT).

Thanks to the immense changes brought about by computer technology, many more facets of IT soon, or simultaneously, appeared in manufacturing systems, human resources data, and sales systems—transforming all these and more corporate functions. ROLM rode this vast wave of change and was the first company to present the opportunity for corporate telecommunications departments to gain control of voice communications, applications, and expenses.

These capabilities were not all present with the first CBX in 1975, but

## Tales from the Field—
## Solomon Wu and Don Armstrong

(Solomon Wu, engineering manager)

Early CBX installations gave some customers their first-ever experience with electronic equipment. In the days before hard drives, the system configuration and call detail records were recorded on cassette tapes, and later on floppy disks. Disks particularly seemed to baffle customers. When asked to ship the floppy back to Santa Clara to be checked out, one customer folded it up and stuffed it into a regular envelope. Another customer, when asked to mail back a copy of the disc, photocopied it and sent the paper copy.

(Don Armstrong, technical support)

Here's another floppy disk story—a customer kept complaining that his CBX floppy disks had a very short shelf life. When I went to check out the problem, I found the disks attached to the CBX's steel cabinet with a big horseshoe magnet strong enough to grip the floppies. The problem cleared up after I explained that magnets erase the data from the floppies.

were rolled out with software releases over the next two years. Kasson took this bit of reality in stride, saying, "It's better not to know some things. If I'd known at the beginning everything the CBX was going to have to do, I would have called the project impossible and never signed up." Every time a new requirement came along, the development team swallowed hard and figured out a way to make it happen. Kasson felt ROLM had asked its engineers to come up with ten times the productivity that had been the standard at HP—and the core group delivered. Having a team that was "way too small" meant they spent far less time coordinating with one another than if one hundred engineers had been working on the project.

Part of the initial sales pitch to prospects was that more features would be available in the future and those features could be easily incorporated into their system by means of a simple software upgrade. This demonstrated the vast capability and flexibility of computer technology. It could grow and change after installation, quite unlike electromechanical systems. This adaptability took the telecommunications industry by surprise.

Many customers, like Shell Oil and Montgomery Ward, selected the ROLM CBX because of its flexibility and manageability. Tyson Foods of Springdale, Arkansas, had additional reasons: The CBX, significantly smaller than the company's old electromechanical system, saved on office space, and the sleek new console eliminated its old plug-in switchboard.[20] ROLM's message to the telecom community at large was: *Welcome to the digital age—a whole new world of capability.*

## The Field Is on Fire

The first system shipped in April 1975, eighteen months after the ROLM board approved diversification into telecommunications. Product development had cost $1 million ($4.6 million in 2013). Ken Oshman remarked in a taped interview that a large Canadian company that had been given a nondisclosure preview had said it couldn't be done for less than $80 million. "They were wrong," he said. "It was just a matter of being willing to take risks and figure out what to do."[21]

The second software release adding capability came out in early 1976. The upgrade was free for the fifty systems that had been installed. Soon after the upgrades, system failures started popping up. Some were catastrophic—the system stopped cold, shutting down phone service—while others were random, momentary shutdowns.

Oshman received almost daily calls from irate customers, one saying he was calling from a payphone because his CBX was dead. Another said he was going to put his CBX out on the street with a *Junk* sign on it.

"The field was on fire," said Maxfield years later. "We were just getting a foothold in this business, and suddenly we were on the brink of disaster." To stabilize systems experiencing catastrophic failures, the software upgrade was pulled and the old software reinstalled. Simply providing dial tone took precedent over any other CBX capability or feature.

ROLM engineers jumped on the problem. The culprit turned out to be the semiconductor industry's new 4,096-bit dynamic RAM chips, produced by Intel and Texas Instruments, that had become available just months before the first CBX shipment and were incorporated into the system. The original software was stable—until the upgrade was installed.

Software programs consist of precise sequences of 1s and 0s, each called a "bit." A random change to any bit can cause serious problems. Some of these new RAM chips had a few defective bit locations in which a 1 would inexplicably and randomly flip to a 0 (but not vice versa) after a short time. If the upgrade had put a 1 into a defective location that had been a 0, that minute change could cause a stable system to fail. The failure could appear in seemingly unrelated ways: an inappropriate response to a command, no response to the command at all, or a total system failure. That inconsistency—where would the failure manifest, and how?—made the problem very difficult to diagnose.

Unfortunately, ROLM was among the first in the world to discover the phenomenon of soft memory errors in early dynamic RAMs. The semiconductor companies denied the problem at first, according to Maxfield. Then they too began seeing it, but ROLM didn't have time to sit back and wait until they came up with a fix. "This was just one of many products for them," Maxfield said. "For us, it was the company."

## *"This was just one of many products for [the semiconductor manufacturers]. For us, it was the company."*— Bob Maxfield

New CBXs, after extensive factory testing to replace chips that did not function correctly with the system software, continued to ship and operate reliably, provided the software was not upgraded in the field. But software upgrades that delivered new or competitive capability were critical to the CBX strategy. ROLM decided that it could not afford to second-guess how long the semiconductor companies might take to find a fix to the problem. ROLM had to deliver a solution quickly, which meant it had to redesign the memory system to add error-correction logic—the ability to automatically detect and repair bit errors. It was an expensive, urgent development effort.

Hardware engineer John Edwards led the memory redesign. Gibson Anderson jumped over from Mil-Spec to help out. No expense was spared. Oshman held ad hoc meetings two or three times a day in his office. When a new PC board layout was needed, two parallel efforts were started and the one that finished first was used. Anderson's first prototype memory controller worked at turn-on, which almost never happens. He was particularly delighted because it was the first digital logic design he had done in years. Oshman, focused on expediency, was less enthusiastic: "Then you probably spent too much time designing it."

Anderson later recalled being speechless: "Probably twenty years went by before I could see his point of view."

Nine months lapsed between problem detection and final solution. A number of other early problems needed to be fixed, like power supplies and software bugs, though none nearly as catastrophic as the memory issue. All the fixes were tossed into one upgrade program.

By then more than one hundred installed systems needed to be addressed. Maxfield later admitted, "The situation was a very serious threat to our survival in the telecom industry." ROLM sent a tiger team into the field to upgrade the whole installed base, and extended the system warranties. The company did everything it could to rebuild its customers' confidence, and in the end, ROLM's responsiveness gained their respect. Its distributors too gained confidence that when things went wrong, ROLM would make them right.

## First Let's Kill Competition

Until ROLM launched itself into the arena, AT&T and, to a much smaller extent, GTE had controlled the PBX business. AT&T was the world's largest corporation. With almost a million employees, it had a larger workforce than any other U.S. employer except the government.[22] Fiscal year 1978 revenue was $3.4 billion from twenty-three operating companies. Its local telephone companies—New England Telephone & Telegraph, Pacific Bell—provided local phone service to 90 percent of the nation. Revenue also came from AT&T's Western Electric manufacturing company, which independently was the nation's eighteenth-largest industrial firm.[23] AT&T's Long Lines division reaped profits from handling almost the entire nation's long-distance calls. Its Bell Labs, one of the world's largest, most respected research institutions, in Murray Hill, New Jersey, held thousands of patents.[24] AT&T had controlled the telecommunications departments of the Fortune 500 companies for fifty years. ROLM had $10 million in revenue and just under two hundred employees. It controlled nothing. The magnitude of the David-versus-Goliath challenge suited Oshman to a tee.

AT&T had no new-technology PBX with which to compete immediately, only its old electromechanical standby. It used digital switching in many of its central offices, of which there were thousands all over the

United States, processing calls as they transited around the nation and beyond. A digital PBX was under development at Bell Labs, but there was no plan to turn this technology into a PBX product for perhaps five more years.

Because AT&T could not immediately compete on product, technology, capability, or manageability, it fought every way it could. Not only was it losing PBX sales, but interconnect telephones and equipment of all kinds were replacing AT&T products more and more often in the millions of U.S. offices and homes of customers that AT&T had assumed it had securely in hand.

Being a monopolist, AT&T had options no company in a competitive market could employ. So it launched a legislative battle against competition, despite the antitrust suit filed against it by the U.S. Justice Department just one year prior. With a million employees and three million shareholders, AT&T had constituents in all congressional districts. When AT&T lobbied senators and congressmen, they listened.

A bill that AT&T had essentially drafted, called the Consumer Communications Reform Act of 1976 and intended to override the *Carterfone* decision of 1968, was introduced in the House of Representatives. This proposed law would made it illegal for ROLM to offer its CBX, and for any other company to manufacture and sell telecommunications equipment that hooked up to AT&T's or any other telco's telephone lines. When the bill was introduced, it had several hundred congressional sponsors, all demonstrating that they would protect the interests of AT&T stakeholders in their districts.

In hopes of blocking approval of the bill, ROLM and other new equipment manufacturers joined forces to educate Congress on the value of competition and innovation. Walter Loewenstern, ROLM's man in Washington, met with a congressman from Southern California who was on the House Telecommunications Committee. He explained that a monopoly could cross-subsidize whatever it wanted to shut out competition, inhibiting technological progress, innovation, and improved service. The congressman replied, "AT&T usually provides someone for my re-election committee and puts an executive on the Telecom Committee. These folks are my friends. I don't see any need to interfere with their business."

Nonetheless, the bill failed by a narrow margin. ROLM breathed a huge sigh of relief and stuck to implementing its CBX business plan. The uncertainty of legislative action, however, discouraged some large companies, such as IBM, from entering the PBX market. ROLM had only one giant to fight—for the moment.

AT&T turned to an age-old competitive measure: slashing its prices. It could even offer PBXs below cost by subsidizing that part of the business with its highly profitable long-distance and local telephone service. The reduced revenue and profit had little impact on its enormous bottom line. "AT&T could subsidize whatever it wanted to," pointed out Maxfield. "It was a monopoly."

⏻

### "AT&T could subsidize whatever it wanted to. It was a monopoly."— Bob Maxfield

This move by AT&T stretched out ROLM's CBX payback period. "We had to compare our pricing to their new, lower pricing," explained Maxfield. "So we made our sales pitch even more sophisticated." ROLM began promising that a digital switch could always be upgraded to whatever new capability might come down the road. Maxfield summed up the company's approach: "With an AT&T system, you were locked in the past. When you bought a ROLM CBX, you bought the future."

## The Black Box

Soon after the Carterfone decision, AT&T had claimed that interconnected equipment would damage the telephone network and cause deteriorated phone service or even a full network crash. The company went into action at the state level. Each AT&T subsidiary, such as Pacific Bell in California, bombarded its state's public utility commission (PUC), which regulated telephone service as a utility, for approval of a measure requiring every non-AT&T piece of equipment to have an AT&T-provided "network protector" coupled to it. No evidence ever surfaced that any damage had occurred, yet the PUCs in every state in the union appeased Ma Bell. The device was a little black box (called a CDH, in the case of a PBX) that consisted of a few resistors and capacitors, costing a few dollars to make. The local phone company charged all its customers who installed non-AT&T equipment a monthly rental fee of between $5 and $50 for each black box, whether for a business or a residence.

"It was a sham," said Maxfield. "It cheated every customer for years. The phone company charged whatever rental fee each state's PUC could be talked into permitting. It was basically the customer's fine for choosing to install non-AT&T equipment."

ROLM was barred by law from touching AT&T equipment on the customer premises. When a CDH failed, ROLM service techs were called in, but when tests showed no problem on the ROLM side, they had to call AT&T for service. And AT&T customer service was notoriously unresponsive. At times ROLM techs had to wait on-site a full day before someone showed up to service or replace a $3 piece of equipment.

## The Giant's Service Philosophy: "We Don't Care"

Comedienne Lily Tomlin famously and repeatedly parodied AT&T service on the wildly popular television comedy *Laugh-In*. Ernestine, Tomlin's phone company operator, would answer a service call: "A-one-ringy-dingy, a-two-ringy-dingy. Hello?" She would roll her eyes in boredom and exasperation while listening to an apparently raging customer, then say, "Sir, we're the phone company. We don't care. We don't have to." Then she'd hang up and look quite satisfied. Posters and bumper stickers showed up everywhere with the Bell insignia and the words *We don't care. We don't have to.*

Bell-bashing was a major theme of the first few years of ROLM's CBX advertising campaigns. According to Bruce Skillings, no one at ROLM said, "We can't do that."

This bumper sticker publicized what seemed to be the monopoly's service philosophy. Photo courtesy of Bob Maxfield.

Instead, they said, "Let's try it. How do we get it done?" One ad that read *Does Your PBX Work Like This?* showed an old AT&T pay phone with piles of coins to pump into it. "There were no holds barred," said Skillings. "It was very edgy stuff for the time." Some later ads depicted AT&T as a big blue dinosaur or the Trojan horse. ROLM won many awards for its ads, including the Association of American Advertising Agencies' gold award for creativity for the first year's campaign. "ROLM humanizes telecommunications with humorous yet informative cartoon ads," said *Computer & Electronics Marketing.*[25]

Many customers remained wary of buying anything but AT&T products, despite bad service and outdated equipment. The black box requirement fomented the fear that telephone service would worsen. Some customers even feared that AT&T would retaliate against them by providing especially poor phone service, Maxfield recalled.

ROLM underestimated the reluctance, even fear, businesses felt about the prospect of turning their backs on AT&T. ROLM had to assure them that because the system was digital and offered total redundancy, it would reduce their phone bills, provide better service and care, and be more reliable. Not only that, but ROLM had to provide impeccable references—other companies that could verify its claims of cost savings and functional benefits. Maxfield described the pressure the people in field sales and service were under: "Our interconnect distributors were on the firing line daily."

## Obstructive Delays

AT&T employed even dirtier tricks in the field. The bulk of ROLM's early customers were new businesses going into new facilities or existing businesses that had outgrown their inflexible old systems. Almost all ROLM installations required that AT&T first install new telephone trunks—cables from the central office that provided multiple incoming phone lines for service. A local AT&T subsidiary, such as Bell Atlantic, would often make and break repeated installation appointments. Dial tone service for many ROLM systems was painfully delayed.

## *"AT&T couldn't compete on product, so they fought whatever dirty way they could."* *— Bob Maxfield*

Charles (Bubba) Yates, a high school friend of Ken Oshman, experienced this tactic firsthand. ROLM installed the CBX in Yates's new medical complex in Houston in mid-December 1976. As the year ticked toward its close, AT&T had still not provided dial tone. Yates called Oshman to complain. Oshman knew that Texas law, like most states, required utilities, including phone companies, to treat loss of service to medical facilities as an emergency. He called the Texas legislator from his hometown and convinced him to invoke the law. "I think Ken actually called the president of AT&T at home," Yates said in an email. "Two truckloads of the most pissed-off AT&T employees and one truckload of equally tempered ROLM techs spent New Year's Eve in our facility." ROLM's head of Houston service later called Yates and asked that he please complain directly to him in the future.

These tedious battles were fought with almost every system ROLM sold in the first few years. "AT&T couldn't compete on product," Maxfield said, "so they fought whatever dirty way they could."

In at least one case, the saboteur was an AT&T fanatic within the customer's company. In 1976, ADP (Automatic Data Processing, Inc.)

in Clifton, New Jersey, installed a CBX. For weeks afterward, however, incoming calls randomly went elsewhere, such as to the local time and weather recording. Larry Gary, then a field service engineer in Santa Clara, caught a red-eye for an early meeting at ADP. Gary was in an ADP conference room with the corporate telecommunications manager and two Bell Atlantic vice presidents when the tech for the interconnect company that had sold and installed the system came in. Just moments prior, he'd been working, unnoticed, in the back of the console room when he overheard ADP's chief telephone operator instruct the attendants who worked the consoles to randomly forward calls to various off-site phone numbers. The woman had vehemently opposed the ROLM purchase and was determined to see it pulled. She was fired and the CBX hummed along after that.

"It was an uphill battle every step of the way in those early days," said Maxfield.

## More Distributors, More Funds

Despite the abundant obstacles, enough companies selected the CBX as their telecommunications solution that ROLM expanded into other geographic areas, selecting the best independent distributor in each major U.S. city.

Norstan Communications signed up as a ROLM distributor in late 1975 because the CBX was the leading-edge product—"the greatest thing since sliced bread," said Paul Baszucki, cofounder (with Sid Cohen) and former chairman of Norstan. For the next fifteen years, Norstan focused on selling ROLM products within its market: Minnesota, Wisconsin, Iowa, and Nebraska. Because of the annual sales meetings, distributors like Norstan got to know ROLM execs—Oshman, Maxfield, Dick Moley—personally. "The company was a first-class operation," said Baszucki. "It was a prosperous and pleasant relationship."

ROLM's distributor meetings, held in sunny locales like Hawaii and the Caribbean, featured distinguished speakers. One was "ROLM's own" astronaut, Jim Lovell, who was CEO of Fisk Telephone Systems, the CBX distributor in Houston. Many ROLMans still remember the talk he gave about his harrowing experience trying to bring the hobbled Apollo 13 spacecraft safely back into Earth's atmosphere in 1970. Michael Davis, a Fisk technician who installed and serviced ten of the first twenty CBX systems sold in the country, said in an email in 2013, "We received stellar support from ROLM, and we certainly needed it."

ROLM obtained its second round of venture capital, raising $1 million, in August 1975 by selling 80,000 shares at $12.50 each to Burt McMurtry's Institutional Venture Associates (IVA). ROLM's stock split again in August 1976, this time two for one. Each of the five founding shareholders now had six times the number of shares they started with. The funds were needed for the ramp-up of CBX manufacturing.

In 1973 McMurtry had left Melchor's Palo Alto Investment Company, which over subsequent years was an active seed venture investor in more than one hundred companies in the Bay Area, including 3Com, Software Publishing, Triad Systems, The Learning Company—and of course, ROLM. McMurtry joined with Reid Dennis to start their own VC company, IVA. In 1974, they successfully raised their first fund of $19 million, with $5 million from American Express and $14 million from six other investors. IVA's fund represented about one-eighth of the $150 million raised by all private venture funds that year, a boom compared to the $22 million raised the year before. The economy was so bad that IVA had held off making any investment for fifteen months. ROLM was its first. McMurtry was pleased to back the company founded by guys he'd believed in since they'd graduated from Rice. McMurtry became a director on ROLM's board.

In 1980 McMurtry went on to become a founder of Technology Venture Investors, TVI, which was the only pre-IPO outside investor in Microsoft. TVI's other successful investments included Altera, Compaq, Intuit, Sun Microsystems, and Synopsys. McMurtry, ever modest about his success, said in an interview, "For every one of those, there were about ten duds." In 2004, he was elected chair of Stanford's Board of Trustees, serving the university that helped lure him and many others to the West Coast.

Continental Capital, an investor in ROLM's first venture round, remained unhappy about the company's diversification into the PBX market. But it had not been able to find a buyer for its illiquid ROLM stock— until McMurtry's IVA stepped forward in 1975 to buy half of its shares at $12.50 a share. Wells Fargo SBIC, another investor in that first round, probably would have sold also, and McMurtry probably would have bought. But Rice graduate Dan Tompkins convinced his boss at Wells Fargo to hang on, believing that ROLM stock would have more value in the future.

ROLM revenue again grew 70 percent, to $17.5 million in fiscal year 1976. The big difference this time was that one-third of it was from telecommunications. But Mil-Spec's annual revenue surpassed the imagined cap of $10 million. Net income was more than $1 million. ROLM's increased credibility enabled it to entice revered Silicon Valley executives Les Hogan and Ed van Bronkhorst onto its board of directors. Hogan, former chairman and CEO of Fairchild Semiconductor, was vice chair of Fairchild's board and had solid footing in both the science and the business sides of the technology industry. HP's VP and treasurer, Ed van Bronkhorst, also joined the board. ROLM added these seasoned directors just in time for its public stock debut.

## A Lackluster IPO

By the summer of 1976, ROLM had a pristine track record, with continuous, remarkable sales growth; consistent profits growth; the ability to self-finance growth; and no bank debt. Preparation commenced for an initial public offering of stock. ROLM's secretary and corporate securities attorney was Larry Sonsini, a young lawyer who had joined McCloskey, Wilson, Mosher & Martin in 1966. Sonsini drew up the registration statement, which contained the prospectus listing these goals:

- "To exceed $100 million in revenue by fiscal year 1982" (ROLM achieved that goal by 1979 and had achieved almost four times that figure by 1982.)

- "To be the dominant independent competitor in our market segments" (ROLM was second only to AT&T in telecommunications and was a major provider of mil-spec computers.)
- "To make sufficient profits to be self-financing" (Profits and secondary stock offerings funded growth.)
- "To maintain our reputation for highest quality of equipment and customer support" (ROLM did.)
- "To maintain leadership in technology" (ROLM did this, too, with some struggle.)
- "To be a great place to work" (ROLM's employees could attest that it was indeed.)

The prospectus contained a caveat: "A number of bills have been introduced in Congress which would modify the existing structure of regulation in the telecommunications industry. Some of these bills may have an adverse impact on ROLM's ability to market the ROLM CBX competitively to interconnect companies." That was no minor risk for anyone contemplating buying ROLM stock as AT&T tried to knock out its competition.

Oshman and CFO Carollo headed out for the "road show" to prime the pump for the IPO, with visits to financial analysts in San Francisco, Chicago, and New York. The afternoon before ROLM was to go public, Stanley Sporkin, the chief enforcement officer of the Securities and Exchange Commission (SEC), raised a last-minute objection. Oshman and Sonsini met with him at the break of dawn. Sonsini has said he will never forget sitting in front of Sporkin about an hour before the opening bell. Sporkin asked about the registration statement: "Who wrote this thing?"

"I did," replied Sonsini.

"Turn to page so-and-so." Sporkin pointed to a name: *Adnan Khashoggi*.

Khashoggi had been an investor in Jack Melchor's Triad Ventures. When the fund closed out, the stock had been distributed, and now Khashoggi held ROLM's stock. He was listed as a selling shareholder—his stock would be sold in the public offering. But Khashoggi was under investigation for alleged kickbacks on the sale of military equipment to Saudi Arabia. Sporkin didn't want him to receive U.S. dollars from selling shares while he was under investigation by the U.S. government.

Sonsini, knowing ROLM was not legally bound to list shareholders who owned less than 5 percent of the company, suggested, "How about we just remove him as a selling shareholder?" He waited to hear the reaction, knowing that it was up to the SEC man whether to allow it.

Attending ROLM's IPO in New York on September 16, 1976, were, from left, Sandy Robertson; Norma and Jack Melchor; Ken, Barbara, and Peter Oshman; Bill Friedman; Tony Carollo; Larry Sonsini; Jeff Melchor. Photo courtesy of Barbara Oshman.

"Sounds good," replied Sporkin, handing Sonsini a pen. "Here, sit at my desk and mark it up."

Sonsini amended the filing papers by hand, Sporkin signed off, and the IPO was ready to move forward—just in time for the opening bell.

On September 15, 1976, ROLM sold 410,336 shares of common stock at $14 per share, raising $5.7 million in over-the-counter (OTC) trading with the symbol RM.

Continental Capital, a 1970 investor, sold its remaining holdings at the IPO and finally got itself clear of that risky ROLM stock. Wells Fargo, also a 1970 investor, sold half of its shares. Both had made a return of more than ten times their original investment.

On paper, the founders were suddenly millionaires. Many employees who had received stock options of varying amounts along the way in appreciation for their hard, smart work fared very well. Neither Oshman nor Maxfield had ever received stock options. But long before the IPO, the board had offered them the option to buy stock outright. With unshakable faith in the company's future, but lacking cash for the transaction, both had taken out bank loans far larger than their salaries to take advantage of the offer.

The world barely noticed the IPO. The *New York Times* listed it without comment. Technology company IPOs were rare in the mid-1970s. Most, like Intel and Advanced Micro Devices (AMD), both founded within a year of ROLM, were semiconductor firms—companies whose products were fueling development of technology products but whose stock held little interest for the press or the broader public. ROLM was not even well known within Silicon Valley. When Jim Kasson told a friend he'd gotten a job offer to work at ROLM, she said, "That's great! I love Italy." The initial stock price of $14 held for a few days before slowly dropping to $10 and holding. The stock first appeared in the *Wall Street Journal*'s Over-the-Counter Markets report on November 5, 1976, priced at $10¼.[27] Oshman received calls from disgruntled shareholders. He commented years later, "It was not a greatly successful IPO. But it was a great buy."[28]

## Product C

ROLM was on a roll, transforming two industries by applying digital technology to provide tangible solutions. By the mid-1970s, mini-computers were impacting many functional departments of the business world, but their reach was not yet ubiquitous. The phrase *personal computer* had recently surfaced, but the concept was primarily an intriguing topic among computer hobbyists, like those who participated in the Homebrew Computer Club, which first met in March 1975 and soon spawned Apple, Silicon Valley's first general-purpose computer start-up.[29]

Ken Oshman envisioned tackling a third industry, an unknown potential he called "Product C." In mid-1976, Oshman asked Gene Richeson, the absent *R* in ROLM, if he would come back to guide the search for Product C. After all, Richeson had been the one back in 1969 to come up with the idea of ruggedizing a mini-computer for the military market. Maybe he could foresee the next big thing. The IPO, just three months away, may have been another component of enticing Richeson back into the fold. Stating while on the road show that all four founders were still with the company beat the alternative of explaining the absence of *R*.

A hesitant Richeson asked Oshman why he should come back. "ROLM was the worst experience of my life," said Richeson. But he had ROLM stock, Oshman pointed out. Didn't he want it to succeed?

Richeson rejoined the company in the spring of 1976 as VP of business development—but since he had become involved with Creative Initiative Foundation, working for world peace, he refused to do anything involving the military. Oshman agreed. "I suppose by then I was mature enough to handle going back," Richeson reflected later.

At the time, the U.S. was in the throes of a major energy crisis. Electricity and gas prices surged. Lines at gas stations wrapped around city blocks. People who could afford to do so hired others to take their cars and sit in line, sometimes for hours, just to fill the tank. Plus, roughly 40,000 U.S. supermarkets were experiencing skyrocketing energy costs for freezers, refrigerators, heaters, lighting, and general electrical demands. Richeson figured computer smarts and flexibility could bring considerable intelligence and management capability to the energy industry, just as the CBX had for business telecommunications.

A smart system, Richeson knew, could help corporations control their energy costs, turn lights off and on automatically, and control heating and air-conditioning to maximize efficiency. He found a two-man start-up company called Entech that was developing an energy management system for supermarkets. Richeson drew up a business plan and presented it to the board. Buying Entech or acquiring the rights to its products would be ROLM's initial step into broader applications of corporate energy management. The board approved the entry into a third industry. Entech's assets were bought for 10,400 shares of ROLM stock. The two founders joined ROLM to complete development and get the product out into the marketplace.

Then a third Entech partner, whom the two founders had failed to mention, sprang forth—while ROLM was in the process of going public, a generally vulnerable three-month period when any company dreads unpleasant surprises. The man sued. ROLM retained attorney Bart Jackson, who was astute in technology and had successfully defended Motorola. Jackson felt certain the case would be dismissed. But the judge in the San Jose court stunned him and ROLM by saying that because the case pitted a "big company" against just one individual, it would stand.

Rather than be snared in a messy lawsuit just prior to going public, ROLM paid the man $250,000 to drop the suit. The two other founders were bound by a "hold-harmless" clause in their agreement: If it turned out they didn't fully own the company as they had represented, they would assume the liability rather than ROLM. Their only means of paying back the $250,000 was to return the vast majority of their ROLM stock—which "effectively gutted them of the incentive to help ROLM succeed," said Richeson.

Several years later, Oshman and Maxfield were sitting on a plane when a man stopped in the aisle next to them and loudly said, "Aren't you the ROLM guys? You paid me big-time." He thumbed through his wallet until he found a worn copy of the settlement check to wave in front of them. Maxfield said about the incident, "Some people, you just don't ever want to encounter again."

ROLM established new stock options for the Entech founders based on performance milestones. Dennis Paboojian was named general manager of the newly formed Energy Management Systems Division. But development of the smart system progressed slowly and needed considerably more investment than had been anticipated. And the market was sluggish despite the energy crisis. While supermarkets spent a great deal on energy costs, their margins were so low that few wanted to invest in new technology to manage those costs if it did not promise an immediate return.

Within a year, Paboojian recommended that the project be shut down and that ROLM focus on its two thriving product lines. "Thank God for Dennis," said Maxfield, who felt that the diversion into a new industry was one of ROLM's biggest mistakes, though he admits that he was complicit in approving it all along the way. "We were too full of confidence and thought we could pull it off again, succeeding in yet a third market," he explained. "Who knows how things would have turned out if we hadn't chased a third product line?" Instead, the project diverted resources from where they were needed: taking care of ROLM's early success in telecommunications and focusing on what should come next in that arena.

Paboojian's role in calling a halt to the energy enterprise was admirable. Maxfield pointed out, "Not many general managers would recommend that their own division be shut down. Most would put their own success ahead of the good of the company and fight for more and more resources to sink into a losing proposition." Paboojian soon went to work for Maxfield, bringing internal information systems up to speed to handle anticipated growth.

*"We were too full of confidence and thought we could pull it off again, succeeding in yet a third market."*
*— Bob Maxfield*

## Products A and B Grow—and Divide

The CBX, meanwhile, had grabbed the attention of Plessey, an English telecommunications manufacturer, which approached ROLM in early 1977 to discuss licensing the manufacturing rights to the CBX for sale in several European markets. Plessey was run by Sir John Clark, a "pugnacious" man who flew the company's helicopter himself and "rode and shot" and played "bashing" tennis in his spare time. Richeson and Chamberlain went to England and negotiated a five-year contract for $1 million up front plus royalty on sales. They returned pleased, because the deal meant that Plessey had essentially covered the CBX development costs.

"Oshman, however, told us we'd left money on the table," Richeson said. Plessey set up a manufacturing facility in Beeston, central England; called its version of the CBX the Private Digital Exchange (PDX); and hoped to ship the first five systems by the end of 1977.

Richeson also investigated the possibility of manufacturing in Puerto Rico, which was nixed. He left the company in 1977, this time permanently. He said, "I have to admit, I didn't much enjoy the experience the second time around either."

Mil-spec products continued to evolve while ROLM bounded into telecommunications. Mike Gilbert, a software manager at Syntex Pharmaceutical working on Data General–based equipment, was recruited to ROLM in 1974 after attending DG users group meetings held at ROLM, to build up the software group. Gilbert's first job was to design the microcode, while Stan Tenold did the hardware, for a computer that would exceed the performance of the new DG Eclipse and still be compatible with all earlier ROLM computers—the 1664, which was introduced in 1975. It was a tri-processor computer—with one processor that was micro-programmed as a general-purpose computer, one for variable precision floating-point processing, and one for direct memory access. In a typical computer, a floating-point add, subtract, multiply, or divide command—with the answer extending to a variable number of decimal points—could take thirty to forty microseconds to execute. A demanding function such as launching a warhead, however, could involve many thousands of mathematical instructions, and each one had to be executed within a few microseconds. This latest RuggedNova delivered that speed. It substantially increased computational power and system throughput and was used in applications requiring high-speed computations and real-time numerical analyses.

Gilbert hired engineer Rex Cardinale right out of Santa Clara University to design software for the new 1650, which was launched in 1976. The 1650 was a compact version of the 1602 but with a new CPU. The number of CPU modules was reduced from nine to one, and the whole thing weighed less than 30 pounds, a remarkable achievement at the time.

It was for applications that required small physical size, low weight, and reduced electrical power requirements, such as for tactical communication, navigation, and weapons management systems.

Gilbert considered ROLM's Mil-Spec section an ideal environment in which to work and develop. "Bob Maxfield was the best mentor anyone could have and protected me from all the junk," he has said. "Stan Tenold was the best hardware guy in the world to work with, and I had Rex Cardinale and a few others who made the software really sing."

ROLM was now operating two very different businesses. Mil-Spec had salespeople selling directly to the military and military contractors; telecom had salespeople motivating distributors to sell. Mil-Spec products had minimal service requirements; when a computer failed, it was replaced within minutes by a spare and repaired later. Telecom was highly reliant on responsive, on-site service for systems that could last decades. Mil-Spec products progressed as technology progressed; telecom was not as technology-driven as it was market-driven, with competitors and customers demanding new applications. Mil-Spec sold several hundred small boxes a year, costing in general no more than $50,000 each; a CBX system sold for no less than that amount, and several thousand large systems were likely to move out the door annually, many priced in the multimillion-dollar range. A new corporate structure was needed to deal with the two discrete, demanding businesses. Oshman decided that the right approach was to create two divisions, each a separate business with its own general manager.

When Ken Oshman first talked to him about stepping up as general

Mil-Spec's most compact computer, the 1650, weighing *only* 30 pounds, came out in 1976. This stop-motion ad of a champagne bottle christening the device demonstrated its indestructibility. Photo courtesy of Bob Maxfield.

manager of the Telecommunications Division, Maxfield declined, feeling he wasn't ready for it. He had learned a lot about manufacturing and felt comfortable with product development, but not with marketing and sales. Then Oshman pointed out that Dick Moley, a "true marketing genius," would back him up where he most needed it. Oshman said Maxfield was the only one who could do this job. "I don't know if that was true," Maxfield commented later, "but when Ken said '*frog*,' you jumped."

In spring of 1977, Maxfield became general manager of the Telecommunications Division, and Leo Chamberlain was named GM of the Mil-Spec Computer Division, both reporting to Oshman as president and CEO. The Energy Systems Division under Dennis Paboojian as general manager was also designated at the time, though its existence was short-lived. ROLM had a new corporate structure and focus—which the company would need if it had any hope of overcoming the diverse challenges that lay ahead.

CHAPTER 5

# BARELY MANAGEABLE GROWTH

...................

By 1977 it was becoming clear that Oshman's push for the company to enter a huge new market that would provide unlimited opportunity for growth had paid off. ROLM had hit the proverbial home run with the CBX product. Revenue in fiscal 1977 was $30 million, making three years in a row of more than 70 percent growth. Net income was $1.92 million. For the first time, telecommunications sales surpassed mil-spec sales, though the Mil-Spec Computer Division's profits still surpassed Telecom's. At the quarterly meeting at which the Telecom Division's profits first topped Mil-Spec's, the management team realized that the company had entered "a new realm," said Maxfield. It had taken almost seven years for ROLM to get to that level with Mil-Spec, even at a steady growth rate that would satisfy any start-up. Within a little over a year, Telecom shot past it.

In ROLM's first annual report as a public company, Oshman wrote, "Our Telecommunications Division grew by almost 300 percent during the last year. That growth rate was difficult to manage, but we succeeded."

## Doubling Every Year

ROLM had more than 600 employees at the end of fiscal 1977, up from 400 the year before. And the company would continue to grow: to 1,100 within twelve months; 2,200 a year after that; 4,400 two years later, in

1980. That made for a lot of new cubicles, phones, conference rooms, copiers, and parking spaces—and a whole lot of products being engineered, launched, manufactured, and serviced—plus significantly more space in which to accommodate all of it.

To make the growth happen, ROLM needed many top-notch engineers. Yet ROLM couldn't find enough good engineers with experience, so it needed to tap into raw talent coming out of the best engineering schools in the country. Gibson Anderson agreed to go recruit from Rice, Stanford, UC Berkeley, MIT, Caltech, Carnegie Mellon, and the University of Illinois. He had a great product to sell: a successful, growing Silicon Valley company . . . private offices for all engineers . . . state-of-the-art projects to work on . . . very competitive salaries . . . stock options . . . remarkable engineers to learn from . . . access to Stanford's Honors Co-op program. MIT's director of college recruiting advised Anderson that if ROLM started giving MIT students summer jobs now, one or two of them might be willing to join the company in a few years.

Anderson made five full-time offers that first year—and hired five excellent MIT engineers. He met with similar success at Stanford, UC Berkeley, and other schools. Said Anderson later, "I loved recruiting. It was great fun. And it was very satisfying to watch these bright, new engineers develop their careers." After a few years, with good engineers from all the schools now working inside the company, Anderson stepped back from personally recruiting and instead managed the process, enlisting ROLM engineering managers to go recruit at their alma maters just as Burt McMurtry had done at Rice for Sylvania.

ROLM added two new capabilities in mid-1977 that opened new markets for the CBX. Both were customer-driven—high on ROLM's customers' wish list—and were optional applications handled by software in the CBX's central processor. Automatic Call Distribution (ACD) efficiently managed a very large volume of calls for business applications such as hotel and travel reservations, catalog sales, credit card authorizations, insurance claims, and newspaper classified advertisements. Time was money for these businesses, and it was paramount that each call be professionally completed as quickly as possible. ROLM's ACD handled calls on a FIFO basis—first in, first out. The salespeople pointed out to prospective customers that competitive products were based on the FISH plan—*first in, still here.*

Centralized Attendant Service (CAS), the second new application, was directed at companies that had several facilities within a single geographic area, like retailer Macy's. Each Macy's store had its own telephone system, but calls to that store and to all the stores within a region would be answered at one location using CAS. Attendants would answer the call and route it to the appropriate department in the appropriate store, reducing the cost of employing attendants at each store who often had idle time between calls.

Both ACD and CAS made the ROLM CBX appealing to new types of business customers. The applications reduced operation costs, offered extensive call management reports, and provided tighter control over the quality of service.

Dick Moley hired Bob Nugent in 1977 to "maraud among the national accounts," according to Nugent. His broad charter was to handle these nationwide companies in such a way that they thought of themselves as ROLM customers, not AT&T customers. That meant providing them with standardized pricing and presentations, assuring top-notch service, and representing their issues at headquarters. Nugent's early presentations were flip charts done on an IBM Selectric typewriter, illustrated and colored by hand, slid into plastic sleeves, and presented from a propped-up binder. Distributors were nervous that ROLM was developing a national accounts program. In their experience, this was how manufacturers stole big accounts out from under them. ROLM, however, worked with the distributors, not in lieu of them. Early successes included Shell, Westinghouse, Sears, Allied Stores, Montgomery Ward, and IBM.

Nugent's first experience with Ken Oshman was memorable. His customer, Automatic Data Processing, had a CBX that was not working properly. ADP's telecommunications manager flew from New Jersey to Santa Clara and demanded to meet with ROLM's CEO. They gathered in Oshman's elegant office, where contemporary paintings graced the walls. Nugent recalled that the ADP manager started in right away, practically raging. Oshman sat expressionless, silent, never once interrupting him. When the man finally stopped, Oshman just looked at him for a moment. At last he said, "It sounds like you've got some big problems. And it sounds like we're at the heart of them. It seems to me that the only solution is to remove the system so that you can put in something that works."

Nugent's heart just about stopped. Here he was, in his first few weeks on the job, on the verge of losing a major account. The ADP man also seemed dumbfounded. "After what felt like an hour of silence," Nugent said, "the guy practically begged Oshman for help so they could keep the CBX." Even with only a few months' experience with the CBX, this telecom manager, like many other early customers, had experienced the system's significant benefits and cost savings.

ROLM had installed just 300 CBXs by 1977. That statistic too would double the next year, and triple the year following. And yet in 1977 it was barely a dent in the U.S. market of almost 40,000 PBX systems of target size, most of them obsolete electromechanical systems in need of replacement. ROLM expanded to twenty-three interconnect distributors, including Compath of California, Electronic Engineering Co. (EECO) in the Midwest, Fisk in Texas, General Communications & Electronics (GCE) in Tennessee, IBT in New England, Jarvis in Virginia and the South, Norstan in Minnesota and Wisconsin, TLC in North Carolina, TSI in Florida, UBS in Colorado, and United Telecommunications (UTC) in New York.

ROLM was eager to get "independent" telephone companies (that is, independent of AT&T—meaning GTE and the small telcos) to distribute the CBX. They were as reluctant as AT&T to have their customers install smart systems that could control telephone costs. Much of their revenue and profit came from the fees they charged for local phone service, which they provided, and long-distance service provided by AT&T Long Lines, from which they received a cut. "It took years to nourish the telcos before they signed up as distributors," said Moley. "They weren't used to pushing product—they just took orders. We had to go around them to create demand pull from the customer."

Sales manager Dave Sant did just that to corner GTE into signing on as a ROLM distributor. GTE was by far the largest independent telco, providing phone service and telecommunications equipment to midsize cities such as Cleveland, Honolulu, Santa Monica, and parts of Dallas. Like AT&T, GTE was a monopoly with its own manufacturer, Automatic Electric (AE), and it wanted to rent or sell only AE products. According to Nugent, Sant went directly to GTE's large customers and said, "You can have this high-powered CBX and control one of your biggest expenses, or you can have this clunker you're renting from GTE and keep sending dollars down the phone line." Customer pressure mounted until GTE relented and signed up to sell the CBX, effectively killing its own product. "It was one of the greatest sales feats of all time," said Nugent.

GTE embraced the CBX so thoroughly that it became a valued partner in ROLM's development of trunk cards, which provided the interface between the CBX and the phone company's central office. There were many varieties of trunks, and as ROLM developed an interface to each of them, the prototype cards would be sent to the GTE lab in Southern California, where they would be tested using GTE's own trunks.

Once GTE signed up, many small telcos followed suit. Thirty-seven telcos became ROLM distributors, including Centel (Illinois) and Winter Park (Florida). They could no longer resist the tide of demand for computer-controlled PBXs that permitted the customer to control costs.

The ACD application was particularly relevant for handling reservations, and many CBX sales were made in Las Vegas after the local telco United Telephone Company became a distributor. Nugent recalled a unique situation there that left him thinking, 'Only in Vegas . . .' A tech proposed that the best time to cut over from the old phone system to the new, when phone service would be down for an hour or two, would be

1:00 a.m., as it was for most cutovers. But apparently 1:00 a.m. is prime time in Vegas. "Evidently," said Nugent in an email, "that's when guys give up on getting lucky in the bars and casinos and get on the phones to try to get lucky in other ways. Eight in the morning worked better."

Distributors and ROLM headquarters worked together to land new accounts. In the spring of 1978, a plumbing leak killed the old PBX at the Bank of Babylon on Long Island. Bank officials decided this emergency was an opportunity; it would test the speed of responsiveness that ROLM's New York distributor, UTC, had been touting. UTC took the order for a new CBX and faxed it to Santa Clara, which configured the system and shipped it in one day. UTC received it, installed it the next day, and cut over to dial tone the next. The CBX was operational three days after the order was taken. CBXs soon went into Babylon's other branches.[30]

Fiscal year 1978 revenue was up 67 percent, to more than $50 million, with Telecom responsible for two-thirds of it. Net income was $3.6 million, almost double the year before. The company had no bank debt. Leo Chamberlain compared Dick Moley's 1973 CBX Business Plan against actual performance every quarter for the first three years the CBX was on the market. All objectives were met, he said, except revenue, which was "vastly underestimated."

ROLM stock moved from OTC to the New York Stock Exchange in July 1977, having met NYSE's threshold for such things as volume of trade and consecutive profitable quarters. Eighteen months after the IPO, the stock price started ratcheting up. Phone calls to Oshman from disgruntled shareholders ceased.

## Serious PBX Competition

By June 1978 more than 750 customers had defied AT&T and bought ROLM CBXs. They represented most major industry segments: oil and gas, retail, medical and health care, financial, transportation, government, law firms, utilities, and more than twenty colleges and universities.

Word was getting around that the CBX offered truly relevant cost savings and productivity benefits. "It was a snowball effect," as the *New York Times* reported a few years later. "One hospital buys a phone system and winds up saving $250,000 on its phone bill. Then it goes to a hospital convention and tells other hospitals about it"[31]—the perfect word-of-mouth advertising.

ROLM continued to evolve the product, expanding the CBX range from both ends of the spectrum—something the marketing folks had wanted since the CBX first came out. The small SCBX provided an economical digital phone system for companies with between 48 and 144 telephones. It was housed in a new cabinet—smaller but, of course, still Burnt Orange and River Bottom Brown. The larger LCBX, purportedly engineered by Dave Ladd over a long weekend, serviced up to 1,500 phones by seamlessly connecting two CBXs.

The California PUC finally permitted the installation of the CBX without AT&T's "protective" electronic devices, bringing considerable cost savings to the customer. More PUCs followed and allowed direct interconnect. The FCC set up a process using the Electronic Industries Association to establish uniform national standards for the interface between a PBX and the nationwide telephone network. The result was RS-464 and companion standards for telephones. The infamous CDH black box was dead at last.

ROLM's digital PBX had caught AT&T by surprise. A year and a half later, AT&T introduced its new Dimension PBX, computer-controlled but based on an archaic, analog backbone. "They just couldn't move fast enough to get a digital switch out," said Maxfield. "Thank goodness. Otherwise, we might've been seriously clobbered." In the Dimension, voice was transmitted by analog means rather than digitally. That meant the product was less flexible, which made it harder to implement advanced features like the ability to connect multiple calls into a conference. Plus, the component costs would not decline, because the world was moving away from analog circuitry. In spite of the world-class technical capabilities at Bell Labs, AT&T had misjudged how rapidly digital technology would progress.

Northern Telecom (NT) of Canada had not misjudged. It had reacted quickly after the Carterfone decision opened the U.S. market to competition, introducing the SL-1, a digital PBX, in the U.S. market shortly after ROLM introduced the CBX. The SL-1, however, was targeted at customers with more than 1,000 phones and so was not a direct competitor . . . yet.

The total non-AT&T PBX market was estimated at $334 million in 1978, and grew to $485 million in 1979. ROLM's market share surpassed Northern Telecom's, even though NT was selling larger, and therefore higher-revenue, systems. GTE's market share was half of ROLM's. ROLM, NT, and GTE comprised more than 50 percent of the non-AT&T market. The remainder was splintered among eighteen other companies, including Anaconda, Chestel, Ericsson, Hitachi, Mitel, Oki, Siemens, Stromberg-Carlson, Womack, TeleResources, Executone, and ITT. The PBX market was becoming crowded, with these smaller manufacturers competing on price with systems that lacked the features, capability, and technology of ROLM's CBX. ROLM dominated in the midsize range, and NT dominated in the larger systems. To continue to differentiate itself, to provide a better user experience, and to increase revenue and margin, ROLM began to manufacture its first user telephone.

## ROLM Makes Telephones

Ninety percent of telephones on a typical CBX system were standard push-button phones with a template overlay. With the exception of one or more attendants' consoles, the rest were multiline phones used by secretaries to handle calls for several managers or by managers to juggle multiple calls. Some situations required separate intercom units for the secretary to communicate with the manager (e.g., "Call on line one"), but most could do no more than put a call on hold.

The ETS 100 (Electronic Telephone Station) was ROLM's first desktop telephone for the CBX, and probably the world's first desk phone that had a display and incorporated a built-in microprocessor. It was introduced and first shipped in 1978—and it was revolutionary.

ETS 100 was an "executive phone," a sophisticated, multi-extension telephone and intercom combination targeted for use by managers and their assistants. The display showed the phone number dialed, how long the call had been under way, and whether the call was on hold. The original units used a red lens over red LEDs. Com-

The ETS targeted manager/secretary situations, with built-in intercom, multiple lines, and single-button access to features. It quickly displaced "key sets" and comprised about 10 percent of lines on a CBX. Photo courtesy of Bob Maxfield.

plaints came in that some phones arrived with the display not working. "It turned out that there are more red/green color-blind executives than you might expect," said Ron Raffensperger, ETS product manager at the time, "and the red-on-red display was the perfect test." A prompt fix was implemented: the ETS 100A with a transparent lens.

Four of the ETS's sixteen buttons could be programmed as line keys, with the rest as one-button access to features that the individual user wanted, such as *do not disturb* or *conference call*. Intercom facilitated communication between managers and assistants. Within a year, the ETS 100 had displaced other vendors' multi-extension keysets on the CBX, and represented 10 percent of the phones on a system.

The ETS 200 for ACD and the ETS 300 for CAS came out in 1979. Citibank ran an advertisement in prime press like *BusinessWeek*, featuring the ETS—"Easy talking with Citibank"—and highlighting how effectively this technological wonder enabled good customer service. ROLMans were thrilled, three years after the ETS came out, to see its appearance in Natalie Wood's last movie, *Brainstorm*.

Also in 1980, ROLM introduced the FlashPhone, the company's private label of a flash phone made by Stromberg-Carlson in Charlottesville,

# Tales from the Field—
# Don Armstrong

A lot of ETSs went into the White House when ROLM won the contract for 1600 Pennsylvania Avenue in 1983. Anyone who worked on the system had to have a top-secret clearance. The CBX itself required considerable alteration for security purposes. The Russians, from their embassy up the street, were bombarding the White House and the Old Executive Office Building with microwaves to foul things up and were using all sorts of sophisticated listening equipment to eavesdrop. So all the wiring to every telephone and location had to be contained in fully connected and grounded conduits to prevent leakage of signals from conversations. And the cabinet panels and doors had to be coated with a special blue paint, and a special woven-metal seal was placed around them. The cabinets were then tested in a facility where they were bombarded with microwaves to see if that bothered

Virginia. This standard push-button phone had an extra button on the bottom right that facilitated using a single-line phone like a two-line phone. When pushed, that extra button simultaneously put the existing call on hold and answered an incoming call. The user could juggle between the two calls or conference them. A message-waiting lamp was incorporated in anticipation of future messaging capability.

CBX capability increased with each new software release. Management of telephone costs and calls was an important CBX asset that continued the function. Next, every form of listening equipment was used to see if any signals could be picked up electronically through the cabinet. The cabinet passed with flying colors.

The cutover—when phone service on the old system is shut down and simultaneously turned over to the CBX—went smoothly, and the ETSs were installed. We heard nothing more until several months later, when a Secret Service agent showed up at the Tyson's Corner Technical Assistance Center with an ETS in a paper bag. Confidential conversations that had taken place in a specific room on this specific ETS had been recorded, he said.

I was given a pair of gloves so I'd leave no prints on the phone as I checked it out—someone had deliberately bent the talk leads but not the data leads. I pulled the design drawings and used a pointer to explain that, because of this, all conversations on this set could be monitored from the main frame without being observed. I made copies of the design drawings for him to take. We never heard anything else about it.

to gain sophistication with the introduction of the ROLM Analysis Center and CBX Management Reporter. The Analysis Center was a subscription service that provided companies with monthly usage reports, whereas the Management Reporter permitted corporate telecommunications managers to run those reports themselves, showing information such as how many calls came in to or went out of each extension on the system, including the dialed number and the length of call. Using this information, ROLM even cooperated with the police investigation of a ROLM employee suspected of making obscene phone calls. CBX call detail reports verified that the individual had called the target number on specific dates and times. The employee was arrested on the job.

As employees of all CBX customers came to understand the system's reporting abilities, abuse of the corporate phone system declined significantly, whether for lengthy chats with local friends or calls to relatives in foreign countries.

## Distributor Turbulence

Now that ROLM had twenty-three interconnect distributors, problems were bound to arise. If a distributor failed to adequately penetrate its geographic market, no independent solution was apparent, because ROLM already had what it considered to be the best partner available in each region. Management began to contemplate building its own sales force to address these problem areas. But taking over a territory by opening a ROLM-owned sales and service office was a touchy proposition. Distributors everywhere, not just in that region, might feel threatened, thinking that it was only a matter of time before ROLM did the same to them. Feeling threatened might cause these other distributors to back off on the energy and focus they put into CBX sales.

ROLM's distributor in Chicago, the third-largest market in the country, had failed to sell a single CBX by late 1978. After considerable discussion, a decision was made: ROLM would open its own sales and service office there. A wholly owned ROLM subsidiary—ROLM Illinois—was set up, headed by Alan Kessman. "We sold a lot of CBXs in Chicago after that," said Maxfield.

Soon afterward, Boston distributor IBT had financial difficulties. ROLM acquired the company and set up ROLM New England, headed by IBT founder Bob Fabriccatori. In New York, the distributor Coradian was doing a great job upstate but not faring so well in the largest U.S. metropolitan market, New York City. ROLM attempted to acquire the company, but no deal was sealed. Coradian's contract was not renewed in Manhattan in 1981, and ROLM New York was established. "Coradian will be hard-pressed to compete against a product line widely viewed as the Cadillac of the industry," reported the *New York Times.*[32]

The pattern was repeated in other regions. A ROLM direct-sales office was established in Detroit—ROLM Michigan, headed by Andy Anderson. The distributors in Virginia and Philadelphia were bought. ROLM Canada went into Toronto.

For its subsidiaries, ROLM sought salespeople who knew how to sell high-price systems. Very few hires "in the field" came from AT&T. For Ma Bell, a "sale" was a lease contract with no analysis of the payback period. Instead, IBM and Xerox salespeople—like George Platt, who quit Xerox to run ROLM Texas—were targeted as having good potential.

ROLM was now on the front line of sales and service in a major way. It grouped the new offices into a new ROCO (ROLM Operating Companies) Division, responsible for increasing telecommunications systems sales and providing high-quality service. Tony Carollo, ROLM's CFO, was made general manager of the ROCOs. He explained in 2013 why Oshman chose to put a CPA in charge of the sales offices: From Ken's perspective, there were a lot of financial implications and contract negotiations to each of these acquisitions. Plus, Oshman didn't want to fold the ROCOs into the same organization as independent distribution sales. Instead, Carollo said, "He wanted a champion for each." Bob Dahl, formerly a key financial officer at Measurex, became the new ROLM CFO.

An underlying principle regarding direct sales had shown up in a 1972 memo from Ken Oshman. Apparently, before deciding to go solely with ROLM's own direct sales force for mil-spec computers, there had been discussion of adding distributors. "The problem with distributors," Oshman wrote, "is the distance between us and the customer. Knowing the customers' needs requires a stronger marketing capability to identify end-user requirements than the distributor is capable of." The Mil-Spec Division had always had direct sales, with no middleman between ROLM and the customer. Yet in the Telecom Division, where understanding demands in the market was far more complicated, distributors stood between product marketing and the customer. Setting up the ROCO Division closed that gap. ROLM could now have close contact with the customer, which would facilitate understanding and anticipating customer needs.

Competition in PBXs was fierce. Manufacturers that didn't offer a digital PBX—yet—were competing on price. Others, like Hitachi, Mitel, and ITT, said they would have one soon. A sale based on price resulted in low margin. The more complex, benefit-based sale reaped higher margin, but required understanding of each prospective customer's present and future needs and knowledge of how the system could fulfill those needs. This market complexity that relied on close customer contact helped guide ROLM as it began to extend its direct telecommunications sales force.

## Hot Stock

Sales for fiscal 1979 reached $114 million, up an astounding 127 percent over the previous year. Net income was 10 percent of revenue, at $11 million, with the Telecom Division now representing 80 percent of the company's total sales.

The 1,000th CBX was cut over at AMF in White Plains, New York, by interconnect distributor United Telecommunications in January 1979. It was AMF's fifth CBX, each in a different location, with five more going in within the next twelve months. By the end of June that year, ROLM had installed 1,800 CBXs in 140 cities—more than 1,000 in the past year. Each new system sold for $50,000 to $3.5 million. The company now had 2,200 employees.

The financial market and the press noted this explosive growth. Investment firm Drexel Burnham Lambert selected ROLM as one of its eight outstanding growth stocks for the coming 1980s, citing the repeated reports of record revenue and earnings. *BusinessWeek* ran the following headline: "A hot new challenger takes on Ma Bell: ROLM's computerized phone equipment hits it big with major corporations."[33] *The New York*

*Times* wrote that ROLM "is one of the fastest growing of the fast-growing electronic companies in Silicon Valley. It is one of the leaders of the booming market for PBX."[34] *Electronic News* wrote, "Betting on risky markets paid off for ROLM. Snatching crumbs from the lion's plate can be very dangerous, but that's just how ROLM became great."[35] *Dun's Review* spotlighted the young, entrepreneurial founders at ROLM, Apple, Four-Phase, and Tandem for "proving there's a place for ideas and energy . . . in the tough data-processing world."[36]

⏻

## "I once met a man who introduced himself as the R in ROLM."— Gene Richeson, the R in ROLM

ROLM was probably the hottest stock in Silicon Valley from 1978 to 1982. In June 1978 Oshman took to the podium again, standing on a table in the cafeteria to announce to employees the board's decision to split the stock two for one. He lauded the employees for their hard work and dedication. On January 2, 1979, the price was at $42. A month later it was $59; two months later, $68. On March 23, 1979, the stock again split two for one, dropping it to $34. By the end of that year, it again was up to $42.

ROLM topped the *Wall Street Journal's* annual Nifty Fifty list in August 1980. The Nifty Fifty provided investors with a strong affirmation of those companies' future prospects. By then ROLM's stock was just above $70 a share. It again split two for one—so one share bought for $14 at the IPO four years earlier was now eight shares, each $35. ROLM's price-to-earnings (P/E) ratio of 32 represented only the second time since 1976 that investors bid stocks up that high.[37]

Stock prices of local Silicon Valley companies were announced on radio stations several times daily, especially during commute hours.

Maxfield would listen to the radio while driving to work on Lawrence Expressway and shake his head in amazement at his stock value. But in those early days, he never quite fathomed what it meant. "My salary took care of my family and needs," he explained later, "admittedly in progressively nicer style, like a Porsche for me and family vacations at Kona Village in Hawaii—but stock never felt like money in the bank."

*Inc.* magazine included ROLM in its *Inc. 100* list of fastest-growing companies in 1979, 1980, and 1981, saying, "These one hundred companies are a symbol of true human achievement. During a year [1981] of economic turbulence marked by sky-high interest rates, punishing inflation rates, and a pseudo recovery, the entrepreneurs who run these one hundred companies pushed their people to outperform all other business groups by every measure."[38]

ROLM hit number 77 of the Venture 100 in 1981, which represented the one hundred largest entrepreneurial companies in America, ranked according to sales. To qualify for this award from "the magazine of entrepreneurs," the company had to be founded from scratch (rather than through a buyout or merger) and had to still be headed by the founder or founders.

Oshman and Maxfield were the Silicon Valley darlings of *Newsweek*, *BusinessWeek*, the *San Jose Mercury News,* and the telecommunications press. The founders became known by their letters—"the *O* in ROLM" or "the *M* in ROLM"—and were often introduced that way. A sort of fame descended on them, although of the many who knew their names, few would have recognized them by face. Richeson once met a man who introduced himself as "the *R* in ROLM." Maxfield once told

One car in many states of the Union sported a license plate like this one, or without the S, or AROLMAN. One that said AROLMA had a bracket that read "The Sweet Smell of Success." Photo courtesy of Johnnie LaJolla.

someone he'd just met that he worked at ROLM (a typical understatement). The man replied, "Great company. I'm good friends with all the founders." False claims like these reflected the famous line: *Success has many fathers, but failure is an orphan.* ROLM's success, Maxfield reminisced, "was a hell of a fun ride."

## Ramping Up "The "Line"

Orders for CBXs exploded. More CBXs shipped out the door in fiscal 1979 than had shipped since the launch, with growth forecast to nearly double over the next few years. Accurately forecasting ROLM's meteoric growth in new orders presented a serious dilemma. Purchasing, for example, had to order adequate supplies of thousands of parts to be on hand to meet assembly needs. Each new hire in manufacturing had his or her own learning curve. Fifty new hires might not be fully up to speed for, on average, a month or more; output commitments had to reflect that fact when a lot of new hires were coming on board. To help fine-tune forecasting, Telecom's manufacturing manager Wayne Mehl presented Dick Moley, head of sales, with a new computerized tool—a microprocessor chip glued to a dart, along with a dart board. The gift was memorably humorous, yet emphasized a key point—forecasts that were wildly off could break the company, as could failure to meet forecasts that came true.

ROLM had prided itself on promptly getting orders out the door under a conventional manufacturing plan that used a sequence of activities performed by three different functional groups. The first group built the cabinet, including the racks, power supplies, and cabling. The second assembled and tested the printed circuit boards, which varied (in the number and types of trunks, phones, etc.) depending on each unique customer order. The third group put the boards into the cabinets and hooked up cables. The fully assembled system then went to system test, which installed the customer-specific software configuration data and performed a full set of diagnostics. The whole process culminated in a "burn-in" that made sure the system functioned error-free for twenty-four hours. Then out the door it went.

In mid-1978, however, delivery times moved out. Manufacturing couldn't keep up with the growth. If ROLM was unable to deliver in a timely fashion, it was in danger of losing orders. Manufacturing had to ramp up production capacity quickly while still controlling costs of goods and maintaining ROLM's reputation for quality. The task went to Wayne Mehl, head of manufacturing. He and a select team studied Japanese manufacturing techniques. "The Japanese," recalled Maxfield, "had been thrashing the U.S. for the previous decade or two in manufacturing." They had perfected "just-in-time inventory," producing goods faster at reduced costs and with higher quality than was typically achieved by U.S. manufacturers. Mehl found that many Japanese manufacturers employed a modular, decentralized format to achieve this.

Mehl considered a conventional, centralized approach of ramping up manufacturing by enlarging the existing manufacturing line. He also considered the decentralized model typical in Japan, which would involve multiple production lines operating in parallel.

The risks seemed highest with the centralized model. As he currently did, Mehl would continue to oversee the whole line, making all the decisions about how to allocate investment in people and equipment among functional groups to keep the whole operation properly balanced. Three functional group managers would report to him, and layers of supervisors would report to them. The overall performance would be highly dependent on each functional group doing its job well and growing in sync with the others. One functional group performing badly, for whatever reason, could dramatically reduce the whole capacity, diminish quality, or increase costs. A production stoppage anywhere along the way would shut everything down. Any quality problems would have to be solved very quickly. Increasing quality and lowering costs through innovations within a functional group would depend heavily on the manager of that particular group.

The decentralized approach, on the other hand, would begin by adding one production line, called a module, running at the same time as the established line. Each module would have its own three functional groups building systems from scratch. Another module would be added when both those lines were stable. Each module manager would make independent decisions about how best to get the job done, and where resources should be allocated within the module's three functional groups. One module's effective innovations would be quickly shared with the others, so best practices would continually evolve. If something went badly wrong in one module, causing it to shut down, only a portion of the production capacity would be affected.

The decentralized approach was proposed and approved. More than 1,000 new employees were hired within twelve months. ROLM rented space throughout the nearby area and went from one manufacturing facility to seven. The performance of each line was carefully measured and the results were compared, creating a natural competition to be the line that shipped the largest number of problem-free CBXs. "It was a microcosm of the marketplace—competition stimulates innovation," said Maxfield.

Within less than a year, production capacity tripled, the per-unit manufacturing costs decreased, and quality held steady at a high level. The decentralized approach made heroes out of supervisors and managers who took risks with bright new ideas and succeeded with their lines, providing visibility and career growth for Dirk Speas, Jim Koepf, Bill Rae, and others. By the end of fiscal 1980, 6,200 CBXs were installed—4,400 new systems within a two-year period. By 1984, there were 15,000. Throughout this explosive growth period, ROLM remained known for having a high-quality, reliable product. As new products were added, the company found that it could have one production module hone in on how best to build the product. Then the product would be introduced into other lines as demand ramped up.

Dr. Steven Wheelwright, then professor at Stanford School of Business, wrote a business case that studied ROLM's manufacturing ramp-up strategy. A previous case study, highlighting the factors involved in the early CBX distribution decisions, had been written by Dr. Adrian Ryans, also of Stanford School of Business. ROLM's style of strategic decision-making was getting attention and being taught to the next wave of bright young managers.

The rapid growth occurred. In 1980 ROLM revenue was just above $200 million, 80 percent of it coming from Telecommunications, with net income above $17 million. The annual revenue growth was a stunning 75 percent. The ROCO Division had grown to comprise twenty-four sales offices in thirteen states and accounted for 23 percent of telecom sales.

An important aspect of managing the company throughout this period of rapid growth was management's determination to develop and nourish an environment that facilitated innovative, nimble approaches to challenges; that shared the company's success with the employees; and that blurred the line between work and play, to provide stress relief and "out of the box" thinking. As time went on, many policies, certain guidelines, and the facilities themselves coalesced to shape ROLM into a Great Place to Work, or GPW, as it was known in Silicon Valley.

CHAPTER 6

# A GREAT
# PLACE TO WORK

...................... .

All four founders had worked for large companies before breaking out on their own. In the early days of ROLM, they often discussed what they had liked and not liked about their former employers. They particularly disliked the regimented approach to advancement opportunities and the lack of attention to individual contribution. All employees were reviewed at the same time and typically received the same annual raise at the same time with little regard to contribution. Promotions too could occur only at specific times of the year. Seniority was protected—some positions could be applied for only after the employee had a certain number of years of experience in the existing job. ROLM's founders believed that rigidity not only dampened individual creativity and commitment, it seemed to thwart success of the company.

"We knew we needed to hire a lot of people," said Maxfield in an interview, "and we wanted them to have values similar to ours. So even when we were on Forge Drive we talked about what it would take to hire people like that and keep them happy and productive." Ken Oshman putting the pay-cut vote before the full staff in 1971 reflected the idea that the company belonged to everyone—the feeling that *We're in it together.* Beer busts created an important sense of fun and camaraderie. But no one in the early 1970s, except perhaps Oshman, had the vision that it would grow into a remarkable corporate philosophy and work style that would permeate the entire company even after ROLM achieved Fortune 500 status. That philosophy would deeply influence the culture of Silicon Valley for decades.

## Pioneering a Corporate Lifestyle

Hewlett-Packard, founded in 1939, was certainly the original Silicon Valley pioneer in establishing a rewarding work culture for its employees. In 1966, HP published the second version of its seven objectives regarding "profit, customers, field of interest, growth, employees, organization, and citizenship."[39] When ROLM was forming personnel policies and deciding on benefits in the early days, the prime question was always, *What does HP do?* According to Maxfield, "We offered whatever they did, and often exceeded it."

Oshman shaped his own notions of employee satisfaction and productivity into something larger—a set of guidelines, not hard policies or rules, that reflected the kind of work environment he wanted ROLM to have both physically and philosophically. He informed the board in 1977 of his vision to firmly establish the company's reputation as a great place to work—a meritocracy, not a bureaucracy, where individuals were motivated to contribute their best and most creative and were welcome to share in the company's success. Oshman identified four principal goals, which he said would be the foundation of the ROLM Philosophy:

- Earn a profit
- Grow
- Offer quality products and customer support
- Maintain a work environment based on an attitude of individual accountability

The final point eventually became simply "Create a Great Place to Work"—which didn't take long to be recognized by its shortened form, GPW.

Oshman took his workplace philosophy so seriously that he disclosed it to shareholders in the 1977 annual report:

The ROLM Philosophy is not a set of directives and rules but rather an attitude to guide work and working relationships. ROLM provides opportunity and challenges so that the employee can grow and be promoted. We treat each individual fairly, respect personal privacy, provide encouragement to succeed and opportunity for creativity, and evaluate based on job performance in the context of the ROLM Philosophy. In turn, ROLM employees are expected to respond by being individually accountable, enhancing teamwork, performing to the best of their abilities, and understanding and implementing the ROLM Philosophy.

This philosophy and the attributes that characterized the type of employees and managers who would implement it were developed, documented, distributed to all employees, and reinforced at all levels of the organization and at new employee orientation. The attributes described shared values such as "Focus on substance, not form." and "Don't point fingers; find the solution." Their simplicity and concreteness provided clear guidelines of the work ethic management hoped for—and expected.

The evolution of this philosophy was fed from the ground up, according to Maxfield. "We'd distribute the documents, get feedback, and amend," he explained. "It wasn't something that one day sprouted forth full grown." This process is illustrated by a 1978 copy of "Attributes of a ROLM Employee," in which one item reads, *"Don't cover your ass or look for fault in others. Solve problems."* The language was amended; the message remained unchanged.

These documents were unusual in American corporate culture at the time, and they were exciting. Today they reflect the work style of most Silicon Valley companies and indeed many companies throughout the United States. ROLM not only laid out these principles but also lived by them.

# ROLM Philosophy[40]

Four goals comprise the ROLM Philosophy and define the ROLM environment:

*1.* To earn a profit

*2.* To grow

*3.* To offer quality products and customer support

*4.* To create a Great Place to Work

The first three goals are not unique. The fourth one is. There are few companies that have made a corporate goal [of] and strong commitment to the creation of a Great Place to Work.

The desired corporate environment at ROLM can be characterized by respect and individual accountability. There is a partnership between the Company and the Individual. ROLM provides an environment conducive to the individual's personal and professional growth. In return, the employee is expected to demonstrate accountability by devoting effort, energy, and commitment to his or her personal success and to the success of the Company.

All ROLM people are expected to understand and practice the Philosophy. Furthermore, selection of new people should be done in such a way that they fit into our environment to promote and strengthen it. The heart of the ROLM Philosophy is not a set of directives or rules but rather an attitude that should guide work and working relationships.

The ROLM Philosophy provides a foundation for the total corporate environment we are striving for. We recognize that our environment is not perfect. ROLM Philosophy represents an ideal we are aiming for.

# Attributes of Success
# for All **ROLM** People[41]

1. Avoid bureaucracy; keep practices simple, but make sure they are communicated, understood, and effective.
2. Freely communicate ideas and suggestions.
3. Show initiative to assure you understand the performance expectations of your job.
4. Avoid "finger-pointing": when you see a stalemate, encourage discussion to get the problem solved.
5. Discourage rumors by communicating facts upwards, downwards, and sideways throughout the company.
6. Use written communications when it makes sense to do so. Recognize the value of face-to-face communications.
7. Focus on substance; it is always more important than form.
8. Take a large view of your job; do whatever it takes to make your tasks succeed, whether or not it is part of your job.
9. Solve problems; don't make excuses or look for fault in others. Don't act "on the record" to prove someone wrong; help make it right.
10. Focus on the important issue; let the inconsequential slip.
11. Build teamwork inside and outside your work group; it avoids the need for bureaucracy.
12. Fix problems as we grow; don't stop growing to fix problems. Don't fix things that aren't broken; try to anticipate things that may become broken.
13. Set personally challenging and difficult goals that support departmental and corporate objectives.

## Attributes of Success for ROLM Managers[42]

1. Level with people. Communicate your expectations—encourage honest response.
2. Get decisions made as close to the action as possible; don't second-guess them unless you have good reasons [that] you communicate. Let people plan and control as much of their own work as possible.
3. Ensure that people understand job performance expectations; then encourage their individual initiative to expand.
4. Promote from within whenever feasible; seriously consider ROLM people if they want promotion.
5. Identify and create an environment that motivates all ROLM people.
6. Maintain equal opportunity and affirmative action practices that meet the spirit as well as the letter of the law. Assist individuals to compete and succeed, and reward them on the basis of merit.

## New Work Style on Old Ironsides Drive

Management knew even back in mid-1975 that far more space would be needed if ROLM were to grow in both its markets. Oshman wanted the physical and philosophical principles of a Great Place to Work to meld into one, so ROLM's corporate lifestyle would be facilitated by the space that its people and buildings occupied. This was not likely to happen in

7. Recognize individual accomplishments in and out of your immediate work sphere. Praise in public; criticize in private. Don't point to third parties to rationalize your failures.

8. Help ROLM people build their self-image; treat them as individuals.

9. Ensure that people are paid fairly considering the labor market, internal equity, and individual worth to the Corporation; then give merit increases only.

10. Communicate praise to individuals in the group; buffer them from group criticism; make sure they are aware of any real shortcomings.

11. Give salary and performance reviews on time.

12. Document practices, policies and guidelines for routine tasks critical to the smooth functioning of the organization. If the documentation doesn't reflect reality, rewrite it.

13. Follow important projects and take continual corrective action, if necessary, to keep them on track.

the ubiquitous multistory, featureless cubes that passed as architecture in Silicon Valley at the time. Only a ROLM-inspired facility would do.

In late 1975, the company signed a forty-year lease on twenty-one acres near Great America Parkway in Santa Clara that were owned by Jack Melchor. Among fifteen competing architects who submitted design proposals, some of them revised versions of previously successful projects,

Oshman selected the only one who had no previous industrial experience—Goodwin (Goody) Steinberg, who had been a student of Bauhaus architect Ludwig Mies van der Rohe. Steinberg described his approach to designing the ROLM headquarters in his book about architecture in Silicon Valley:

> [I applied] the residential model to the workplace as I painted a picture of integrating indoor and outdoor space for maximum enjoyment and utilization. I addressed security issues not with locks and alarms but with pools of water and landscaping that limited authorized access . . . My sketches reflected the innovative philosophy and principles of the ROLM business plan itself.[43]

Oshman hired Don Smith to be ROLM's construction project manager. Steinberg, Oshman, and Smith worked closely to design and build a contemporary, employee-friendly, park-like campus unlike any other in Silicon Valley at the time, a campus that would be compatible with the vision of ROLM as a very appealing place to work.

In August 1977, ROLM's two newly formed divisions moved into 4900 Old Ironsides Drive in the city of Santa Clara. Phase one—buildings 1, 2, and 3—was complete. The ongoing construction of buildings 4, 5, and 6—phase two—and laying of the landscape for another year and a half made the place look more like a huge construction site than an elegant new facility. But by 1979 the stunning campus had been fully built and encompassed six single-story buildings.

Gingko, decorative plum, and almond trees shaded paths that wound around grassy lawns. A brook spanned by arched wooden footbridges meandered through the property. Boulders were added to the stream to create the pleasing effect of a babbling brook. Koi, water lilies, and papyrus plants thrived in a pond that later became home to a beloved bronze alligator. The stream was stocked with young trout in the spring. Just walking between meetings from one building to another amid the lush landscape provided a respite of serenity in an otherwise intense workday.

Inside, expansive windows provided a light, airy work environment. Managers' offices were

The new ROLM campus at 4900 Old Ironsides Drive near Great America in Santa Clara in 1978, before trees grew tall and vines covered the arbors. Photo from ROLM 1977 Annual Report.

located in each building's interior space, with no windows—instead they were surrounded by wood-and-fabric cubicles where staff benefited from abundant sunshine and a view of the outdoors. A recreation facility and a cafeteria that opened to allow outside dining were remarkable perks. External gathering spaces encouraged "an ambience conducive to interaction, interdependence, and integration."[44] Plenty of parking spots ringed the outside perimeter. As visitors walked from the parking lot to Building 1, they passed a pond with a tall fountain and billowing, blooming shrubs, but motorists driving by glimpsed little of the unique, park-like serenity that employees experienced daily.

Leo Chamberlain (in addition to his role, by then, as executive vice president) became ROLM's champion of GPW. He worked with human resources to further develop the GPW concept by documenting the ROLM Philosophy, Attributes of a ROLM Manager, and Attributes of all ROLM Employees. Even now, these are worthy guidelines for employees, managers, corporations, and organizations that aspire to a productive, innovative, and invigorating work environment.

Chamberlain took his GPW role seriously. His managing style included walking around, a lot and everywhere. He chatted in his cheerful, friendly way with everyone and regularly took the pulse of the workforce in order to understand how employees were feeling. Even eighteen months after he retired, he penned a letter to the VP of human resources with feedback on a new ROCO personnel brochure: "The only attribute I found missing is 'Focus on substance; it's always more important than form' . . . It discourages politics, or writing pretty memos, or 'blowing in ears.' It allows an informal yet serious atmosphere."[45]

In 1978, Oshman phoned Loewenstern in D.C. and asked him to return to headquarters to head up the human resources department. Loewenstern objected that he knew nothing about HR. Oshman said, "That's good. I don't like having personnel professionals in charge. They're fine inside the department, but not in charge."

Loewenstern agreed—he felt that too often, professional HR people tell others what they can't do, rather than how to do what they want to do. He moved back to Santa Clara and ran human resources until 1980, when he went half-time, spending one week a month in Santa Clara and one week lobbying for ROLM in Washington, D.C.

Gibson Anderson, who had joined ROLM as an engineer and had done a great job recruiting young engineers, followed in Loewenstern's HR footsteps. He told *Time magazine*, "Turnover among engineers [at ROLM] is less than half the average in Silicon Valley," an accomplishment he attributed to the company's benefits and its position as a technology leader.[46] One of the most famous benefits was an unprecedented twelve-week sabbatical.

## A Lonnnnng Vacation

As if taking your lunch break beside a gurgling brook and being recognized and rewarded for individual contribution weren't enough to entice top engineering minds to join ROLM, Ken Oshman proposed a sabbatical policy to the board of directors: three months of continuous, fully paid vacation after each six years of service. According to Maxfield, one director asked, "This applies only to key management, right?"

Oshman answered, "Nope. Everyone."

"Even the assembly line workers?"

"Absolutely."

That egalitarian approach was revolutionary among U.S. companies. The employee was guaranteed his or her job upon return; someone would be trained to do the job in the interim. The first person to take a sabbatical was Vineta Alvarez, the first assembler of the RuggedNova 1601. Some ROLMans used time off to remodel a home, travel with families, or pursue passions such as antinuclear activism or painting. Most employees returned refreshed, ready to adopt new approaches.

Oshman offered this inside-out perspective: "[The sabbatical] proved to you that you weren't so darned important. The company went on. Someone else could do your job."[47] To Ken Lavezzo, the sabbatical brought both bad and good news: "The bad news was that I realized I was expendable. The good news was that being expendable was very freeing. It helped me let go of the small things and focus on ever bigger issues."

Sabbaticals occasionally had unintended consequences. When Jim Kasson returned from his in 1979, when he was running telecommunications engineering, the first week back was miserable. "Work had been fun before," he recalled thinking, "and I couldn't figure out what had changed, until it hit me: All the easy decisions had been made while I was away, but the no-win, painful ones had been saved for my return. Once I got those taken care of, I felt a lot better and got back into the swing of things."

Some employees were unable to get back into the swing and left within a year of their sabbatical to seek a less intense work environment. So management came up with an option to the twelve-week sabbatical at full pay: six weeks off at double pay. For employees who lacked savings, it provided the financial cushion to travel. Still, the option was seldom selected. Jim Kasson said he counteroffered: "How about twenty-four weeks at half pay?!"

The egalitarian atmosphere extended to many facets of the workplace. In the parking lot, for example, even Oshman had no reserved space. From his perspective, if you wanted a good parking spot, you should arrive early. Casual Fridays was a no-brainer in this company's culture:

jeans, polos, and sandals. And executive breakfasts, where small groups of ROLM employees from all levels could meet with top executives in an intimate setting—with no questions off limits—were common. This egalitarian, open approach stood in stark contrast to traditional U.S. companies, which maintained an invisible but firm barrier between the ranks of employees.

## The Fittest Company in Silicon Valley

Corporate athletic facilities were rare but not nonexistent in the mid-1970s. For decades, Firestone Tire and Rubber Company of Akron, Ohio, had had a bowling alley and golf course—for executives only. Years after ROLM completed the most revolutionary element of GPW—the athletic center—Oshman reflected on the decision to build it:

> We had always had a Christmas dinner dance. It was fun when we had fifty people, but not when it got to be 3,000 and we had to have five parties and you didn't know half the people. We said, "What if we didn't have this? Maybe we could use the money to put in a parcourse or a basketball court instead."

The employees voted on whether they wanted athletic facilities or a Christmas party. The gym won by a wide margin. "The amazing thing?" said Oshman. "It cost no more than all these Christmas parties."[48]

The athletic complex turned into far more than a fitness trail or a couple of basketball hoops. It included a twenty-five-yard, six-lane lap pool and a second "fun" pool, plus saunas, steam rooms, tennis courts, racquetball courts, a jogging track, and a weight room. Aerobics, kickboxing, and yoga classes were offered before, during, and after normal work hours. Employees were free to attend at any time, provided their work got done, and could bring their families on weekends.

In fact, management encouraged sports. The employee handbook said,

"If a sufficient number of employees express an interest in an approved activity, and are willing to organize and maintain the program, ROLM will back the group and provide the necessary equipment." Employees were quick to take advantage of this opportunity: A ski club, a chess club, a running club, a basketball league, a volleyball league, and a flag football league all sprang up.

*Management Review* devoted a five-page article to ROLM's environment and style of management, with considerable space given to describing "the four-acre, $1.3 million indoor (known by locals as the ROLM Dome) and outdoor athletic complex . . . The operating budget for all activities runs well over $150,000."[49]

The lap pool wasn't built for Bob Maxfield as some people said—but it probably would not have been built without him. "When I started at Rice," he said, "it became clear that I couldn't swim competitively *and* get the grades I wanted, so from then on I swam for fitness." He did one hundred laps twice a week, usually at about 6:30 a.m. It was cool to brag, "I swam with Maxfield this morning."

Wes Raffel was twenty-seven years old when he joined ROLM in 1983. He'd been a nationally ranked swimmer for Harvard only a few years prior. A crowd had gathered when he found himself up against Maxfield in the team tryouts for who would represent ROLM in the butterfly stroke at Silicon Valley Corporate Day. Raffel said Maxfield was in great shape and didn't look close to being the forty-something Raffel knew he had to be. When they swam the tryout, Raffel didn't even glance back to see how far behind Maxfield was. "I figured I'd blow him away," he said. "But when I touched the wall at the finish and looked around, there he was, coming right into the wall.

ROLM's athletic facilities set a high benchmark for other Silicon Valley companies, with a 25-yard lap pool, a swimming pool, Jacuzzi, sauna, parcourse, tennis courts, a gym with a full basketball court, and an exercise room for fitness classes. Photo courtesy of Evelyn Cozakos.

The crowd went nuts. They saw a good race." At Corporate Day that year, Raffel won the butterfly for ROLM, Maxfield won the back stroke, and ROLM won overall first place as the fittest company in Silicon Valley.

## Great Food, Abundant Coffee

Understanding that nutrition and caffeine fuel hard work, ROLM provided plenty of good food and hot coffee. Break stations were positioned throughout the buildings with free beverages and snacks. A sign on coffee machines read: *If you take the last cup, please make a fresh pot. If you're too busy, call me and I'll come do it.* It was signed *Ken*. Needless to say, there was always a fresh pot.

Food service in the cafeteria was set in stations by type of cuisine—an innovation then, a standard now. Outdoor dining decks and massive skylights acknowledged "that lunch could be more than a sandwich; it could be a respite, an opportunity to recharge one's batteries."[50]

Employees raved about the food offered in the cafeteria, serving early breakfast to early dinner. They loved how pleasant it was to dine al fresco at tables and chairs scattered on patios, under trees and umbrellas, and beside the brook—unless the timing on the sprinklers had gotten out of sync. With great food, a convenient location, and prices subsidized by the company, employees tended to eat in rather than go off-campus.

Ken Oshman, a gentle extrovert, sometimes approached a table with tray in hand and asked, "Mind if I join you?" Leo Chamberlain, an exuberant extrovert, plopped himself into the midst of a different group for breakfast each morning for two years, asking everyone how they liked working for ROLM, what they liked best, and what they would change if they could. Bob Maxfield, the quiet introvert, fixed a breakfast smoothie with enough calories and nutrition to hold him till dinner.

At breakfast one morning in late 1977, GPW champion Leo Chamberlain sat with a young man and woman who asked him about ROLM's pregnancy leave policy. He answered their questions and then asked where they worked.

"Across the street" came the reply.

"No, I mean which department," Chamberlain said. "Are you in manufacturing or what?"

"Oh, we're not with ROLM," the man said. "We work at the company across the street."

The woman nodded. "We come here because the food's so good and cheap."

Chamberlain didn't miss a beat. "So, tell me, how do you feel about stealing from a company?"

They looked at him dumbfounded.

He explained that the prices were subsidized by the company for the benefit of employees and asked them to leave.

"Can we finish our breakfast?"

"No. I'd rather you not."

The cafeteria's excellent food at subsidized prices and the opportunity to dine alfresco convinced many employees to arrive early for breakfast and remain on campus for lunch. Photo: BusinessWeek, November 19, 1984, p. 166.

After that, ROLM employees were promptly issued their first name tags—no tag, no lunch. Despite this episode, no perimeter security fence surrounded the twenty-one acres, and for years all the buildings remained unlocked during the day. In about 1981, state-of-the-art ID badges with photos were issued to permit automatic entry to the specific buildings to which an employee had authorized access. On Facebook's ROLM Alumni page, many former ROLMans post photos of the badges that they held on to for the sake of good memories.

## Trick or Treat?

ROLM was an early adopter of flextime and job sharing, subject to the approval of the immediate supervisor. ROLMans could arrive and depart for work or use the gym at any time, as long as their work got done. Earlier risers would be at their desks before dawn; night owls could be found in their offices after midnight. The benefit was called "flex-flex time" because of the dual flexibility to arrive and depart *and* exercise at will.

The gender glass ceiling, an even tougher barrier in technology than in other industries, was perhaps not shattered at ROLM, but it cracked. The company had many women in mid-management roles. Janice Carnes headed marketing for the Office Systems Division, formed in 1979. Heidi Schoolcraft was one of many female engineering managers. Val Gillen left Memorex to become controller of the Telecom Division and was much happier in her new role. "ROLM was like coming out of the dark into sunshine," she said. "We worked so hard. But it was so fun."

ROLM met or exceeded the standard benefits that could be found at nearly all companies, such as comprehensive family medical and dental insurance coverage. In addition to the Stanford work–study program in technology, partial tuition reimbursement was available for undergraduate and graduate education at other universities. Whereas many companies offered no vacation until the employee's second year on the job, ROLM employees could take two weeks of paid vacation in the first and second years; another week was added in the third year. Children of employees viewed the annual family picnics, with clowns and old-fashioned competitions like the three-legged race, with the sort of enthusiasm typically reserved for Christmas and birthdays. Ken Oshman's turn at the Dunk Tank was widely attended; he would sit in the trigger seat above the cold water wearing a suit and tie and smoking a cigar.

Perhaps the most distinctive benefit enjoyed by ROLM employees was the Halloween celebrations, which were epic at all ROLM facilities. In Santa Clara, the winners of each building's costume competition went head-to-head at an all-hands outdoor competition where the finalist judges were founders and senior management. Development teams and departments often competed with elaborate skits. In 1983, ROLM's top management came as Snow White and the Seven Dwarfs, with six-foot-six Bob Nugent fully decked out as Snow White. Off-the-charts-smart Maxfield was Dopey. The always observant, ever alert Oshman was Sleepy.

The ROCOs relished bringing potential customers to the West Coast to ogle the campus and meet with executives. One Wall Street firm insisted that Halloween was the only time its people had available for a visit. The firm's visiting execs and their rep from ROLM New York, all in dark, three-piece suits, arrived the year that all the women in accounting chose to dress up as "ladies of the night." The visitors found it distract-

Halloween was raucous, with competitions for best costume and skit, by an individual, building, department, or development team. The sign on the green toga on the right said, "Once a ROLMan, always a ROLMan." Photo courtesy of Don Armstrong.

ing enough as the ladies—not to mention bears and full-grown babies—filed past the glass wall of the conference room. And then Supermanager arrived for the meeting—Leo Chamberlain in a Superman T-shirt, red tights, and a red cape. The discussion seemed to go well, but the prospect ultimately declared it could never do business with such a flakey company. Customer visits on Halloween were subsequently banned.

## Sharing the Bounty

While keeping employees happy and healthy was a major goal of GPW, ROLM management knew that tangible rewards for smart, hard work were even more important: They wanted to do whatever was in their power to keep employees invested in the company's success. Management believed that employee ownership in the company motivated employees to help the company succeed. Stock options and a stock purchase plan fostered that goal.

Stock options were established right from the start. The board annually approved the total percentage of stock that could be distributed to employees each year as options. Annual company-wide management reviews determined how that pool of options was distributed based on who was contributing to the company's welfare. ROLM expanded on HP's example of generosity by extending options not only to key management but to individual contributors as well. Options often layered on annually as long as the employee remained a productive member of the corporate team, providing a significant incentive for employees to stay with the company. Oshman and Maxfield never received stock options, though; they felt that they were thoroughly incentivized to succeed and that the entire allocation should be directed toward others.

Stock options gave the employee the right to purchase stock in the future at the "strike price"—the fair market price of the stock on the day the options were granted, regardless of what the stock was selling for on the day the option was exercised. For example, say a four-year option on 1,000 shares of stock was given to an engineer on April 15, 1978, when the price on Wall Street was $20 per share. On each anniversary of that date for four years, that employee could exercise 25 percent of the option. That is, he or she had the option to buy 250 shares at $20, even if the stock was trading for $70 a share on Wall Street. Those shares could be sold for immediate gain or held in hopes the stock price would further increase. Of course, if the strike price was underwater—that is, if the market price was lower than $20—the employee would not exercise the option at that time.

Judging whether to cash in the stock to fund current wants or needs, or to hold it and wait for future gains, presented a dilemma for many employees. One marketing manager exercised his options and sold the stock to buy a house for his young family. Six years later, he told friends that based on the stock's growth, it was the most expensive home in the Valley.

The employee stock purchase plan was established in 1971. After six months with the company, any employee could purchase shares of ROLM stock each calendar quarter, up to 10 percent of his or her annual gross salary a year. When the plan was established, the purchase price was the market rate, but in the mid-1970s that was changed to a 15 percent discount off market value. On ROLM's tenth anniversary in 1979, each employee received one share of stock for each full or partial year of employment.

ROLM also followed HP's example of sharing profits. Each employee received a portion of fiscal year-end profit as a percentage of base salary, which could add thousands of dollars to a person's annual income. Profit sharing was above and beyond whatever raise came as a result of the employee's annual salary review. At the end of fiscal 1979, for example, profit sharing distributed among 700 eligible employees represented a bonus of almost 15 percent of salary.

Division-wide quarterly meetings were held, during which management reviewed progress and thanked employees for their hard, smart work, and employees asked whatever questions they wished about operations and strategy. Many questions focused on cost control. According to Oshman, "Most employees were stockholders, so they should be concerned about costs."[51] The quarterly meetings wrapped up with a beer bust or an ice cream fest.

Start-ups, IPOs, and stock options fueled the job-hopping frenzy of Silicon Valley from the late 1970s until the dotcom bust of 2001, and in the resurgence after 2010. Everyone in Silicon Valley was hoping to work for the next big hit, a company that would blast from start-up to Wall Street success. In exchange for this potential success story, employees were willing to work well beyond forty hours a week. Many received lower salaries than if they had worked forty- or fifty-hour weeks for IBM or Sylvania or any other large, traditional company that did not offer stock options but had retirement plans. That work ethic fueled dreams and possibilities and created Silicon Valley's risk-taking, "Wild West" reputation, along with its workaholic lifestyle. As a result, financial security, even great wealth, became reality for hundreds of thousands of Silicon Valley residents.

## *The* Place to Work

From 1978 until 1984, ROLM was *the* place to work in Silicon Valley. Dozens of resumes were received for every job opening. The number of employees tripled between 1978 and 1980 and nearly tripled again by

1984. Monday morning orientation sometimes had as many as fifty new employees selected from among the best and brightest workers available. With that many new hires, the ROLM Philosophy could easily be unseated. Orientation was where it was instilled in each new employee.

Bob Maxfield spoke at most of the Telecom Division's orientations. He looked so young that one newbie thought he must be the son of the *M* in ROLM, there to represent his father. Every orientation held a mix of assembly line workers, administrators, techs, engineers, and managers. Maxfield shared a similar message with them all, which he encapsulated in an interview:

> You're coming into ROLM at an amazing time. We're grow-ing very fast, grabbing market share, doubling manufacturing capacity. We have lots of exciting products in the wings. There's far more work that needs to be done than can possibly be done. If you see something you can do, jump in and do it even if it's not "your job." Work as hard and as long as you want. Be as innovative as you can possibly be. Do the best you can. This experience can really make a difference to your career. But if you just want to work eight to five, that's fine too.

Maxfield explained his thinking behind this message:

> I hoped that some of them would really dig in. We were in great need of smart, motivated people. ROLM's situation was rare— that kind of growth doesn't come along often. Their performance could really make a difference to the company and to their own careers. I'm sure many, especially in manufacturing, had never been in the same room with top management of any company until they attended orientation at ROLM. I wanted them to see the face, the openness of ROLM management, so they knew a bit more about who and what they were working for.

Many ROLM employees grabbed hold of the opportunity to do something more than their job called for—and succeeded as a result. Multitalented employees had the opportunity to explore possibilities: Gibson Anderson moved from engineering to head of human resources. Janet Gregory went from being an administrative assistant to a sales rep to a product marketing manager and on to VP of sales at other companies. Tony Carollo was ROLM's CFO who became general manager of the ROCO Division. Bill Friedman, ROLM's general counsel, became Western Region manager for the ROCOs. Ken Lavezzo, an engineer, moved into manufacturing management and later became general manager of the newly formed Phones Division. Keith Raffel, Ken Oshman's assistant, followed Lavezzo into Phones Division management. Fawn Alvarez worked as an assembler at ROLM right out of high school; then became a manufacturing line lead; went into build forecasting, finance, and marketing; and joined the crisis management team solving acute customer problems. Her sister, Bobby Alvarez, also started as an assembler right out of high school, but soon started keeping track of software revisions and eventually became a systems engineer. ROLM was willing to take chances on people who showed smarts and initiative. The company benefited from their talent and dedication, without which success would've been impossible. As for the employees, ROLM gave them the opportunity to stretch beyond their grasp.

Photo courtesy of Evelyn Cozakos.

ROLM's willingness to give young, smart people room to grow extended to vendors as well. Bruce Skillings, ROLM's account manager at Standbro Drummond from 1973 to 1978, was one of those people. He stated in a phone interview, "I was just recently out of college, and ROLM listened to me!" Thanks to insights he gained while working with ROLM, Skillings added HR departments to his ad agency's focus, saying:

At that time, the *San Jose Mercury News* want-ads section was

## Betting on People—Bob Finocchio

After I received my MBA in 1977, I went to work at Bank of America, in a group that made loans to emerging high-tech companies. ROLM was one of my clients, and I got to know Ken [Oshman], Walter [Loewenstern], Bob [Maxfield], Tony Carollo, and Joe Graziano. One day Bob took me to lunch and asked why someone like me would want to work at B of A. That got me thinking.

In 1978 I went to Fairchild Semiconductor, but only very briefly, because ROLM made me an offer to do corporate credit and handle financing issues with the independent distributors, before the ROCOs existed. I accepted.

In 1979 our distributor in Colorado was having troubles. Ken and Tony told me to "go buy it." I had never done anything like that before and hardly knew what I was doing, but they took a chance with me. Then they told me to buy the distributor in Salt Lake City, which also had problems. Tony soon asked me to go start up ROLM Colorado and be VP

sometimes seventy-five pages long, with columns and columns of engineers needed. It's hard to make your company jump out in that environment. We applied marketing and advertising techniques and helped a lot of companies hire the best people they could—people like those I'd encountered at ROLM. I learned that it's not all about the product or service you offer; it's more about the people who do the work.

ROLM was among the companies cited in the 1984 book *The 100 Best Companies to Work for in America*, with special attention paid to finance there. I knew little about how to do any of these things, but I got them done.

In late 1980 Tony asked me to replace the president of newly formed ROLM Michigan, who'd died suddenly. I had never sold anything or managed sales or service. Again, ROLM took a chance with me.

In 1981 Tony asked me to get ROLM Canada going, concurrent with my Michigan duties. After several months I hired George Harvey, who became president of ROLM Canada and later VP of marketing for ROLM.

In 1983 I became president of ROLM Northern California. Soon after that Tony and Ken asked me to "fix service" for the ROCOs. I certainly had no experience at that, but I did it. I had about 2,700 people working for me.

Every step of the way, ROLM took a chance on me. I suspect many people at ROLM have stories like mine. It was funny, though—I spent very little of my career in finance, but Ken always saw me as a finance guy.

the company's athletic facilities, flex-flex time, and lack of hierarchy. The downside of the increased publicity these facets attained was the superficial appearance that ROLM was a cool, laid-back company, as if employees could sit in the hot tub or work—their choice. But as Gibson Anderson noted in the book, ROLM had a very competitive atmosphere: "This is no loosey-goosey, hip California place . . . We fire people. We do not guarantee lifetime employment. We believe it's bad for morale to have deadwood around."[52]

*Time* magazine's cover article on the "new breed of risk takers" in Silicon Valley acknowledged that ROLM was one of the earliest companies to rise above the inevitable problems of fast-paced growth and technological change:

> Executives in the valley face a few acute problems because of their highly competitive environment: keeping workers satisfied in order to reduce job hopping, and maintaining the small-company entrepreneurial spirit as firms grow larger. ROLM has been a pioneer in developing a new corporate life-style that encourages worker loyalty and innovation.[53]

The ROLM Philosophy was built on a fundamental belief that any individual, when properly prepared, would be able to assume responsibility for his or her work with as few controls as possible. Broad goals were established: have the competitive analysis done by September, for example, or the new finance system online by the first of the year. But there was leeway in how those goals were accomplished, as long as they were accomplished within the set budget. This lack of micromanagement meant that individuality was given room for expression. As Oshman told the *San Jose Mercury News,* "If we had all our people marching to the same drumbeat, we couldn't get much innovation."[54]

## *"If we had all our people marching to the same drumbeat, we couldn't get much innovation."— Ken Oshman*

Teamwork, collegiality, and an attitude of "whatever it takes" marked the environment. This approach led naturally to a decentralized workforce, an open and flexible structure that motivated colleagues and encouraged participation. Part of the goal of GPW was to avoid bureaucracy, which Oshman hated: "Whenever we see it, we squash it," he said.[55] In 1983, the company had only sixteen vice presidents for 5,000 employees; ROLM was "the most bottom-heavy company in the high-tech industry."[56]

This unbureaucratic approach emphasized keeping things simple and avoiding the encumbrances of a bloated administrative structure. Naturally, as the company grew, this became more difficult. But flexibility remained a fundamental part of the ROLM philosophy.

Opportunities abounded in Silicon Valley. Technology companies were popping up everywhere. Nonetheless, ROLM was *the* place to work because people enjoyed heading to work there. Geoffrey Kirsch of the distant ROLM New England told *BusinessWeek*, "It was no problem getting up at 5:00 a.m., because every day, you felt like you were on a mission."[57] GPW permeated all ROLM facilities.

## Ken's Unique Style

Much of ROLM's success emerged from Ken Oshman's unique ability as a leader. Yet his style had interesting contradictions. At times he seemed to foster divisiveness, and at other times he sought consensus. He often asked for and listened to differing opinions, but made the final decision on his own—sometimes announcing it as a "management" decision and sometimes as his own. Either way, there was never uncertainty that responsibility for the decision lay with him.

Oshman was a visionary and a crystal-clear communicator. He greatly appreciated the hard work ROLM's employees performed, and he let them know it in broad messages. Yet one-on-one he could seem demanding, as if the person he was addressing had not yet put his or her whole mind and heart into the issue. "Ken constantly challenges the thoroughness of your thinking," Leo Chamberlain once told the press:

When you go to him with a super idea, he'll listen, compliment, and then immediately come up with something you hadn't thought of . . . Your first reaction is to talk a mile a minute, but if you do that with Ken, you're dead, because he's so smart. Instead, you need to say, "Interesting question," and get the hell out of there to think it through, and then come back.[58]

Some considered Oshman a complicated man. Jim Kasson claimed he never quite figured Oshman out: "He was a contrarian. He'd pick your ideas apart. But even with that, he somehow had a way of really making you want to please him. Sometimes he'd come back a week or two later with your own point of view, and then you knew you'd won." According to Kasson, Oshman and Dennis Paboojian would "really go at it sometimes." On the other hand was Dick Moley, who with his quick insights and dry wit handled Ken well.

As for the relationship between Oshman and Bob Maxfield, Kasson never saw Oshman publicly disagree with anything Maxfield said. "If Bob said it, Ken believed it," Kasson explained. "Bob was clearly number two in the company, not from any way in which he behaved—I never saw him act like he had big executive power—but more in how Ken behaved toward him." Maxfield didn't recall being treated any differently than other employees were. "Ken sure as hell pushed hard in our one-on-ones," he responded.

Before becoming Oshman's executive assistant in 1982, Keith Raffel was legal counsel to the Senate Intelligence Committee in Washington, D.C., where he had surely encountered challenging, demanding individuals. But he called Oshman "a tough boss" and said, "His expectations of you were so high that reporting to him was fraught with anxiety. He rarely said *Good job* right to your face. There was always a little something you could do better."

What was it about Oshman that inspired such hard work and loyalty from his employees and even his peers? Former ROLMans might say it was his vision—somehow he made you see it too. Surely his own loyalty to his employees was a large component. Dick Moley said, "I learned a great deal from him. He was a superb businessman and a great leader of people. He was far from being a micromanager—he gave you room to roam. He was loyal almost to a fault, but that engendered tremendous loyalty and commitment in return."

Oshman wanted to surround himself with people who had an entrepreneurial spirit, who were willing to try new methods or think about issues in a new way. In a taped interview, he said:

> I think entrepreneurs are born, not made. Some people are naturally risk takers and eager to go try something new. I enjoy new challenges. Someone said, 'You might fail.' And I say, so what's wrong with failing? The most important thing is to have more successes than failures.[59]

That was the philosophy with which he encouraged his employees.

## Reinforcing the Goals

A thousand or more new employees joined ROLM annually after 1978. These new hires were suddenly dropped into the midst of the Great Place to Work rather than growing with it. Ken Oshman, who composed his own memos, felt it was important to bring them into the fold by periodically emphasizing the company's objectives. The opening paragraph of his 1980 memo to all employees said about these four goals, "They're all we need, and there's no priority. Each is very important." Oshman laid out each goal in plain English:

- **Goal #1: To earn a profit.** "It's the major reason any company is in business. But why? Not out of greed. It's out of necessity to finance the business. We need more capital equipment, test equipment, increased inventories. As we sell more products, we have more money that is owed to us by customers. As a company, we've never distributed our profits to shareholders. They can gain by stock price. Our employees have benefited by the distribution of profits through our profit-sharing program. Profits enable us to make the right decision for the company. If you've ever been around a company that is not making profit, the decisions are short-term, not logical, and are aimed at finding a way to make the next penny to finance the business. We've always made a profit, and our profits have steadily increased year after year."

- **Goal # 2: To grow.** "We need to grow; we can't be stagnant. Because we're competing against major large companies—[against] IBM and Sperry Univac in Mil-Spec, and in Telecom against AT&T, a company whose revenues equate to a number of world countries. A theory said that the more you do of something, the more likely you are to do it well, and the better you do it, the less it should cost you. This theory of economies of scale means that the company that can generate more products will have a cost factor that can drive competition out of business. What it means as it applies to ROLM is that the only way we can survive is to gain market share against competition. Growth also provides opportunity for employees to grow. The environment we're trying to create means new opportunities for people. We're a substantially different company from the one we started, and that change has brought a lot of opportunity for our people to try new things and do new things."

- **Goal #3: To offer quality products and customer support.** "We're distinguished for our quality products and services. The product that goes out the door is only a small fraction of our quality. The way we answer the phone, process orders, respond to the needs of our customers are all quality. We've done a good job on quality. It's the reason we can grow. Our reputation improves, our profits improve, and the quality of our products and services improve. Quality is closely linked to our other objectives."

- **Goal # 4: To create a Great Place to Work.** "That's so we can attract the finest people we can. We have an outstanding, distinguished group of employees. You can look to your right and your left and see people you're confident are contributing to major factors of success. Making ROLM a great place to work is at the heart of almost all of our decision making. After all, we can have great products and great facilities, but none of it is worth anything unless it's translated into new ideas, products, and services by our employees. Without these employees, we can't make our profits, or great products, and we can't grow."

In the memo, Oshman admitted these objectives were quite general, saying, "It's hard in day-to-day decision-making mode to always tie each decision to those objectives, but I hope they're in the bedrock of where we're headed and where we come from. I hope they help each of us better understand why we do what we do."

## GPW: A Competitive Edge

ROLM's timing was impeccable in establishing the GPW philosophy simultaneous with moving into its new home. A strong synchronicity developed between the culture and the very appealing campus in Santa Clara. Job-hopping was rampant in Silicon Valley in the late 1970s through the mid-1980s. Engineers especially moved rapidly between companies, sometimes staying only a few months on the job if they found that being on the inside was not all that it had appeared to be. Perhaps the company's prospects for success did not seem as good as they had appeared to be, or the work environment was grinding without the relief of camaraderie or a sense of success. Perhaps they simply got a better offer of stock options elsewhere. This rapid turnover resulted in the transfer of inside knowledge; in high costs of repeated recruiting, training, and break-in periods; and a work environment rife with a sense of impermanence.

Yet in the midst of this turmoil, the combination of the ROLM Philosophy and the company's new campus generated stability and calm in the eye of the storm. Word spread quickly throughout Silicon Valley about the unique work style at ROLM. The company was able to attract and retain the best and brightest employees in the area.

That competitive edge worked as ROLM expanded geographically. The ROCO Division had grown to comprise twenty-four sales offices in thirteen states and accounted for 23 percent of telecom sales. Offices included ROLM Colorado, ROLM Intermountain, ROLM Texas, and ROLM Atlantic. GPW went wherever ROLM went.

Bursting at the seams of Old Ironsides Drive, the Telecom Division leased facilities all over the surrounding area. Mil-Spec too was growing and feeling squeezed. Plans got under way for a Mil-Spec facility at One River Oaks, in nearby San Jose. Growing cost-effectively in the Bay Area, however, had become more and more difficult due to the high cost of living and increased government unfriendliness toward business in general. ROLM purchased land for two facilities outside of California—an early example of the exodus of Silicon Valley firms to more corporate-friendly states.

In 1980, sixty acres were bought in Colorado Springs, Colorado, at the base of the scenic geologic wonder, Garden of the Gods. Plans began for seven buildings that would house research and manufacturing. A few months later, ROLM purchased 120 acres in Austin, Texas, for manufacturing and product development.

Considerable planning and execution were required in order to undertake all these new plans and facilities within such a short period of time. Expanding from ROLM's campus-like headquarters presented management challenges. *BusinessWeek* reported on the success of ROLM's approach, comparing it to similar expansions at other companies that had caused management problems and predicting that ROLM would not fall prey to these types of difficulties:

> ROLM has managed to avoid the manufacturing and financial snags that often confound fast-growing companies. An analyst from Merrill Lynch said, "They have done as good a job managing the company as they have in designing and building their products."[60]

Word of ROLM's style spread beyond the United States. In 1980, a magazine titled *America,* distributed in the Soviet Union and aimed at illuminating the American way of life, ran an article in Russian about ROLM's egalitarian culture. ROLM eventually hired tour guides to answer questions about the company's award-winning grounds and its philosophy for the many press visitors and focus groups from other companies wanting to emulate ROLM's style and success.[61]

In 2004, in front of a large audience gathered at the Computer History Museum to hear the four founders talk about ROLM, Bob Maxfield said he thought this new notion of culture was the company's greatest contribution to Silicon Valley. "The four of us couldn't make it happen or create it," said Maxfield. "It developed because we knew the kind of employee we wanted, the kind of place we wanted, and the kind of creativity we needed. We tried to get out of the way and let it develop from the employees up. It was unique."[62]

Years later, when ROLM's legacy was becoming apparent in the growing number of companies that tried to embody GPW, Oshman commented in a taped interview, "A lot of people say that employees are the most important, but we really believed that. We did innovative things to keep, attract, and manage people."[63] Its philosophy, casual style, amenities, perks, and strong sense of accountability and commitment permeate Silicon Valley companies to this day—and many companies elsewhere.

Photo courtesy of Dean McCully.

And it resulted in ROLM being *the* place to work in Silicon Valley. Its informal style softened the boundaries between top management and lower echelons. The appealing grounds, cafeteria, and gym blurred the lines between work and play. Architect Goody Steinberg said, "The result was the transformation of corporation into community. A unique spirit developed at ROLM, a spirit of companionship, collegiality, friendship, and mental stimulation . . . If the ROLM campus became a model for the Silicon Valley workplace, the risk tolerance there soon became a mantra for Silicon Valley success."[64]

ROLM would draw heavily on the willingness of its employees to work hard and smart as it moved out of the 1970s and into the whirlwind of the 1980s. The company would soon face technological and strategic challenges far greater than battling AT&T.

CHAPTER 7

# TELECOM'S PARADE
# OF PRODUCTS

......................

Competition in the telecommunications market had significantly intensified by the late 1970s. AT&T still had the largest market share of sales,
despite its analog PBX, with ROLM and Northern Telecom neck and neck
at about 20 percent each. The rest of the market was splintered among the
two dozen other companies, several of which offered or had announced a
computerized PBX. Differentiation between products based on user phone
features and system manageability became more difficult. Price competition was intense. ROLM's fine reputation for reliability and service held
firm and won many bids.

More competition was on the way. The *San Jose Mercury News*
reported weekly on start-ups that had received venture capital funding.
Three or four PBX start-ups had been funded to the tune of $30 million to
$40 million each. These start-ups would likely be using cheaper and faster
contemporary hardware components than ROLM's, but they would have
considerable difficulty developing the software for the rich array of features and management capability that the CBX had. However, that would
not keep them from stepping into the marketplace with a basic system and
further increasing price pressures.

## Lengthening the Runway

ROLM was under the gun to reduce COGS (cost of goods sold) and/or increase the revenue per system by offering new, optional functionality. Many new capabilities had been delivered, most of which no one had foreseen back in 1975. More than 200 user features were available, many stemming from user feedback. But there was a limited array of new voice features that the customer would be willing to pay for. "We were running out of feature runway," said Maxfield.

⏻

## *"The good news is, every company needs a PBX. The bad news is, they only need one."* —Dick Moley

Dick Moley, head of sales and marketing, summed up the problem: "The good news is, every company needs a PBX. The bad news is, they only need one." Market research firm Dataquest estimated that by 1982, 70 percent of all offices would replace their old electromechanical PBXs with new models.

ROLM had grown rapidly by gaining market share from AT&T. But Moley knew getting 50 percent market share was unrealistic. "Unless we could dramatically expand the size of the market," he said, "we would inevitably slow down."[65] Straight voice communications was becoming a commodity market. ROLM had to step forward soon with something that would pull it ahead of the pack.

## The Hub of Integrated Voice and Data

Today, smartphones and blazingly fast computers provide immediate access to resources within the company and around the world. Back in

1980, though, corporate information was retained on paper, stored in manila folders in desk drawers, credenzas, and file cabinets that, if stacked atop one another, would reach miles high. Adventurous companies were adopting computer capability to store finance records and to control some manufacturing processes, though individual programming by computer experts would be required in order to crunch that financial data and present it on spreadsheets, or to automatically adjust the right valves as the pressure changed. Commercial applications that standardized word processing and spreadsheets, like WordPerfect and Lotus 1-2-3, wouldn't be widely available for another few years. Besides, typically the only people in a company who could type were secretaries.

Back then, sitting on the desks of some courageous employees were large, boxy CRT (cathode ray tube) data terminals, which accessed data stored in the corporate mainframe or the departmental mini-computer. A few years later there might even be an early personal computer. No interconnection existed between departmental minis, as local area networks (LANs) were not yet available. If the worker needed to access information from more than one mini, a second terminal had to be used, which was also sitting on the desk or a credenza, or was a shared terminal in an open space.

Terminals typically had to be located within fifty feet of the host computer—beyond that, the signal deteriorated. For greater distances, slow, expensive modems were placed both near the terminal and near the mainframe. The fastest available modem was 2,400 baud—which means that, loosely, 2,400 bits were transmitted per second. For example, each letter of a word is a "byte"; each byte has eight "bits." So a four-letter word like *like* would have 32 bits. The bottom line: Data transmission was painfully slow.

Most terminals had 25-pin RS232 connectors—a tight bundle of 25 pairs of copper wires that ran from each device to wall sockets, then snaked through the walls to the host mini or mainframe. This cable for data transmission was separate from the cable that ran from the phone to the PBX.

With data being transmitted—digitally, of course—between the mini and the terminal, and voice being transmitted digitally within the CBX, the possibility of transmitting both data and voice through the CBX had been part of ROLM's thinking since the original business plan of 1973. Five years later, rumors circulated about forthcoming products that would combine both voice and data, like Northern Telecom's alleged OCS (Office Communications Systems). IBM was rumored to be working on a PBX for the U.S. market, with the implied threat that the resulting product would process both voice and data. AT&T was thought to be interested in developing and selling computers, but because it was a telecommunications monopoly, FCC regulations barred it from entering a new industry due to the potential of unfair advantage via cross-subsidizing. Computer companies wanted into the telecom market. Telecom companies wanted into the computer market. Everyone began scheming about how to combine the two.

Voice in the CBX—in any digital PBX—was digitized into 1s and 0s once it was inside the CPU (not at the telephone), making it just another form of data that could be transmitted and handled with relative ease, technologically no different from the data passing between terminals and computers. ROLM realized from the beginning that the CBX could combine Data Switching with voice switching by collecting data from a user's terminal, transmitting it through the CBX, and sending it off to its relevant mainframe or mini. The CBX had the potential to handle all corporate needs for voice and data communications; it would interface with desktop products and devices as well as telecommunications networks of all kinds. ROLM's early product development road maps had envisioned introducing Data Switching as soon as all the important voice features had been completed, first for capabilities such as Least Cost Routing and Call Detail Recording and later for Automatic Call Distribution and Centralized Attendant Service. While Data Switching was on the back burner, the CBX marketing pitch began to emphasize that it was important for companies to invest in digital voice technology so their systems could be upgraded easily as advancements involving data came along. The implication was that ROLM would have some groundbreaking products in the future but was not yet prepared to announce them.

In 1978, with the marketplace buzzing about voice/data integration, ROLM management decided the time was ripe to promote Data Switching, by positioning the CBX as the "hub of the office." Moley, in 2013, said, "With that, we would dramatically expand the market and our competitive position along with it."

The corporate structure of most Fortune 500 companies made the prospect of voice/data combination awkward from a sales perspective. The corporate telecom department managed phones and phone systems, and the corporate data or computer department managed mainframes, minis, data terminals, and the data communications between them—and "never the twain shall meet," Maxfield pointed out. In most companies their responsibilities did not overlap, and the two managers typically had no reason to communicate or even consult with each other. A power struggle was inevitable between the two communication departments as their functions gradually merged. ROLM wanted the telecom manager to win that struggle, to evolve into the powerful corporate communications technology officer who would purchase ROLM products that provided solutions for both voice and data needs.

ROLM management also realized that combining voice and data solutions within the CBX would enable other path-breaking products, including integrated voice/data desktop devices and related office applications, thus providing another path for continuing the company's remarkable growth rate. To achieve that strategy, ROLM's Telecom Division outlined an impressive array of products, including the world's first family of digital telephones, telephone/data terminals and devices, and a digital link that would handily combine voice and data on a single telephone cable to the CBX. By introducing these products, ROLM intended to become a leader in the new world of combined voice and data.

## The Office of the Future

In its initial bid to lead this thrust into new territory, in 1979 ROLM went to its fifth ICA trade show ready to introduce its brand-new concept: the Office of the Future. In this setup, the CBX was positioned as the backbone of the communication network—the hub through which voice and data would flow. The CBX would process the voice and retransmit the data to the relevant mini-computer or mainframe. All this would eventually be accomplished over the same cables used by the telephone, eliminating the cost of labor and materials to run multiple large bundles of separate data and voice wires all over the building. In essence, the CBX would function like a local area network (LAN), though LANs were still in very limited use.

ROLM's starting point for the Office of the Future was a product called Data Switching (DS), accomplished by a small desktop box that connected to the data terminal. The DS box reformatted the terminal's many data and control signals to allow data transmission over a standard telephone cable. The DS was connected to a wall jack the same way a second telephone or analog modem would be. From there the wiring back to the CBX was the same as for a telephone. At the CBX, the data was switched to the appropriate local computer or to a distant computer via dial-up modem. DS eliminated the need for an expensive modem, even if the terminal was far from its host computer.

DS promised substantial savings by eliminating modems and allowing terminals to be placed far from the host without reducing quality or speed of transmission. It made it easy

ROLM's initial step into the Office of the Future—Data Switching—demonstrated that the CBX could be the hub of all corporate voice and data communications. Photo courtesy of Bob Maxfield.

for one terminal to flexibly connect to any computer; terminals no longer had to be hard-wired to a single host computer. DS also simplified internal "moves and changes" among terminals, so they could be unplugged and moved from one desk to another. Employee migration no longer required a wiring change; DS offered the same software flexibility that the CBX brought to telephones.

Data Switching established the important point that the CBX could be the hub into which flowed all of a company's voice and data needs. Signals would be sent from that hub to the appropriate hosts for processing.

The product was especially relevant to financial institutions with their ubiquitous terminals. *ABA Banking Journal* reported that ROLM Data Switching "allows high-speed, direct-digital, switched communication between asynchronous terminals, computers, and transmission facilities. It eliminates the need for modems at each terminal and central processing unit."[66] This product extended ROLM's reach deeper into the finance industry.

The ROLM Electronic Messaging System (REMS), a rudimentary email system, was also demonstrated at the 1979 ICA—an industry first. No commercial email product existed. IBM and a handful of other companies in the world had proprietary text messaging systems, each custom-designed to run on the company's own huge network of mainframes at corporate headquarters. REMS allowed office workers to send, receive, and answer electronic messages from other employees by plugging a terminal into a DS box.

REMS and Data Switching moved ROLM's stake in the game from one end of the field—the voice end—to the center line where voice and data intersected. The press took note of the new strategy. In 1981, *Business-Week* reported, "ROLM is targeting an even larger market: the so-called office of the future. In doing so, the company will have to challenge such giants as International Business Machines, Exxon, and Xerox. Many industry-watchers, however, are betting that ROLM will lead the way in merging office communications and data processing."[67] Management foresaw the potential of heading in this new direction, predicting it would transform the company into a multibillion-dollar organization by the late 1980s.

> ***"We thought text messaging was a nice-to-have feature. No one who'd never used it before thought it was a necessity. But it turns out that it's one of those once-you-have-it-you-can't-live-without-it things."***
> ***—Jim Kasson***

REMS was installed at General Electric as a test. The software for the product ran on the CBX's backup computer, which was seldom needed due to the system's general stability. Kasson said, "The design team figured they may as well put all that idle power to good use. We thought text messaging was a nice-to-have feature. No one who'd never used it before thought it was a necessity. But it turns out that it's one of those once-you-have-it-you-can't-live-without-it things." REMS ran perfectly at GE—just long enough for the people there to get thoroughly hooked. Then one day, the CBX system went down. The backup computer dumped REMS and turned to its real job, providing telephone service until the necessary repairs could occur. REMS was down for a full day, until the technician arrived the following day to restore the main computer. By then, the system had dumped all the previous messages from its memory. "GE was furious," recalled Kasson. "They were actually doing real business using text messaging!" With no alternative messaging solution to offer, ROLM uninstalled the product and even quit mentioning the product. But Kasson said the team learned an important lesson: "The CBX backup computer

## Bill Gates at ROLM—Jim Kasson

We knew future applications and the terminals we were spec'ing needed a word processor, which you couldn't just license off-the-shelf at the time. We signed a contract with a striving, privately held company in Seattle—Microsoft Corporation—that was working on a word-processing program and on a 16-bit operating system. A year later, after delays, miscues, and tightened budgets, we were ready to cut the cord on the project. Some engineering managers told me that Microsoft had not delivered on some items. I wrote the CEO, a young Bill Gates, a letter saying that since the project seemed to be low on the priority list for both companies, how about we mutually cancel the project? I suggested that both parties accept the money ROLM had paid up to that point would be it—no future fees due.

Bill called me the day he received the letter and asked to come to Santa Clara to discuss it—the next day, if possible.

I had an array of managers in a conference room when Bill arrived, alone. When I mentioned the delayed items, he said, "Let's go through each one." He knew the details behind each issue. It turned out ROLM had been the root cause of every delay. I dismissed everyone else and said, "How about we pay you $100,000 to cancel the project?" He said, "It's a deal," and left. He wasn't about to just wipe the slate clean. ROLM's project was too important to tiny Microsoft's survival.

was for that purpose only, and we needed to find another solution for peripheral computing applications."

ROLM's positioning of the PBX as the hub of both voice and data had an impact on market perception of what a PBX should now do. *Business-Week* ran a major perspective on the topic: "Now the PBX is being given an even bigger job—linking all the data processing and word processing equipment as well as the telephones that will make up the office of the future." In the article, Oshman showed no hesitation in making his prediction: "In the future," he said "PBX manufacturers that are not able to integrate office functions will see their sales drop."[68]

ROLM hoped that the hurdles—having to implement all the expected voice features, systems management capability, and data integration, not to mention ensuring reliability that was well beyond what was expected of a computer system—would be too high for any start-ups that had PBXs under development.

## A Top-Down Reorg

In order to cope with ROLM's rapid growth, and to ensure focus on the many new products required to execute the voice/data integration strategy, the company reorganized in early 1980, starting at the top. Ken Oshman, Bob Maxfield, and Leo Chamberlain formed the Top Management Team (TMT), emphasizing the team concept from the top down. Oshman remained CEO and president. Maxfield and Chamberlain were named executive vice presidents. TMT had the responsibility of allocating resources among the divisions, which were to manage themselves from there.

Wayne Mehl became VP and general manager of the Telecom Division, Maxfield's former position. Dennis Paboojian took over the role of Mil-Spec general manager from Leo Chamberlain. And a new division was formed to turn the voice/data vision into real products: the Office Systems Division (OSD), headed by Jim Kasson as VP and general manager. OSD was ROLM's bridge to the integration of voice and data and to important new sources of revenue and profit. Its revenue could potentially surpass the Telecom Division's within five years, as demand for data-based, non-voice products was forecast to skyrocket.

Interconnect and telco sales and corporate marketing were integrated into the new Markets Group Division, headed by general manager Dick Moley. An International Division was created, headed by Wolfgang Schwartz, who reported to Moley. Tony Carollo continued to lead the ROCO Division. All divisions were to report to TMT, without any one of the three individuals having traditional responsibility for specific divisions—an interesting concept, according to Maxfield, though in reality he focused on OSD and Telecom; Chamberlain, on Mil-Spec and HR; and Oshman, on everything else.

The non-mil-spec side of ROLM had three major objectives as this reorganization took hold:

1. Cost-effectively integrate voice and data, starting at the desktop, running both voice and data over one single pair of wires to the CBX's CPU, which would act as the distribution hub, passing signals to the appropriate host computer.
2. Move the CBX toward the current state-of-the-art technology to remain cost-competitive and expand market coverage to multi-thousand-line systems.
3. Provide new voice/data applications, such as voice and text messaging and integrated voice/data desktop devices.

The OSD and Telecom divisions embarked on an effort to accomplish all three, and a remarkable number of products resulted.

## VLCBX: Increasing Capacity

ROLM had long set its sights on selling systems larger than 1,500 phones. Customers of these systems would have larger telecom expenses and would even more greatly appreciate the management capabilities and features of the CBX. They would also likely buy more optional add-ons, raising the price per line and profit margins.

Development of a new multi-node VLCBX ("very large CBX") that would increase CBX capacity to 4,000 telephone lines got under way in 1978, overseen by engineering manager Dave Ladd. It was an enormous undertaking, with dozens of engineers involved, because of the huge increase in computer power required and the need to distribute the processing over a network connecting multiple data-switching nodes.

The original CBX had started with the Data General–based 1603's 16-bit CPU, using its hardware, instruction set, and programming language. The new VLCBX had five development subprojects completely new to ROLM:

1. Its own unique 32-bit CPU hardware design (before the days of powerful microprocessors on a chip)
2. A new real-time operating system
3. A new high-level, systems programming language, dubbed RPL (ROLM Programming Language)
4. A totally new application code base, not a revision of the CBX code
5. A sophisticated communications architecture that tied multiple CBX computers/nodes into a single system using a unique "token-passing bus" local area network (LAN) that was state of the art at the time. (Imagine the network as a bus or subway car that can handle only one rider (bundle of data) at a time—and that rider holds the only token. Complex algorithms determine which queued rider/bundle should be handed the token next. This prevents the subway/network from being jammed and delivers each rider/bundle to the correct destination—so quickly that all riders/bundles seem to arrive instantly.)

Ron Raffensperger was the product marketing manager for the massive project. Bob Dolin was the sole programmer of the VL operating system kernel, which looked a lot like Berkeley UNIX—because he had attended UC Berkeley, and because "licensing real UNIX from AT&T was not an

## Software Development Was Different Back Then—Bob Dolin

Microprocessors in 1978 were only 8-bit computers with limited address space. If you wanted a more powerful computer, you had to build it out of multiple components. There was no flash memory, only disk drives and floppy drives. Ethernet was very new and required thick coax cable to tie together the nodes. No simple twisted-pair solution existed. Today, a real-time operating system consists of a scheduler, support for multiple processes, memory management, interprocess communications, a wear leveling, a journaling flash file system, and high-speed networking in the form of Ethernet support.

So, when we talk about the initial real-time operating system (OS) of the VLCBX, we are talking about only a scheduler, support for multiple processes, memory management, and interprocess communications. That is what I wrote for the VL. Today, that might be called the operating system kernel, because the OS now consists of lots of other services. Later in the VL development, but before the first shipment, we designed support for a hard disk and did a custom-designed LAN, called the internode hub. By then we had a small OS and configuration management group that supported the hub and created a journaling file system so the VL would be protected from power failures and restarts during disk updates. CBXs had lots of data to store—they were very configurable systems, and they needed all the disk storage and protection they could get.

## System Configuration Was Different Back Then Too—Ron Raffensperger

To configure a system back in 1976, the sales technician would fill out Fortran coding sheets with the hardware configuration, the software features desired, the extension numbers of the individual telephones, etc. These sheets were mailed to ROLM, where the information was keypunched onto cards. These cards were then loaded into a program running on a ROLM mini-computer, where the system software and the configuration information were merged—"hard-wired"—into one software program that was copied onto a cassette tape. The cassette tape was then loaded into the customer's CBX during manufacture and was also inserted into a portable cassette reader that connected to the CBX using a 110-baud serial (RS-232) connection. The CBX was then shipped.

Such things as the telephone extension of a particular phone could be changed from a portable terminal at the customer site. The first portable terminals were large and noisy, but then the TI 745 terminals came along, which were much smaller but used thermal paper. The terminals operated at 110 baud to 300 baud—painfully slow.

To update a system with a new version of software, or to add capacity or change any of the optional features

option," said Dolin. Likewise, RPL, developed by Gary Maxey, was very similar to C, the language used to implement UNIX. The software was a fully distributed system, which no one had ever done before, and involved mirroring the state of each call (managed as a transaction) within each

(and some of the regular features), the distributor technician would send revised coding sheets to ROLM, where they
would be keypunched and merged with the cards from the
original configuration, which had been kept in paper files. This
was not a "scalable" solution.

The first step toward scalability was a program that
allowed editing and configuring to be done online using a
mini-computer. The program, written in 1977 by Rich Gerard,
was called THWAQ—rumor has it that it stood for *To Hell
With* some girl whose initials were *AQ*. THWAQ was a big
step forward and was used for all non-VL systems. Solomon
Wu eventually wrote a deconfiguration program that could
read the old backup tape.

VL configuration files were kept separate from the operating software, so one set of operating software could be
used for all VL systems. Every VL was shipped with a blank
configuration, then configured on site using the VL's graph-
ical user interface on dumb VT-100-compatible terminals.
No coding sheets, no cassette tapes. This meant that system
upgrades could be loaded on-site—a major improvement.

Later, with the IBM-ROLM 9751, we moved to a 3½-inch
hard disk. Since this system used the ported VLCBX software,
all systems—no matter the size—had a hard disk and there
was no need for a config/deconfig program at all.

VLCBX node that was involved in that call. The VLCBX was a major technological achievement for ROLM, analogous to the development of the
RuggedNova 1602 back in 1971, a ROLM original—from scratch, but on
a much larger scale.

The VL was announced in early 1979, ahead of availability because very large system sales had very long lead times. It was "the most flexible and obsolescence-resistant system available," according to the brochure. It competed head-on with Northern Telecom's SL-1.

The first system went into electric company Georgia Power in late 1979—3,000 lines, with plans to grow. "It was a disaster initially," said Kasson, "with software that didn't come close to the required reliability." VLCBX orders from other companies, accounting for many millions of dollars of revenue, were held up until Georgia Power became viable. Bill Rae led the support tiger team, with "platoons of engineers" on site, said Kasson. One of the problems involved handling massive numbers of simultaneous phone calls during peak hours. Within a few years, computers would simulate call volume to facilitate testing. But back then, real phone calls were needed, meaning real people would need to assist with the testing. ROLMans responded to the plea for help: Hundreds of employees came in over several weekends to make coordinated calls that would stress the system so engineers could test software solutions for the problem. It took several agonizing months to finally resolve all the problems. But because of ROLM's obvious commitment and massive support, Georgia Power stuck with it, and subsequently used its VLCBX system for more than twenty years.

The VL became a highly reliable product. "Barring a lightning strike," Kasson said, "it would run forever." Within two years, the VL provided telecommunications service to DEC (Digital Equipment Corp.), General Motors, Gulf States Utilities Co., Varian, Universal Oil Products, and many other large organizations. The sales force tapped into a new super-size market niche, and these multimillion-dollar CBXs were a major boost to ROLM's revenue.

## Skunkworks

The system hardware architecture of the CBX, designed by Jim Kasson in 1974, was based on a modular concept—a high-speed digital backplane in each shelf of the cabinet, with the shelves interconnected by cable. The other system modules—line cards, trunk cards, the CPU, conference bridges, and other interfaces—plugged into the shelf backplanes. That modularity was intended to allow the graceful, gradual introduction, module by module, of new technology that could provide better performance, lower cost, or new functionality. With careful design, installed systems could be easily upgraded in the field—by a software upgrade if no hardware was involved, or by replacing old hardware modules with new ones (or adding new ones) that provided new functionality or better performance.

A time would come, however, when the speed and memory capacity of the CBX's CPU would run out of gas. When that occurred, a new CPU would be designed that could be retrofitted to any installed system needing it. That was the plan, anyway.

ROLM had promised upgradeability from day one. The original CBX brochure stated it in no uncertain terms: "ROLM's philosophy is simple— never abandon an installed CBX. The very first ROLM CBX put into operation may be upgraded with the features of the latest software release." Avoiding obsolescence was a key part of CBX positioning, an important sales point in convincing customers to go with the new kid on the block: ROLM's new technology would carry them into the future, whereas old technology was a brick wall. That upgradability had held true for many years as new CBX features and capabilities were introduced.

A serious flaw in the architecture emerged in the late 1970s. The CBX switching was designed around the decision to use 12 kHz 12-bit ($12 \times 12$) voice digitization, which was the most cost-effective technology in 1974. However, by the late 1970s, an 8 kHz 8-bit ($8 \times 8$) approach had become the industry standard, driving down the cost of the $8 \times 8$ approach relative to the cost of the $12 \times 12$. The cost gap would continue to widen. This would affect the cost-competitiveness of not only the CBX but also the digital phones that ROLM planned to develop, where the analog voice would be converted to digital form in the telephone rather than at the CBX.

To remain cost-competitive in the long run, ROLM would have to eventually convert to newer 8 × 8 voice digitization technology. But the telecom engineers could not figure out a way to accomplish this in such a way that systems in the field could be gracefully upgraded. The only solution they could envision was a "forklift upgrade"—roll in a forklift, pick up the old system, toss it out, and bring in a new one.

If word leaked to existing customers that this was how ROLM planned to handle its future voice/data capability, they would become highly perturbed that their investment was less flexible than they'd believed. Prospective customers on the verge of buying would stall their decisions, knowing that ROLM might soon roll out new technology. If that rumor spread throughout the telecom world, the impact to ROLM's revenue and reputation could be disastrous. However, the company had to consider the long run. ROLM had no choice but to remain cost-competitive in the marketplace. Not to do so would eventually lead to ruin.

In early 1980, management decided to undertake a "skunkworks" project so ROLM would be able to introduce a new low-cost design when and if it became a competitive necessity. The project had to be kept secret even within ROLM so people who dealt with customers did not say, "Wait till you see our new system." The project was code-named USCBX, as if the team were designing an ultra-small CBX for ultra-small companies—a new market for ROLM that the sales force had said it wished it could sell into. But what the USCBX group was really designing was an ultra-secret replacement for the CBX, ranging from forty to 1,000 lines. It was a "clean sheet" approach, including not only a new switching design but also a new power supply, cabinet, cabling system, and interface cards, all optimized for cost reduction.

The USCBX skunkworks was established within the Telecom Division, headed by engineering manager Gaymond Schultz, with marketing manager Bill Stensrud. Knowledge of the project's real purpose was on a need-to-know basis only. Yet the USCBX team's leader fostered an elitist attitude that isolated the team even beyond the need for secrecy. Engineering manager Ken Lavezzo once advised another manager to meet with USCBX engineers before proceeding much further with his own project. The manager responded, "That would be a nonstarter," as conversations with members of the USCBX team seemed to be generally unconstructive.

As development progressed, the USCBX project experienced substantial delays and rising estimates of manufacturing costs. Jim Kasson described the USCBX as "scary," saying, "It was disruptive technology that required a broad side step from everything we'd developed so far, rather than evolving technology that would work with what we had."

"That's a problem with skunkworks," Maxfield said later. "It can be very hard to get company-wide buy-in as the launch approaches. And that was exacerbated by the project leadership."

In the meantime, that handful of PBX start-ups sprinkled throughout Silicon Valley, which had looked as if they could present serious cost competition, did not survive to see the light of day, primarily because they could not duplicate ROLM's rich set of software features. Facing only existing competitors, which were also running on aging hardware, ROLM's cost disadvantage was not nearly as acute as it would have been had the newcomers made it onto the field.

Sentiment to kill the USCBX project began to swell in mid-1981, applying increased pressure on the key issue—how would the CBX ever convert to $8 \times 8$ voice digitization? Then engineering manager John Edwards sent out a stunning two-page memo proposing an approach that just might adapt the existing CBX with its 144-kbps sampling rate to new 64-kbps capability and allow for graceful field upgrades—something that had been thought impossible. "It was remarkable," Kasson said. "Everyone thought, 'Why didn't we think of that before?' Sometimes it takes getting cornered before the great idea comes along." Edwards's plan used the existing CBX backplane and permitted module swap-outs to deliver the specific capabilities the customer needed.

The USCBX skunkworks was cancelled. "Everyone breathed a sigh of relief," said Maxfield. The key members of the USCBX team promptly quit to start Sydis, a short-lived company that brought to market an integrated voice/data terminal similar to one planned for the USCBX. Most of the individuals succeeded, wildly so, with a subsequent venture.

Much of the USCBX hardware was repurposed for other projects. The cabinet and power supply were incorporated into the voice message system that was under development. The voice and data transmission link between desktop and CPU became a key to future developments that would bring another technology first for ROLM, and a key to its future success.

A team of engineers promptly dove into turning John Edwards's proposal into a real solution. The approach promised a reasonable upgrade path for installed CBXs and a way of handling the new data products. It could buy precious time, extending the existing CBX life by several years—if it worked.

## PhoneMail: The Killer App

OSD set itself up for a home run in November 1982 when it introduced a major business innovation, a voice message system called PhoneMail. Tape-based message recorders were in use in homes but could not be attached to office phones that were connected to a digital PBX. Instead, almost all office messages were handwritten on a pink pad, usually by a secretary or assistant. Taking and delivering messages consumed hours each day. Connecting with that secretary could be difficult at times—while traveling abroad, it could require middle-of-the-night calls.

A few voice-message systems for businesses had been introduced in 1980, but thanks to cumbersome user interfaces, very high costs, fear of new technology, and the recession, the market had not developed. So while the market for such systems was reported to be only $6 million at the time, it was expected to be $200 million by 1985.[69]

PhoneMail was ROLM's first application to use an attached processor rather than the CBX's CPU—the REMS lesson had been learned. Messages were stored as data within a computer system connected to the CBX. The team included, among many others, Emil Wang as product marketing manager, with Jeff Crowe and Laura Watkins reporting to him, and Julie Holding in engineering. Development cost about $5 million and took two and a half years. The field test at Mrs. Fields Cookies was so successful that other national accounts (Citibank was one) received a PhoneMail launch package that included a case study documenting the success—accompanied by the distinctive red tins full of chocolate chip cookies.

Now messages could be left in the caller's own voice, with complete and accurate information. Greetings could be easily changed. A blinking light on the phone and a distinctive dial tone indicated that a message was waiting. Messages could be retrieved from the desk phone or by calling in from anywhere in the world at any time. They could be forwarded to other extensions, saved, prioritized, or deleted. "PhoneMail introduced an entirely new concept in terms of business communication etiquette," said Laura Watkins. "We wrote an implementation manual to help companies successfully modify their culture and processes for handling incoming calls and messages."

Keeping cost down was the driving factor in packing a large number of lines onto one interface card. The cards were so big that Alan Kessman, by then head of ROLM New York, remarked in a product preview, "I can't sell this. These boards can't be carried on the subway!"

But they did sell, everywhere. The price tag was 40 percent to 60 percent lower than that of competitive systems: about $88,000 for 200 users. Phone-Mail ads touted it as "The end of tele-phone tag"—and while this particular

Ten nodes of PhoneMail were installed at Columbia University, along with ten VLCBXs, and thousands of ROLMphones, after a year of laying 6,000 miles of cable to connect 75 buildings. They remain in use today. Photo by Ben Garcia 2001 from http://www.columbia.edu/cu/computinghistory/rolm.html.

frustration remained an occasional issue, incidences were cut to a fraction of what they had been.

AT&T announced an integrated voicemail system for the Dimension only two weeks prior to ROLM's announcement. But the news did not bring down rain on ROLM's parade. *BusinessWeek* reported, "Gloom usually fills an executive suite when a major competitor is first to announce an important new product. But ROLM Corp. was all smiles late in November after AT&T scooped them . . . Dick Moley said, 'AT&T has a lot more advertising bucks than we do.'"[70] Moley knew ROLM would benefit from AT&T's ability to spread the word about voicemail.

It wasn't long before word got out. In early 1983, as ROLM marketing manager Kathie Hullmann sat accessing PhoneMail from a phone in an airline lounge at New York's John F. Kennedy Airport, she became aware that Oscar-winning actor Michael Douglas had sat down next to her. Douglas was watching intently as she pushed buttons to save, delete, or forward messages, sometimes leaving a message of her own, such as, "Pam, please send this guy the information he needs." When she hung up, Douglas asked, "What were you doing on the phone?!" He looked amazed as she explained PhoneMail. "Wow," he said, "I need that!"

Everyone did. PhoneMail was a huge productivity enhancer, recognized as a "killer app" by late 1983. Universities bought VLCBX systems because of PhoneMail. Students—notoriously poor message takers— could now reliably receive messages from friends and family. The university could send all phones an urgent message within moments, such as, "Classes are cancelled due to the blizzard."

*This American Life* by *WBEZ Chicago*, on January 11, 2002, did a 20-minute segment based on a five-second PhoneMail message. In 1990, a Columbia University student whose greeting referenced the movie *The Little Mermaid* received this message from his mother, who was angry that he hadn't called her: "You and the Little Mermaid can go f _ _ _ yourselves." On the program, the now-adult student mentioned that the university had this ROLM phone system. "You could forward messages to people," he said. "You could forward messages to everyone on campus if you wanted."

The moderator said, "Sort of like a precursor to the Internet."

The former student said he forwarded it to a few friends (*Can you believe my mom said this?*), who forwarded it to their friends, and within days everyone on campus heard his mother's infamous Little Mermaid message. It was probably the earliest example of something "going viral."[71]

Voice-message capability became a requirement for many phone systems. ROLM management debated a major strategic departure—decoupling PhoneMail from the CBX and selling it as a stand-alone product, allowing it to be attached to any PBX. Other companies, such as Octel, would soon fill that void. But at ROLM, OSD had many development projects in the works, demanding precious resources, and this was not a priority. The notion of a standalone voicemail product was scrapped—for the moment.

## CBX II: The Upgradeable Superhighway

John Edwards's proposal turned out to be solid. The new approach would accommodate both 8 × 8 and 12 × 12 voice digitization, the key to being able to upgrade installed systems. As the team dove into development, it decided to include two important new capabilities:

1. A dramatic increase in the total communication capacity (bandwidth) of the system, from 74 Mbps to 4,400 Mbps, by means of a new inter-node fiber-optic link with capacity of 295 Mbps—named ROLMbus 295
2. Much-higher-speed connections between two devices, up to several Mbps, by means of super-multiplexing time slots

These capabilities would handily accommodate the increasing data communication requirements on the horizon, while providing a solid obsolescence-free platform for the future. They would also allow the VLCBX capacity to be expanded from a maximum of 4,000 to a maximum of 10,000 lines.

All this could be accomplished with a cost-effective upgrade path as customer needs changed, from adding a few 8 × 8 digital telephones to providing very-high-speed connections between computers. The existing cabinets and 12 × 12 line and trunk cards could still be used, avoiding a forklift upgrade.

To fully realize the cost and functional benefits of the new architecture would require several years of development. Smaller projects within the major project were prioritized. Interface cards for the planned line of digital desktop devices with the 8 × 8 voice digitization took immediate priority. Redesign of other modules to reduce cost could be done over time, as could the design of new modules to enhance the bandwidth, since customer needs would develop relatively slowly.

ROLM would typically announce new capability publicly only when it was immediately available or would soon be available for purchase with a committed ship date. However, the market situation in this case demanded a more aggressive approach. Pressure from the press and investors mounted for the company to make good on its Office of the Future concept. ROLM, concerned about the start-ups that had been funded, had felt compelled to announce early that it would be a player as voice/data integration evolved. But the days of rapid development for major projects were long past. The press was breathing down ROLM's neck to put up or shut up. The stock fell 50 percent, sales were growing more slowly than in the past, and operating margins were declining.

*BusinessWeek* ran a troublesome article in the summer of 1982. The title stung: "Why ROLM's Star Isn't Burning as Bright." The article complained that although the company had announced in late 1980 that it would diversify into office automation, it had "yet to produce any such products . . . ROLM also needs to update its seven-year-old line of PBX equipment (85 percent of sales), now facing increased competition from new companies."[72]

Oshman's response, printed within the article, reflected the cool confidence that ROLMans admired in their leader. "It has taken a lot of effort to find the place where we can make the best contribution," he said. "Office automation and telecommunications revenues could be comparable in four years—or if it's six, that's fine, too."[73]

ROLM needed to counter the perception in the industry, fed daily by competitors, that its product line was rapidly becoming obsolete and customers would be left high and dry. A major market impact was needed. The decision was made to package all the planned capability into a new product line called the CBX II, which would be announced at a major event. The CBX II's impressive package would not only turn around market perception but also leapfrog the competition, none of which could match the enhanced data capabilities of the new architecture.

The distinctions between SCBX, MCBX, LCBX, and VLCBX would disappear, replaced by a single product spanning forty to 10,000 lines. If the customer needed a single-node system of up to 800 lines, the solution was the 8000 CPU—the CBX II 8000, a faster version of the original 16-bit processor that could also address more memory. If a multi-node system of up to fifteen nodes was needed, the answer was the 9000 CPU— the CBX II 9000, which was the original 32-bit VLCBX processor, with either the standard VLCBX inter-node communication links or the new fiber-optic ROLMbus 295 links (depending on the number of phones and amount of data to be transmitted through the CBX). The VSCBX remained unchanged, because it was rare for a very small system to need more expensive, sophisticated applications. Installed systems with the original DG 16-bit processor would henceforth be referred to as 7000s. "We put everything we planned to do into the CBX II announcement, with staggered availability," said Maxfield.

ROLMLink and CBX II capabilities were seen as strong ROLM assets when IBM and ROLM confidentially explored the possibility of a significant alliance in the spring of 1983. That market-rattling partnership grew out of a number of strategic and business issues—and had far-reaching consequences.

Meanwhile, the CBX II was launched on November 17, 1983, utilizing a new technology to achieve maximum market impact: satellite broadcast. A live videoconference that originated in the ROLM headquarters auditorium was seen simultaneously at one hundred sites by more than 10,000 viewers made up of ROCO employees, interconnect distributors, customers, and analysts. The Santa Clara High School marching band in full regalia paraded onstage to herald ROLM's renewed position of market leadership.

The marketing campaign was precisely timed to simultaneously inform the world that ROLM now had high-speed data capability and to assure customers that their CBX investments were sound. The day of the launch, all customers received a brochure whose cover said, *We're leaving our competition behind.* Inside, it read *Not our customers . . .*

CBX II is a fully available, totally digital, absolutely expandable centerpiece for the business communication system that can take you into the next century. The good news for you is this: The 13,000 systems we've already installed can be upgraded to CBX II capabilities very easily, very painlessly, and very, very cost-effectively.

The following day, a ROLM ad appeared in the two-page centerfold of the front section of the *Wall Street Journal,* the most expensive ad placement the company had ever purchased. The dreaded impact of forklift upgrades had been successfully, and privately, avoided. ROLM's own industrial designer Ben Yamada handcrafted about fifty miniature CBX II models, one for each CBX II team member.

The press lit up, including the front page of the *Wall Street Journal*, in the "What's News" column: "ROLM introduced a switching system able to transfer large amounts of data between phones and computers."[74] *BusinessWeek* praised the capability of workstations and computers to communicate at high speed, saying, "ROLM is converting the insides of its existing PBX from a one-carriage country lane into a fast superhighway . . . 'It enables us to leapfrog the competition,' said Moley . . . 'If our competitors have anything further to say, it will be a whimper,' said Oshman.'"[75]

Canadian *Globe and Mail* agreed with Moley that ROLM had leapfrogged its competition.[76] *Information Systems News* said, "The ROLM switch is designed to handle more traffic than any other product currently available . . . New users of the system will be able to easily upgrade to the new system."[77] *Think* magazine ran an article titled "How do you spell connectivity? ROLM."[78]

The *San Jose Mercury News* quoted Jim Carreker, vice president of high-tech market research firm Dataquest: "They've blown away any problem of blocking in data traffic. . . . They've got an architecture that will support applications for the next fifteen years."[79]

The launch of the CBX II achieved its objectives: ROLM put to bed any doubts about its commitment to avoiding obsolescence and to its vision of the CBX as the hub of voice and data communications. The CBX II had arrived. There was only one thing left to do: make it work.

## The Digital Desk

Back in 1980, ROLM management had decided that ROLM-built telephones and terminals would be important components of the company's voice/data integration strategy. That same year, at the computer industry's premier trade show, National Computer Conference, dazzling graphics systems that could automatically generate pie and bar charts from a ten-year forecast were displayed to gawking crowds. Hot items at the show were tape drives, platter-size Winchester storage disks, daisy-wheel printers to produce high-quality print, and "the latest models for hooking up computers to telephones."[80]

If ROLM-built phones replaced the 80 percent of phones on a CBX that were currently standard push-button phones, the revenue per line for each CBX sold would increase. The end-user experience would be greatly enhanced by an ergonomically designed phone that provided single-button access to features. This could drive CBX sales as stories of happy users circulated among telecom managers.

ROLM-developed phones would be designed to directly provide data-switching support to data terminals and personal computers. Instead of the extra box required for the DS product, the terminal would connect directly to the phone, and the cable from the phone to the CBX would combine voice and data communications. And it would be important to cost-effectively provide much higher data rates than were available from modems. Reasonably priced analog modems were limited to less than 10,000 bps (10 Kbps); the goal was to achieve several times that speed.

The next logical step for the integration of voice and data at the desktop was to combine the functions of both a sophisticated telephone and a data terminal into one desktop device. Not only would this reduce the footprint on the crowded desktop, but it would permit a whole range of new, user-friendly features, such as one-click dialing from a contacts directory displayed on the device's screen—a remarkable convenience compared to searching for a phone number by flipping through business cards in a Rolodex™ file or scattered in a desk drawer.

Projects were initiated to develop a family of digital phones, to be called ROLMphones, and an integrated voice/data terminal, code-named Cypress. These products, and the high-speed, digital link that would connect them to the CBX, would be positioned as fundamental to the Office of the Future—the core of the Digital Desk.

ROLM-developed desktop devices would be "digital"; that is, the voice would be converted from analog to digital form in the telephone, rather than at the CBX. This was now economically practical, due to the rapidly decreasing prices of $8 \times 8$ analog-to-digital conversion chips, and it allowed for innovations in desktop-to-CBX communications, since all information would be digital, not partly digital and partly analog.

The decision to convert voice to digital form directly within the phone opened the way for reducing the number of wire pairs running from the desktop to the CBX, since one pair dedicated to the analog voice would not be necessary. Perhaps the three pairs required for the DS box plus phone could be reduced to two or, even better, one. Every desktop already had at least one pair of wires for the telephone. So if one pair were enough, data communication could be added with no additional wiring required— a very cost-effective solution.

The conversion of analog voice into digital code right in the handset occurred using an off-the-shelf A-to-D (analog-to-digital) chip. But the transmission over one pair of wires of that data—not to mention the power for the phone and the additional data that would be needed when a data terminal was connected to a digital phone—required ROLM's first custom-designed integrated circuit. The project was overseen and largely accomplished by engineer Greg Dumas, with the considerable guidance of Professor Marty Graham. After one year of layout design, he sent the schematics off to be prototyped. The prototype came back within a few months. At the next development team meeting Dumas, flushed with excitement and pride, reported in his typically quiet voice that it had worked and only one revision was needed. Within eighteen months, from start to finish, ROLM's first custom IC was ready, manufactured by ZyMOS in Sunnyvale, California. The capability was called ROLMLink and provided a crucial high-speed, high-bandwidth link to the CBX on a single pair of wires.

In May 1983, ROLM launched the Digital Desk at a video teleconference that originated in the auditorium at Old Ironsides Drive. Announced were ROLMLink, Cypress, the ROLMphone 400, and ROLMphone 400D, the latter providing for high-speed data connection to any data terminal at speeds of up to 64 Kbps. The market for integrated office automation products was in its infancy but was expected to grow at 85 percent a year.[81] ROLM wanted a reasonable share of that.

## ROLMLink—Bob Maxfield

Consolidating the voice and data digital signals and the phone's electrical power could be done over three pairs of wires connected to the CBX, but could it be done over one? This would permit voice/data desktop devices to be connected to the CBX with no additional cabling required, which would be a major benefit. The engineers asked Marty Graham to take a look at the issue.

Professor Martin Graham had taught all the ROLM founders an undergraduate electrical engineering course at Rice University before he moved to UC Berkeley in the late 1960s. For ROLM, he often acted as a consultant and technical advisor, even traveling to customer sites, both domestic and international, to solve particularly prickly problems. He was a wizard at coming up with innovative solutions to difficult circuit design glitches and at troubleshooting thorny technology issues. When ROLM called him in to resolve the voice/data integration question, he came back in a couple of weeks with an astoundingly innovative design, which was dubbed ROLMLink.

The company made its initial bid for integrated voice/data terminals with Cypress. The product combined into one unit a number of items that were normally separate on a manager's desk—a digital telephone, a calculator, a Rolodex™ business card file, a speakerphone, an intercom, and a computer terminal to access databases—at a lower price than the combined price of all these devices. The cost of installation would be cheaper

On one pair of wires, ROLMLink enabled a 256,000-bit (256 kbps) per second data rate in each direction simultaneously. The 256 kbps was divided into four subchannels: 64 kbps for the voice, two channels of 64 kbps for data (which could be combined into one 128-kbps data channel), and 64 kbps for sending commands back and forth from the CBX to the desktop devices. ROLMLink also provided power to the telephone over the same wire pair. ROLMLink would work on standard telephone cables at distances up to 1,000 feet.

As far as we knew, this had never before been accomplished, and there was a great deal of skepticism until the feasibility of the scheme was proven. To make this cost-effective, ROLM would have to design a custom integrated circuit to implement the technique. The company had never undertaken a custom integrated circuit design, and it would add to the many risks already at play in the development of ROLM-built phones and terminals. But everyone agreed that ROLM-Link would make an incredibly powerful demonstration of the enormous potential of the CBX to integrate voice and data communications. So we jumped into the project.

due to lower material and labor costs, and the user would face a simpler world by dealing with one integrated device for all communication that wasn't face-to-face. Also included were many personal-productivity applications, such as a personal contacts database, the ability to see who had called while the employee was away from the desk, and an appointment calendar. And it reduced complex, to the push of a single button, lengthy

This publicity photo of Bob Maxfield using a Cypress with the pull-out keyboard retracted was signed by members of the Austin development team. Photo courtesy of Bob Maxfield.

log-on procedures to remote computers. This made life much easier for users who often had one hand on a keyboard and the other holding a telephone, such as stockbrokers.

The Digital Desk was on the market, with more to come—very soon.

## ROLMphones on Parade

The ROLMphone 400 was introduced in May 1983 as if it were a single product, a technological leap over the ETS 100. But in fact it was the premier member of the world's first family of digital phones, though no mention was made of that. The ROLMphones development project had begun back in mid-1980. It took three years from concept to ship. The process of development of these phones serves to illustrate how the team format functioned at ROLM and how the company handled issues that arose during a typical product development.

Two key characteristics of successful development teams at ROLM were open communication and respect among team members for one another's differing skills and opinions. With these factors present, unanimous team decisions could generally be reached on key issues, even after intense and wholehearted discussion with the company's and the product's (rather than the individual's) best interest in mind. ROLM's phone team, like most other development teams within the company, embodied these characteristics.

The phones were initially conceived to function only with the USCBX. The development team started small within the Telecommunications Division, with product marketing manager Kathie Hullmann and USCBX hardware engineer Bruce Prentice nailing down specifications.

When the USCBX project was cancelled, the scope quickly shifted to the CBX, and a fire was lit—these phones were needed sooner rather than later. The initial team expanded to include representation from all facets of the product's life cycle, from concept to specifications to design, implementation, manufacture, ship, and service. Marketing added Cheryl Booton and Janet Gregory, both reporting to Hullmann. Team meetings were held almost weekly. Team leadership shifted throughout the project, depending on which issue or phase of development was most relevant at the time. The precepts of *design to manufacture* and *design to service* were always priorities—they lowered costs to make the product and maintain it after it was in use.

A hardware engineer, probably Bob Sheppard, remarked in a team meeting in 1981, "You know, someday everyone will have a portable, wireless telephone. We'll talk on the phone walking down the street, in the grocery store, everywhere." Such a futuristic notion sidetracked the business at hand as the team speculated on the technological developments that would be needed to make such a wonder happen. And yet within two years, Motorola offered a two-pound, brick-size cell phone for $4,000 (equivalent to $9,400 today, compared to smartphones the size of one's palm that now cost a few hundred dollars).

ROLM's family of phones would have three models. The smallest had twelve programmable feature buttons in addition to the twelve-button dial pad. The feature buttons provided single-button access to features, so users would not have to combine keys to create codes, such as # and then 7 to transfer a call. The middle-of-the-line phone had twenty-four keys that could be configured as lines or feature keys, and the high-end model had forty. They were christened the ROLMphone 120, 240, and 400, respectively.

The 120 was a single-line phone, and the 240 and 400 had multiple-line capability. The 240 and 400 had integrated speakerphones. The 400 had an LCD display. The custom ROLMLink chip was embedded in all ROLMphones. Utilizing the data capability of the chip, however, was

*ROLMphone 120*

*ROLMphone 400*

*ROLMphone 240*

an extra-cost option. Initially, a terminal or personal computer could be connected only to a ROLMphone 400D, which had a connector for the terminal's cable. Later, all models had a data option available.

Ben Yamada did the industrial design of the phones—their shapes, color, look, and feel. He was originally hired to design a good-looking, efficient USCBX cabinet. Of course, this was before computer-aided design (CAD) existed. Yamada's tools for sketching and rendering were pencils and magic markers. He used drafting machines to make the mechanical drawings for each manufacturing part. Appearance models and prototypes were fabricated out of wood or plastic and required considerable sanding and painting. Numerous handsets and phone cases were crafted this way. "No one was even making models out of foam then, much less using computers," he said in a later interview.

The ROLMphones business plan proposed that the most basic model in the family, the 120, would be priced at only a small premium over a standard push-button phone. That aggressive pricing would result in such a high volume of sales that ROLM, for the first time, would need a high-volume assembly line. Manufacturing manager Dirk Speas was assigned to make that happen. Bob Michael, manufacturing engineer, kept a close eye on the manufacturability of hardware designs.

The manufacturing line was established in a dedicated facility in Building 7 on the corner of Patrick Henry Drive and Tasman Drive at Santa Clara headquarters. Robots and a computer-controlled process made it very different from the meticulous, manual assembly of CBX system components that took place in Building 3. The ROLMphone production line used the latest best practices coming out of Japan, incorporating statistics and Taguchi Design of Experiment methods. Said Ken Lavezzo, "We got so good at it that we eventually competed for the Japanese Deming Prize"—the gold standard for manufacturing, which emphasized continuous improvement through the process of total quality management (TQM).

In the interest of cost savings, hardware engineer Walter Bell proposed eliminating the switch hook. All phones had a small switch in the handset cradle for the user to toggle in order to terminate one call and get dial tone for the next call without putting the handset into the cradle. Bell proposed, without a switch hook to toggle, that the user lay the handset into the cradle for a second, where it would be detected by magnetic relay—or if the phone was multiline, that the user push another line button, which would disconnect the first line. The proposal was studied for many weeks before the team agreed that the lack of a switch hook would cause no user resistance. Though no customer objection ever surfaced, the feature did not become a trend and phones today still have a switch hook.

The 120 was to be priced so corporate decision makers would choose it over a $75 standard telephone almost all the time, which meant a price target no higher than $100. Despite considerable efforts to bring cost down, the initial cost of goods (COGS) of the ROLMphone 120 was $111. Cost was forecast to drop, however, as volume built up. Three months prior to launch, Hullmann presented the sales forecast under various pricing models for Top Management Team review. With aggressive pricing of $100 for the ROLMphone 120, the family of ROLMphones was forecast to generate a combined $75 million revenue within one year of the first shipment. Oshman seemed to think this was overly optimistic—upon hearing the figures, he exclaimed, "You're smokin' something!"

Much discussion ensued regarding ROLMphone 120 pricing. Aggressive pricing could have a ripple effect: the low price would grab the attention of the sales force and the marketplace and would drive sales—and more volume would drive costs lower. Also, more CBX users with the 120—a good-looking, elegant phone that made features handy and accessible—would be happy users. And happy users might drive CBX system sales as word got around. But of course, until COGS came down, the more successful the 120 was, the more money would be lost.

ROLMphones 240 and 400, on the other hand, were high-margin products. Their volume of sales based on the projected mix, however, could not completely compensate for the loss ROLM would sustain on the high volume of ROLMphone 120s until sufficient cost reduction was achieved.

Engineering committed to being vigilant about fulfilling an electronics truth—that the component costs would come down with each design iteration of the ROLMphone 120. Speas asserted that costs would also decline as ROLM gained experience with the high-volume manufacturing process. With these assurances, despite shipping $11 out the door with each ROLMphone 120 initially, top management endorsed the aggressive pricing model.

The phones were tested on the ROLMphone team members first, then field-tested at Mil-Spec's new facility at nearby One River Oaks. A last-minute "showstopper" glitch was detected in the IC, relating to distance of the phone from the CBX. Incredible effort by Dumas and ZyMOS turned around an IC revision in record time.

The ROLMphone 400 and the 400D with ROLMLink were introduced in May 1983 at ROLM's first-ever video teleconference. The 400 cannibalized the ETS 100, and ETS production ramped down as the 400 ramped up. The ETS 200 and 300 for ACD and CAS remained available until the ROLMphone 400 was adapted to those special applications.

At the mega video-teleconference in November 1983 that unveiled CBX II, the ROLMphone 120 and 240 were also revealed, completing the family. Hullmann announced that there was also a remote phone. On cue, a ROLMphone with hidden wheels zipped onto stage, did a perfect 360, and exited, all on its own. "Well, more specifically, *one* remote-controlled phone," Hullmann quipped about the stunt. The cap of the launch was the announcement that a stockpile of ROLMphone 120s had been manufactured and were ready to ship, right then.

Customers were enthusiastic. The phones' appearance, functionality, and pricing were spot on. By January 1984, 50,000 ROLMphones had been shipped.

An unexpected marketing "pop" came from the LCD display of the 240 and 400 that showed the name, not just the phone number, of the calling party when the call came from inside the company. For probably the first time in history, the phone could reliably be answered with, "Hey, Ken, what's up?" The caller's name display brought an element of surprise and delight that lasted for several years.

Users were so pleased with the phones' operation that stories abounded of ROLMphones being stolen and taken home, then sneaked back in when it was discovered that the CBX would also have to be stolen.

The "smokin'" forecast was exceeded. During the first full year that all three phones were shipping, 1984, revenue was $86.9 million, neck and neck with the Mil-Spec Division's revenue. By the end of June 1984, the COGS for the 120 had dropped to $83, then to $68 in 1985 and $52 in 1986. The gamble had paid off. Cost savings came from every possible angle, including moving from a back that was held on by four screws to one that snapped on, eliminating the cost of screws and reducing assembly time.

The Phones Division was formed in mid-1984, headed by Ken Lavezzo as general manager. ROLMphones revenue climbed to $103.6 million in 1985, with 30 percent growth targeted for the year after that.

At the time, U.S. companies were starting to move their manufacturing operations to Asia. But rather than manufacture the lower-cost, lower-margin phones overseas and the higher-cost, higher-margin phones in Santa Clara, which would seem logical, ROLM took the opposite approach by manufacturing the ROLMphone 120 in Santa Clara and the ROLMphone 240 and 400 in South Korea at Samsung. Lavezzo explained that the cost of the 120 was design-driven, and the company needed to turn around the new designs as quickly as possible so it wasn't shipping money out the door with each one. Meanwhile, the ROLMphone 400 was highly profitable from the start, so the product design was never altered. While the team considered manufacturing all the phones in Santa Clara, the decision was made to go with South Korea so Asian manufacturing techniques could be explored.

*"It's amazing what you can accomplish if you're not wasting time cleaning up field problems. I think companies often don't appreciate how important this is."*
**— Ken Lavezzo**

According to Lavezzo, one of the things that made ROLM so successful is the attention that the company paid to product quality. "You just can't afford to have any field problems when you're shipping 3,500 phones a day," he said. "We never had a serious field problem with the phones." As a result, all the division's energy was spent moving forward. "We never idled or took a step backward. It's amazing what you can accomplish if you're not wasting time cleaning up field problems. I think companies often don't appreciate how important this is."

This ROLMphone 120, seen in the Sears store in Manchester, New Hampshire, in spring 2013, is one of many thousands that remain in use out of tens of millions that were sold. Photo courtesy of Don Armstrong.

ROLMphones were an unqualified success. The penetration on new CBXs reached 80 percent, displacing all those plain black phones. The one-millionth ROLM-phone shipped in spring 1986; perhaps up to twenty million were sold over the next twelve years. Thousands remain in use thirty years later. The ROLM Alumni Facebook page was abuzz when a ROLMphone 240 made an appearance in the 2013 film *Jobs* about Apple founder Steve Jobs.

Jeff Blohm, a newly minted software engineer who joined the team in 1982, recalled when his boss, Steve Plant, took him aside after a team meeting and told him to enjoy the moment because there would be only one, maybe two, projects like this in his career. "He was so right," Blohm said, "and I've been grateful all along that he took a moment to point it out to me. I was too inexperienced to have that perspective on my own." A small team of people working productively together had made a significant difference to the company, and the resulting product would prove to enjoy a long, healthy life. Plant and other ROLM management knew well that projects of this magnitude came along only rarely.

## Steve Jobs at ROLM—Jim Kasson

ROLM's Digital Desk products caught the attention of Apple Computer vice president of marketing Floyd Kvamme. Apple's Macintosh computer had a small but devoted market primarily comprised of graphics designers. ROLM had captured the major corporate universe, and Apple wanted a bite. Kvamme arranged for Steve Jobs and Wayne Rosing, a senior Apple engineering manager, to meet with Bob Maxfield and me.

Within moments of arriving in the executive conference room, Jobs announced, "I was sitting on the john this morning"—though that's more polite than what he actually said—"and I realized your PBX architecture is all wrong. Here's how a PBX should be designed." He was already at the white board, scribbling an indecipherable schematic. Bob and I sat in silence as he rambled on about something to which he had clearly given only two minutes' thought.

## Integrated Voice/Data Terminals

Voice/data desktop fusion efforts gained momentum. An article in *IEEE Annals of the History of Computing* stated, "In 1984, computing firms saw integrated voice/data terminals (IVDTs) as the solution to the proliferation of new forms of executive communication."[82]

Even before Cypress was launched in May 1983, ROLM embarked on developing two more integrated voice and data products. All three were designed and manufactured in ROLM's Austin facility, within OSD. Matt Blanton headed Austin engineering, Doug Stone headed manufacturing,

Then he noticed a ROLMphone on a credenza. "Is this your digital phone?" He picked it up and turned it over in his hands while I explained its capabilities.

Jobs said, "So how do you accomplish all that?"

I proudly told him how ROLM had put voice, power, and data through a single 26-gauge twisted pair, and said, "What's more, you could hook it up backwards and it'd still work."

"In a few years," Jobs said, "you guys will be laughingstocks because you didn't use fiber optics." It was a rare miss for him. Copper remains the way to connect things at the desktop.

With the ROLMphone still in hand, Jobs said, "You know, I've taken stuff apart since I was a kid. Can I have one?" Bob gave him a polite *No, hell no*, at which point Jobs said, "Well, hey, Wayne'll get back to you and we'll see what we can do together."

As they left, Bob and I gave each other that *Ain't gonna happen* look.

and Carol Wingard led the marketing team that included Phil Pompa and Dennis Haar.

According to the *New York Times*, voice/data workstations were the next big thing in office automation: "At present, a manager wanting stock quotations from a news service needs a personal computer, a telephone, and a modem to link the two. Rigging this gear and signing onto a news service can be complicated and can lead to a jungle of wires on the desk."[83] To meet the forecast demand, start-ups had come on the scene—namely,

Sydis (founded by former USCBX team members), Zaisan, and Davox. Northern Telecom's Displayphone was already on the market. Large corporations—Wang, IBM, AT&T, NEC, Mitel, Compaq, and Xerox—were expected to introduce products within months.

In summer 1984, as ROLM Austin prepared to launch the next two Digital Desk products, several key members of sales staff, on the quiet, were shown one of the prototypes, code-named "Mesquite." Not all of them stayed quiet, however. The press soon reported rumors of ROLM's new Mesquite. Marketing changed the name to the more easily spelled Cedar, and no ROLM product named Mesquite ever hit the market. With Cypress already on the market, the new Cedar and Juniper completed ROLM's "forest family" of desktop devices when they were launched in the fall of 1984.

Cedar combined all the capability of ROLMphones and the Cypress terminal, plus it doubled as an IBM-compatible personal computer. It

Cedar. Photo courtesy of Bob Maxfield.

had 512 KB of memory, two drives for 5¼-inch floppies, a printer port, and a nine-inch graphics monitor. The *New York Times* extolled its pop-up light-emitting diode screen, its disk-drive memory, and its modem. Also impressive was the fact that Cedar, like other IBM machines, could run the top-selling business software programs Lotus 1-2-3 and Multiplan. "It can memorize and dial numbers, set up conference calls, track the length and destination of calls and display messages," the article said. "Many experts agree that the work station could have an important place in the corporate strategy of both ROLM and IBM."[84]

Cedar's single-unit price was a hefty $4,995 (more than $11,000 in 2013). An IBM personal computer, with 256,000 bytes of internal memory, a single disk drive, and a monochrome display, was $2,520, which was $25 more than the new Apple Macintosh. But the Cedar combined a phone and a computer.

Personal computers were beginning to appear on more and more desktops. ROLM's Juniper connected a ROLM-phone to an IBM or IBM-compatible computer so the PC monitor displayed the telephone call and contacts data-base. Juniper comprised an add-in

Juniper. Photo courtesy of Bob Maxfield.

board, software on a 5¼-inch floppy, and a cable to connect the phone to the board. The brochure said it turned the PC into "a powerful management tool, with all the data communications, phoning, timekeeping, and message-taking capabilities of Cedar and Cypress." The card was reasonably priced at $1,495.

Cedar and Juniper made the cover of *Mini-Micro Systems*' November 1984 issue. *Micro Communications* said, "It's hard to see the trees for the forest of micros. But ROLM's Cedar and Juniper stand out in a clearing."[85]

With the "forest products" Cypress, Cedar, and Juniper, ROLM launched itself into the burgeoning IVDT market and hovered at the periphery of the personal computer market. The IEEE article said, "Studies by IBM, SRI, and Booz Allen & Hamilton showed that well-integrated office automation systems could improve productivity by 20 percent per year—meaning the payback period for a $6,000 investment for a manager earning $30,000 per year would be less than 18 months."[86] The *San Francisco Chronicle* reported, "There's enormous potential because now Cedar and other products are out to compete with the huge personal computer market."[87] ROLM's forest products were positioned to grab some of that enormous potential.

Between 1980 and 1984, ROLM nursed the new VLCBX into thriving health; launched PhoneMail, which changed a fundamental aspect of business operations; renovated its telecommunications product line with the CBX II; launched ROLMLink, the key to desktop voice/data integration; crafted five phones (FlashPhone and ROLMphones 120, 240, 400, 400D); released two IVDTs (Cypress, Cedar) and a card that turned a PC into one (Juniper); introduced many new software-based features; and introduced several advanced data networking capabilities (IBM Gateway, T1, D3, and X.25). The products launched in 1983—CBX II, ROLMphones, ROLMLink, and Cypress—polished ROLM's star and made it clear that the company would be a serious contender as corporations moved toward integrating their voice and data needs.

### "Hey, it's a free world. They can come here or stay there. It's their choice."
### — Ken Oshman

It's no surprise, then, that ROLM's engineering staff doubled within eighteen months in the early 1980s. HP was a favored recruiting target. After a number of engineers jumped to ROLM, an HP executive telephoned Ken Oshman and protested that ROLM was poaching its best developers. Maxfield recalled that Oshman's response was something like "Hey, it's a free world. They can come here or stay there. It's their choice."

To accomplish all this, ROLM leased a number of existing buildings adjacent to the Santa Clara headquarters and refurbished them, for a total of nine buildings on forty-three acres, with more than 800,000 square feet for CBX operations. At this point, ROLM occupied much of the real estate west of the Great America theme park.

The Colorado Springs 200,000-square-foot manufacturing facility with a fitness center opened in 1982, run by Dennis Caton, who moved from Santa Clara. ROLM's GPW philosophy was in evidence—the production-line employees, rather than executives, had dramatic vistas of the Garden of the Gods. T-shirts reading *ROLM on the Range*—

ROLM's Buildings 1 to 5, with flat white roofs, are grouped together, with the gym and tennis courts. Buildings 7 to 9 are behind and to the sides. Many other buildings were leased. Photo courtesy of Joao Elmiro Rocha Chaves.

the Rocky Mountain Range—were proudly worn.

By 1984, ROLM had fulfilled all the major objectives the company had laid out at the start of the decade: integrating voice and data, updating the CBX, developing PhoneMail. "Looking back on it," said Maxfield, it's amazing how many products we brought out in that four-year period. The number of things we were doing simultaneously is just mind-boggling. We were working hard to assert a leadership position in a rapidly changing data and voice marketplace, and we had to assume our competitors were going to do smart things."

CHAPTER 8

# MIL-SPEC
# MARCHES FORWARD

....................

By the late 1970s, the military's definition of *rugged* had changed only slightly since ROLM moved into the abandoned prune shed in 1969. ROLM's mil-spec products now met specifications that included vibrations of 10 Gs applied over a frequency range of 5 Hz to 2,000 Hz, shock and impact of 15 Gs for 111 milliseconds, and altitudes of 80,000 feet. These computers would operate in the presence of humidity, sand, dust, salt spray, salt fog, fungus, and, within a few years, electromagnetic radiation. Industrial applications for rugged commercial computers had emerged in the market, such as for snowcats in the Arctic and Shell's oil rigs in the Gulf of Mexico. "ROLM's mil-spec computers were overkill for those," said Maxfield in a later interview. Products like the RuggedDEC came on the market to address these applications, generally at a lower price than ROLM could provide because they only had to operate, for example, up to 70 degrees C (158 degrees F), not 95 degrees C (203 degrees F). The phrase *mil-spec* indicated that a product met the military's *super-rugged* specifications.

Leo Chamberlain had three immediate goals when he took the helm as general manager of the new Mil-Spec Computer Division (MSC) in 1977: First, he needed to continue the division's record growth and profitability to support the nascent Telecom Division. Second, he changed the name of the computers from *rugged* to *mil-spec*, which ROLM's then-largest customer, the military, understood as meeting its intensely rugged specifications. And third, to emphasize that point, he added a phrase to the product ads: *That's why we're number one in mil-spec computers*. Aside from those three goals, said Chamberlain, "We just worked our tails off."

ROLM also met specs for the military's most recent requirements for such things as performance, cost, size, and memory, which had changed enormously over the years. The Mil-Spec Computer Division continued to bring out new products, staying abreast of technology and the demands of the military.

## The Mil-Spec Hits Continue

"ROLM had a presence within the entire Department of Defense R&D food chain," said Tony Gerber, Mil-Spec's VP of sales until 1980. "It was able to follow budget allocation plans for various government-funded programs, influence written specifications as far as possible, monitor the bidding phases, and ultimately contact the winning prime contractors or subcontractors." ROLM's tentacles reached deep into the U.S. military-industrial complex to help the company sense and respond to future needs.

Revenue from mil-spec products in 1977 was $12.2 million, up 10 percent from the previous year, by far the lowest annual growth in ROLM's history, as the U.S. economy approached record-high inflation and unemployment. It was the first year that sales from telecommunications surpassed mil-spec sales, though Mil-Spec's gross profits topped Telecom's. Also that year, the model 1606 and 1666 computers were introduced; both were designed for applications requiring large memory capacity, with the ability to address more than 1024K words of memory. The 1666 also had the hardware floating-point processor that was introduced in the 1664.

The first ROLM Mil-Spec users' group meeting was held in late 1977 in San Francisco with twenty-four attendees, each representing a different customer such as Lockheed, Raytheon, or the Air Force. Chamberlain entertained at the evening banquet by telling a digital bedtime story, complete with sound effects from the movie *Star Wars*, a recent pop-culture phenomenon.[88]

The division regained its momentum in fiscal year 1978; with revenue up 50 percent, to $18 million, it was now contributing one-third of the company total. In 1979, the MSE/30 was introduced, a full mil-spec version of the Data General Eclipse computer system. It was the first system to bring sophisticated file-management capability to military operations at rugged, remote sites. The MSE/30 was used in radar warning systems and in programs to intercept incoming enemy missiles.

The decision to develop compatibility with DG's Eclipse product was made in the mid-1970s. ROLM had licensed DG's Nova in 1969, but DG's 1974 16-bit Eclipse had literally eclipsed the Nova. DG was developing the 32-bit Eclipse MV/8000. ROLM did not have the resources to develop such an advanced computer, and all the software that went with it, specifically for its niche market. To stay abreast of the most current technology, a license was secured to adapt the commercial Eclipse for mil-spec application.

Along with these new family members, MSC was continually upgrading its successful 1602 computer with newer versions—the 1602A, 1602B—each with reduced size, weight, and cost, improving the products' price/performance ratios. ROLM's computers went to U.S. government agencies, industrial customers worldwide, and U.S. military prime contractors, which embedded the computers in their larger systems. Motorola used ROLM Mil-Spec computers in its drone control system, and Raytheon employed them in the Navy's countermeasure system. NASA used a ROLM 1603 in an automatic landing system for helicopters, and the NASA Ames Research Center used it to develop speech recognition for aircraft pilots. Foreign sales were supported by wholly owned subsidiary ROLM GmbH of Germany and by selected distributors throughout the world.

As ROLM reached its tenth year of existence, the Cold War imposed a suppressed rage between the United States and Russia. Intense hot spots around the world kept the U.S. military alert and active. A lengthy civil war in Lebanon practically destroyed Beirut. In November 1979, militants seized the U.S. embassy in Tehran and took fifty-two Americans hostage, holding them in captivity for 444 days. Russia invaded Afghanistan in December 1979. ROLM's MSC products, whether on their own or embedded in the large systems of major contractors such as Boeing and Lockheed, went wherever the U.S. military went.

In 1979 and 1980, ROLM mil-spec computers were considered for use in all ground-launch cruise missile systems being developed by the Air Force and in sea-launched cruise missile systems by the Navy—the GLCM and SLCM programs (pronounced *glick 'em* and *slick 'em*). During the selection process, ROLM demonstrated a full working system to visiting U.S. military contract officials to emphasize that when ROLM said, "Off the shelf," it meant *off the shelf.* The visitors were flabbergasted at seeing a live demonstration, which went far beyond the usual factory tour and line drawings. They kept protesting, "We can't pay you for this demo, there's no money in the budget for this," and Chamberlain kept assuring them that the demo was on ROLM's nickel—that this was how ROLM did things. Mil-Spec got the GLCM/SLCM contract, and Chamberlain broke company rules about no alcohol during work hours by popping open bottles of champagne.

MSC sales returned to previous growth rates, increasing 60 percent in 1979 and 50 percent in 1980, to almost $29 million and $43 million, respectively. Fiscal 1981 Mil-Spec revenue was $51.7 million, up 21 percent—a rate that was very respectable by most standards, yet significantly slower compared to the two previous years. Operating margin, however, was holding steady at an admirable 25 percent.

When Leo Chamberlain moved into the role of executive vice president on the Top Management Team in 1980, Dennis Paboojian took over as the Mil-Spec Division's general manager. Stan Tenold, then head of mil-spec engineering, describes how ROLM's style worked within the Mil-Spec Division: "At the beginning of each quarter, things were usually very hazy on how to achieve the bookings and revenue goals. As the issues became

This ad featured the MSE/30, the first in Mil-Spec's series of products compatible with Data General's powerful, commercial Eclipse computer. Photo from ROLM 1979 Annual Report.

clear, each part of the organization knew what would be needed to hit target." Sales would provide the most likely prospects and the probability of booking them, with specific configurations coming from the individual salespeople. Weekly shipment meetings provided the division's management team with insight on the attainability of the quarterly revenue goals and how to accomplish them. All the functional areas were represented in these meetings—Sales (Dave Pidwell, Peter Licata), Order Processing (Bonnie Heaviside), Manufacturing (Steve Phillips, Don Campodonico, Mike Farnsworth), Production Control (Diane Bokamper), Special Engineering (Bob Jennings), and Engineering (Rex Cardinale and Stan Tenold). Each shipment detail had to be clearly understood, since most mil-spec systems had quite complex configurations—just wiring the motherboard usually required considerable time. Then the manufacturing and testing teams had to organize and schedule the subassemblies. In the test stages, Ron Diehl and Don Williams made sure the systems functioned properly. "Everyone did whatever it took to make the quarter's goal," explained Tenold. "In fact, *whatever it takes* was a key characteristic of ROLM in general."

Three new products were added to the Mil-Spec Eclipse family of computers. In 1981, the MSE/800 was announced; compatible with Data General's Eclipse MV/8000 with a 32-bit CPU, it was the most powerful mil-spec computer system on the market. The MSE/14 offered the best performance-to-price ratio for midrange military computer systems. And the MSE/25, with the strongest software capability of any 16-bit military computer available, was soon to be selected for an industrial application: monitoring the safety of nuclear power plants.

In 1982 MSC introduced the Model 4050 Disk Subsystem, an eight-inch Winchester recording disk that had 35.6 megabytes of mass-storage capacity. With its "small size" (3.2 cubic feet) and "low weight" of 110 pounds—shockingly large and heavy by today's standards—the chassis met strict military specifications. It sold successfully to prime defense contractors in the United States and Europe.

To meet the new mil-spec requirement regarding nuclear radiation, MSC designed a unique circumvention technique that permitted its computers to perform before and after a nuclear event without loss of operating integrity. ROLM was the first company to incorporate this "radiation hardening" into an entire computer system on a mass-production basis. As the strategic and market complications faced by the Telecommunications Division dominated ROLM's top management focus, the Mil-Spec Division's management operated fairly autonomously, investing, developing, and marketing with intent to dominate its market.

## A Home of Its Own

MSC's ability to focus on its own issues brought results. By 1982, sixteen of the twenty largest defense contractors had selected ROLM computers for use in their systems. The Mil-Spec Division's computers played a vital role in national defense, performing such functions as intercept, analysis, jamming, communications, and control. Mil-Spec's computers could be found aboard most U.S. Navy ships and Air Force planes, on a variety of Army vehicles, in McDonnell Douglas's Tomahawk cruise missiles, in Raytheon's SLQ-32 (pronounced *slick thirty-two*) shipboard electronic warfare suite, and in Lockheed's Outlaw Shark, the first system to identify targets over the horizon. ROLM's reputation of being the number-one supplier of mil-spec computers came from its consistent performance and its focus on quality assurance, engineering, manufacturing, and service.

The large procurement programs, such as Raytheon's SLQ-32, McDonald Douglas's SLCM/GLCM, and the Army's ILS (integrated logistics support), were crucial to Mil-Spec's growth and revenue. "These programs took years of dedicated focus and support throughout the organization," Stan Tenold said, citing the work of individual salesmen—Al Miller (Raytheon), Jim Bradley (U.S. Navy), Les Irby (U.S. Army), Brent Neel (Lockheed), Ray Thompson (ESI)—and of the program management (Rich Conley, Larry Stovall, Patty Lou) and systems operations (Steve Phillips, Rich Conley) groups. "The data and documentation require-ments of these programs were immense and required dotting every i and crossing every t," explained Tenold. Each individual contributed signifi-cantly to the progress of MSC's programs, from the competitive phases through procurement.

ROLM's Mil-Spec computers also found increasing acceptance in the industrial marketplace for applications that required near-military rugged-ness, with Halliburton and Dresser Industries, both oil field services com-panies. Shell Oil used MSC computers on oil rigs in the Gulf of Mexico, and International Paper used them in its paper-processing operations. These industrial applications comprised as much as 20 percent of MSC sales.

In 1982, with military budgets tightly constrained, however, MSC's revenue was up less than 4 percent, to $53.7 million. Fiscal year 1983 revenues rebounded, up 43 percent to $70 million. The division consis-tently operated at 25 percent net income, whereas the company's overall net income slid to 7 percent in 1983, diluted by the compressed margins of the Telecommunications Division. The telecommunications business was not nearly as profitable as the defense industry. Telecommunications could generate a lot more revenue than MSC, but those sales did not result in the percentage profit that MSC experienced.

In early 1983, the Mil-Spec Division moved its 800 employees from their cramped quarters at Old Ironsides Drive to One River Oaks, in North San Jose. The new three-building campus, on leased land, sat among a few other corporate facilities, but the surrounding area was primarily thou-sands of acres of undeveloped land, including a longtime working dairy near Highway 237. Mil-Spec's new facility, also designed by Goodwin Steinberg, had 310,000 square feet and capacity for 1,300 employees. The property reflected the lush setting of ROLM's Santa Clara headquarters on

## Ada—Bob Maxfield

By the early 1980s, the Department of Defense (DoD) had more than 1,400 computer languages in use. It decided to standardize on one programming language for developing all applications for militarized computer equipment: Ada, which came out in 1983. Named for Ada Lovelace, the first female computer programmer, Ada was a powerful, object-oriented language designed by CII Honeywell Bull under contract to the DoD.

There was a lot of industry skepticism about whether a new programming language created and driven by DoD would ever be successful. Dennis Paboojian, MSC's general manager, determined that ROLM could have a powerful competitive advantage by taking a leadership role in the issue. Although ROLM had never developed language compilers, he put together a team of subcontractors to undertake an intense effort. ROLM became the first mil-spec computer manufacturer to offer an Ada compiler that could generate run-time code for its entire line of computers. It provided market visibility and enabled the Mil-Spec Division to bid on programs that had an Ada requirement, even if Ada was never actually used on the program.

a smaller scale, with pond, stream, shaded walkways, a sunken outdoor gathering area, a cafeteria, and a gym. For the first time, Mil-Spec was physically distanced from the rest of ROLM. "We had an increased sense of autonomy," said Tenold. "Customers were quite impressed, and no longer confused by the telecom presence." A two-story atrium graced the

The Mil-Spec Division moved to new facilities at One River Oaks, San Jose, in 1981. Photo © Steve Whittaker Photography 1985.

engineering/marketing building, large enough for the high school band that once played "Happy Birthday" there as surprised engineering manager Rex Cardinale entered the main door, and for most of the employees to gather around the railing of the second floor, singing in celebration.

Mil-Spec continued to offer solutions for the military's use of increasingly advanced computer systems. ROLM's third disk drive, the Magnum 4200, came out in 1984. The division was awarded several large DoD contracts: a major Army electronic warfare program, a Navy submarine-based system for weapons monitoring, and for the Air Force, a satellite communications system and an intercontinental missile-launching system. Major defense-industry contractors that embedded MSC products in their large systems included McDonnell Douglas, Rockwell, GTE, TRW, and AEG Telefunken. Mil-Spec sales outside the United States included Germany, Taiwan, Australia, Japan, Italy, and Israel, to governments and to prime contractors that embedded Mil-Spec computers in their systems.

The IBM partnership agreement inked in the summer of 1983 had but one minor impact on Mil-Spec: "We were able to buy of a lot of discounted IBM PCs," said Nadine Grant, then manager of MSC customer service and support. IBM was itself a very large defense contractor, supplying large quantities of its own mil-spec computers to the military. No discussions about potential synergy occurred between the management of ROLM's and IBM's military divisions. MSC remained unaffected by the ROLM-IBM partnership—so far.

CHAPTER 9

# DRINKING FROM
# A FIRE HOSE

.....................

Back in early 1980, ROLM had just introduced the concept of the Office of the Future with its entry product Data Switching. A dozen major ROLM products were being fleshed out from concept or were in development. The USCBX project was still alive. Manufacturing was ramping up, and new facilities were being staged in Colorado, Texas, and San Jose. While the company was experiencing this whirlwind of action, however, the national economy hit the skids.

## A Full-Blown Recession
## and Other Alligators

A recession began developing in early 1980. That year, nationwide unemployment neared 11 percent; the interest rate was 10 percent, with some mortgages as high as 13 percent; and inflation peaked at 13.5 percent. The full-blown recession lasted until late 1982.

Yet in September 1980, ROLM raised $41 million cash in a secondary public offering of 1.2 million shares at $36.25 each. The public's and investors' faith in the company was strong. ROLM repaid about $9 million in short-term debt and banked the rest of the cash to finance anticipated expenditures for new facilities and for research, development, testing, manufacturing, documentation, launch, and training for all the future products that were in the wings.

This positive showing continued, and ROLM rode out the nationwide recession better than most companies. Orders were up. Profits held steady. Nonetheless, a hiring freeze was put into place in early 1981. Fiscal 1981 revenue, at $294 million, had grown 47 percent—a whopping show by almost any standard, but still a significantly slower growth rate compared to previous years that had ranged from 70 percent to 98 percent growth. Net income was $23.7 million. Telecom made up 83 percent of sales.

*BusinessWeek* reported, "ROLM has managed to avoid the manufacturing and financial snags that often confound fast-growing companies." In the article, a Merrill Lynch analyst said, "They have done as good a job managing the company as they have in designing and building their products."[89] The Harvard Graduate School of Business named the four founders—Richeson, Oshman, Loewenstern, and Maxfield—as Entrepreneur of the Year in 1981.

AT&T finally brought out a digital PBX for large companies, the Dimension 2000. Its solutions for small- and medium-size companies remained analog. In an effort to convert its customers to the Dimension, AT&T raised prices on the rental fees of its old equipment. That was good news for all other manufacturers, as it encouraged users to consider alternatives to AT&T. The market was active and volatile, busy with upgrades or replacements of existing systems and news of the new voice/data offerings. The U.S. PBX market was expected to double by 1985, to $3.6 billion.[90]

Considerable competitive shuffling was occurring in the market, with traditional data companies wanting to tap into voice capability and voice companies into data. One of the first challengers from the computer industry was Datapoint Corp., which introduced its Information Switching Exchange (ISX) in spring 1981. Wang Laboratories was said to be developing a voice/data version of its data-only system. Fujitsu acquired a majority interest in American Telecom Inc. Honeywell purchased Action Communication Systems. IBM was selling a large, outdated PBX in Europe for special applications for a few customers. *BusinessWeek* said, "While the IBM model does not handle both voice and data and is not now being sold in the U.S., there is no doubt what direction the computer giant is headed."[91] Meanwhile, AT&T was contemplating how it might blast its way into the data world.

Some shuffling was also happening inside ROLM: Burt McMurtry left the board in 1982. ROLM was a big company by then, and McMurtry felt that the timing was right for him to step down. Bob Maxfield received a handwritten letter soon after McMurtry departed:

> I just want to thank you again for the education I've received watching you, Ken, and others build ROLM. I'm sorry I won't be so close an observer of your future growth, but I hope to be more than an interested bystander. You guys have never needed much help, but please let me know if there's any way I might be of assistance. I hope you'll continue to enjoy building the company.[92]

"That letter meant a lot to me," said Maxfield in 2013. "I thought the world of Burt—still do. Now he's the elder statesman of Silicon Valley. He probably understands the ins and outs of the Valley better than anyone."

McMurtry was replaced by Bob Noyce, inventor of the integrated circuit, Intel cofounder, and one of the "traitorous eight" who'd started Fairchild Semiconductor back in 1957. Besides sharing his considerable business acumen, Noyce could contribute insights into technological advancements that would help ROLM stay on the front edge of the technology curve.

## "Venture capitalists often overstay on a board of directors."— Burt McMurtry

"Venture guys often overstay on a board of directors," McMurtry said later. "They're good when companies are small. But needs change as the company grows, and most venture capitalists don't have the experience needed at that point."

McMurtry wasn't the only longtime ROLM mentor who decided to move on that year. Leo Chamberlain retired in January 1982—"before I get too decrepit," he told everyone. In reality, he had made up his mind long before joining ROLM: In his previous company he'd witnessed the bitter treatment of an older employee as the company tried to force the man into retirement. Chamberlain had promised his wife back then that no matter what situation they found themselves in, they would retire to Hawaii when he turned fifty. "I was having fun at ROLM," he said. "I held her off for two years but finally had to give in."

A week after retirement, Chamberlain answered the doorbell to find Ken Oshman on his doorstep in a jogging suit, panting, out for an evening run. He asked if Chamberlain would temporarily come back and run Mil-Spec, because Dennis Paboojian had just been diagnosed with prostate cancer. "Hell, I would've climbed a tree for Ken," said Chamberlain, "so of course I came back."

Paboojian was back up to speed within four months, after undergoing intense chemotherapy, and Chamberlain retired to Hawaii for good. He, like McMurtry, would be missed. Many Leo-isms had worked their way into ROLM's culture over the years, notably "up to our ass in alligators," a phrase he used whenever the going got tough. Before he retired, he had a placard constructed beside the pond: *Don't feed the alligators*. He hoped that when people saw that sign, they would think, 'That was Crazy Leo for you.'

Shortly after his departure, a six-foot bronze alligator moved into the pond and a chair appeared in the cafeteria: "The Leo Chamberlain Breakfast Seat, Reserved 7-8 a.m. Daily."

As the recession lengthened in 1981 and 1982, the overall business communications market in the United States failed to grow. With military budgets constrained, the Mil-Spec Division's revenue was up less than 4 percent, to $53.7 million, one-seventh of the company's total. Yet ROLM's over-all revenues grew 29 percent, to $380 million in fiscal 1982. Although it was the lowest growth rate the company had ever experienced, it was nonetheless remarkable given the poor economic environment.

*U.S. News & World Report* ran an article on firms that were doing fine despite the recession. ROLM ranked number two with 56 percent average annual revenue growth for the decade 1972 to 1982. Fast-food company Wendy's took first place with 68 per-cent annual growth. "These companies have increased their earnings per share every year since 1972," the article pointed out.[93]

A large bronze alligator appeared in the pond shortly after Leo Chamberlain retired in 1982 to commemorate his oft-repeated, "We're up to our ass in alligators." Photo courtesy of Evelyn Cozakos.

British CBX manufacturer Plessey's five-year licensing contract was due to expire or be renewed in late 1982. ROLM made no effort toward renewal because Plessey's sales were insignificant to overall CBX financial performance. Management assumed the feeling was mutual, since there had been no word from Plessey as the expiration date approached. At the last minute, Plessey CEO Sir John Clark invited Dick Moley, Ken Oshman, and Bob Maxfield to visit the facilities in Nottingham, followed by lunch at his country estate. They assumed the gesture was either a friendly start to new contract negotiations or a friendly finale to the relationship.

The factory tour on Friday was pleasant. On Saturday morning, Clark's limo picked up the three ROLM leaders and their luggage at the hotel, and would deliver them to Heathrow by late afternoon. But first, Sir John escorted them around the local village's annual fair. "The villagers were quite deferential toward him," recalled Moley, "the way they would have been toward the lord of the manor in the old days." Then they headed to Clark's country estate, an old Georgian-style house, with extensive grounds and a stable. "We had a cheery garden lunch," Moley said. "Then he dropped the bomb."

Clark informed them that Plessey would not renew the contract. In fact, Plessey was nearing introduction of its own digital PBX. Within several months, the company would launch in the United Kingdom and Europe, and it would enter the U.S. market shortly afterward—in direct competition with ROLM.

Plessey was not known to have a highly advanced telecom development team. Oshman informed Clark that a lawsuit based on copyright and patent infringement would result if Plessey was serious about this. "Oh, we're quite serious," said Clark, and he bade them farewell.

Oshman phoned attorney Larry Sonsini from an airline lounge. Sonsini would have a saber-rattling letter ready upon Oshman's return to California.

Confident of its position, Plessey invited ROLM's engineers to examine the design. It claimed that any design elements identical to ROLM's were that way simply because it was the only way that made sense. "The avenue to defeating that argument was to find things that were the same that made no sense," said Office Systems general manager Jim Kasson. In December 1982, he and software engineer Joanne Kanow headed for England. Kanow found, verbatim, ROLM CBX code that had been "patched out" (sidelined) but never deleted. Kasson also found unused signal lines on the Plessey backplane with the same names as unused lines on the CBX backplane. "It didn't take an expert to see that Plessey's software and underlying code was essentially ROLM's," Kanow said later. "Comments in the code were easy to spot because of identical misspellings and things like quirky slang typical of [ROLM engineer] David Ladd software."

Faced with these findings, Plessey offered $2 million to settle out of court. The final decision, in summer 1983, was for $10 million ($23 million in 2013) and, according to a summary memo by in-house counsel Michael Morris, "some statement to the world by Plessey, singing ROLM's praises and stating 'we wouldn't be where we are without you.'" Plessey was granted the right to use ROLM's patents, but it was barred from entering the U.S. market for three years. Plessey's PBX found moderate success in the U.K. and European markets. The company was bought by GEC-Siemens in 1989.

## Outlasting the Competition

Thanks to the technology revolution that ROLM had ignited, between 1977 and 1982 many U.S. companies had opted for a forklift upgrade, tossing out their old PBX clunkers and replacing them with new digital systems. ROLM shipped its 10,000th CBX in September 1982. T-shirts celebrated the milestone with a picture of Alexander Graham ROLM on the front and *Ma Bell is the mother of my invention* on the back. The CBX range had expanded to cover all but the smallest companies, from the VSCBX for as few as twenty-four users to the VLCBX for up to 10,000 users.

ROLM's decision to sell directly to the customer had resulted in increased sales and customer satisfaction, and it played a key role in ROLM's understanding of end-user needs and the changes occurring in the telecommunications marketplace. The decision to go into direct sales had proved successful. New ROCOs added in 1982 included ROLM Midwest, ROLM New England (Geoff Kirsch), ROLM New York (Dan Smith), and ROLM California (Dan Shea). A total of fourteen ROCOs with fifty-five offices serving all major cities in North America accounted for 70 percent of sales by 1983. James Carreker, vice president of high-tech market research firm Dataquest, commented on ROLM's success: "Mr. Oshman isn't a quick turnaround manager. He states a long-range strategy and sticks with it . . . That was unpopular with some at the time . . . But it turned out to be an extremely sound strategy, because it allowed ROLM

# Tales from the Field—
# Don Armstrong

The installation of a CBX at the International Monetary Fund required all sorts of special security treatment. Everything in that area was sealed. Even the manhole covers were welded shut. The IMF needed to communicate with a building nearby but couldn't use T-spans, microwaves, or fiber optics because they would interfere with all the other electronic and communication gear in use. Instead, the techs had to set up an infrared link on the roofs of these two buildings. Infrared has an extremely tight beam width, requires precise line-of-sight, and is quite sensitive to heat. So on a hot day, communications would halt when the link fell out of alignment as the building minutely expanded and contracted. We'd go up on the roof to realign the signal, with the Secret Service

to keep control of its products."[94] ROLM's decision to go into direct sales, replacing many of its outside distributors, had been a wise one.

In addition to beefing up the ROCOs, new independent distributors were added in North Carolina, Tennessee, and Hawaii. The national accounts program worked closely with the ROCOs and independent distributors, and provided special service and uniform pricing for major corporations such as Bank of America and Federated Department Stores. Its accomplished sales reps, like Mike Clair, Jack Reich, and Bob Jones, provided the hands-on attention that prevented AT&T from reclaiming these major national firms that had once been its customers.

The ROLM Federal Systems Group had been established in 1980 to hovering over us with their holsters barely hidden. We'd hit the IMF cafeteria afterward, where the filet mignon was only $3.50.

Another CBX, with Release 5 software, went into the federal building that housed both the Social Security Administration (SSA) and Connecticut senator Chris Dodd's office. Senator Dodd's office received many complaints that the SSA phones were always busy and no one could get through to have their questions answered. It took considerable effort to figure out that the SSA operators frequently put all lines on hold for long periods of time so they could take a break from work. The folks in the senator's office didn't believe me when I told them, so I rigged the system so that whenever all the Social Security phones were put on hold, Senator Dodd's office lost dial tone. There was a big turnover in Social Security soon after that.

address the special needs of the federal government. Many installations required system adaptations for security purposes, and anyone who installed or serviced the systems had to have a top-secret security clearance. ROLM won many contracts, including the White House and the International Monetary Fund.

By mid-1983, ROLM offered sales and service in more than 140 cities internationally, including in Canada, Argentina, Mexico, Venezuela, and Hong Kong. Each country had its own telecommunications specifications that required product specialization, a development process called *homologation*. It involved such things as the maximum level of volume permitted on a call, the maximum length of delay permitted after a button was hit until the system responded, how many digits were allowed in the country's dialing plan, and much more. These were nontrivial system implementations that differed by country. International sales were problematic because of the expense of homologation and the difficulty of forecasting the revenue that would result.

The industry was still not a level playing field. Northern Telecom and AT&T, being monopolies, could subsidize their low-margin PBX operations with the high-margin profits of providing local and long-distance telephone service (Nortel in Canada, AT&T in the United States). The top three PBX manufacturers in 1982 held 90 percent of the PBX market, with AT&T around 50 percent, and ROLM slightly ahead of Northern Telecom with around 20 percent each. The remaining 10 percent of the market was splintered among a dozen minor manufacturers such as Mitel. In late 1983, to measure perceptions among telecommunications industry opinion holders, an independent market research firm was enlisted to undertake a blind poll of consultants, research firms, and industry press editors. They were asked to rank fourteen PBX manufacturers on various attributes. ROLM ranked highest in all factors: technological leadership, most advanced office automation products, and best customer service.

ROLM had successfully penetrated the U.S. corporate telecommunications industry and become practically indispensable to all industries and services. CBXs were in use at all the top twenty firms of the Fortune 500, in ninety-one of the top 100, and in 334 of the top 500. All top ten computer companies had CBXs, as did nine of the top ten retailers, and eight of the top ten oil and gas companies. ROLM systems were found in the medical and health care industries, financial firms, transportation companies, law firms, utilities, colleges and universities, and all levels of government.

In early 1983, ROLM's positioning as the hub of voice/data integration was publicly validated by the three largest mini-computer makers—Data General, Digital Equipment, and Hewlett-Packard. They each endorsed the ROLM CBX as the way to interconnect their office automation gear.

*BusinessWeek* reported on the partnerships that blurred competitive lines: "Computer makers have moved into communications to link their machines, while the communications equipment producers have begun making such products as computer terminals to sell their switches. Suddenly these fierce competitors have started working closely together." The article quoted Maxfield, who pointed out that without these cooperative arrangements, computer manufacturers would find it difficult to compete in the market.[95] In fact, the pressure proved too great for Datapoint and Rockwell, which announced they would exit the digital PBX market. The troublesome Silicon Valley PBX start-ups that had worried ROLM had folded, either unable to develop products that could leap over the hurdles of accomplishing full voice and data integration out of the chute, or unable to raise the vast amount of funds that doing so would require.

## The Surprising New AT&T

AT&T continued to stew over the idea of any manufacturer but itself supplying products in the telecommunications arena. It lobbied each new session of the U.S. Congress for a communications reform bill to overturn the 1968 Carterfone decision, hoping to reinforce its monopoly, despite the antitrust suit filed against the company by the Justice Department in 1974. By the early 1980s, many congressional members had at last come to understand the value of competition and continued to resist AT&T's pressure. The Justice Department thought the giant should not be permitted to override competition in the nascent long-distance telephone service industry; further, it was of the opinion that AT&T should divest itself of manufacturing arm Western Electric. Western Electric would then become an independent manufacturer whose products could be offered to AT&T and any other phone service provider.

AT&T, no doubt feeling that the telecommunications business alone lacked sufficient growth potential, was eager to enter the commercial computer industry, a very large, rapidly growing, unregulated market dominated by IBM. AT&T's own Bell Labs, one of the world's premier research institutions, had been designing computers for years, and Western Electric was already manufacturing them for use in many of its central offices, the backbone of the U.S. local and long-distance telephone service. Further, Bell Labs had developed a powerful operating system called UNIX, which it made available under license to government and academic institutions to develop programs for their own use—an "open" system. IBM's operating system was proprietary and unavailable—a "closed" system. "From a technology standpoint," said Maxfield in hindsight, "AT&T had legitimate reasons to believe it could compete successfully in computers."

The Justice Department antitrust suit against AT&T was finally approaching a conclusion in the fall of 1981 when ROLM's Dick Moley was called to testify in front of Judge Harold Green as a witness for the Justice Department. Moley said it was "great fun" to be cross-examined by AT&T's attorney: "Green was clearly going to find AT&T guilty of antitrust—even I could tell that from his questions and body language. That had to be just as apparent to AT&T." If Judge Green ruled as expected, AT&T would be forced to divest of Western Electric and would have to provide equal access to the new long-distance competitors. It would be reduced to holding a monopoly position on local phone service through its subsidiaries, the Regional Bell Operating Companies (RBOCs, also called the Baby Bells, such as Ohio Bell) and to competing with newcomers in the regulated long-distance market.

The telecommunications giant strategized with its legal team about how to negotiate a favorable outcome. "AT&T believed their own propaganda that Western Electric could beat anyone in the world," said Moley. "They thought Western Electric was their magic bullet for competing in the computer industry." Rather than risk allowing the trial to run to its inevitable conclusion, AT&T offered to divest the local operating companies in exchange for keeping Western Electric.

AT&T was still attempting to escape a long-overdue leveling of the playing field. According to Moley, "AT&T's bigwigs at corporate thought they held the political clout." But in reality, Moley said, it was the local guys in the Baby Bells who had the clout: They did the groundwork for congressmen and officials in election campaigns. They advised congressional committees. "So AT&T gave up their monopoly position to compete in a field they knew far less about than they thought they knew and in which they had no political clout to create legislative bias," said Moley.

The government's eight-year antitrust suit against AT&T was settled in January 1982. The lawsuit had generated tens of millions of pages of documentation and had involved hundreds of attorneys. AT&T Computer Systems was promptly formed in order to ready AT&T's eager assault on the computer industry. The Baby Bells had to be spun out by January 1984.

AT&T's formerly lucrative long-distance business quickly came under increasing attack from new competitors MCI and Sprint and many small providers. From this point on, that arena would see a flood of competition, with rates significantly reduced and the variety of services greatly expanded.

AT&T ultimately failed in the computer market. Bob Maxfield said, "AT&T didn't know what it didn't know, which was how to compete in an unregulated market after one hundred years of being a monopoly." Dick Moley called AT&T's divestiture agreement "the worst corporate decision of the twentieth century."

## *"AT&T's divestiture agreement was the worst corporate decision of the twentieth century."— Dick Moley*

Ironically, more than two decades later, in 2006, one of the remaining Baby Bells—SBC, formerly Southwestern Bell, which had acquired other former Baby Bells Pacific Telesis and Ameritech—bought the old remnants of AT&T and formed AT&T Inc. It is now a provider of telecommunications services, including cell phones, wireless, and high-speed Internet, with approximately $30 billion annual revenue. Decades after the AT&T divestiture, one arm of the former monopoly has experienced success in both the voice and data arenas.

But back in early 1982, before the benefit of hindsight, the world suddenly looked different after the surprising court settlement. The former telecommunications giant was entering the computer industry and thought that it was destined to grab hold of the voice and data integration of the corporate world. Huge companies on both sides of the data/voice line were looking to extend a giant leg across to the other side and span the gap. The idea of the PBX playing a key role in a company's overall communications plan was gaining traction.

Data-only IBM sorely wanted to be a player in the combination of voice and data. Although it offered an outdated product in Europe, it had failed at half-hearted attempts to develop a PBX for the U.S. market. The amplified threat was that AT&T would apply its communications expertise to its future data solutions. "IBM was not scared of much," said Maxfield, "but the prospect of competing against AT&T in the computer industry had to be taken seriously."

Soon after the AT&T antitrust suit was signed in 1982, IBM entered into a handshake agreement with small Canadian PBX manufacturer Mitel for joint development and marketing of products. Mitel had minor success in the United States with a small analog PBX in the mid-1970s but held less than 1 percent of the U.S. PBX market. In 1981 it had announced a digital PBX of up to 2,000 lines, the SX2000, right in ROLM's product space. The IBM-Mitel agreement gave IBM the right to market the SX under its own label. Telecom insiders were skeptical that the alliance would result in a real threat, as Mitel had yet to deliver the SX. But IBM certainly had the money to toss at the problem, and that's what it chose to do, though not in the expected direction.

## Mounting Pressure

ROLM's pockets were, to say the least, not nearly as deep as IBM's. In late 1982, margins were being pinched and expenses were high. The Mil-Spec Division's higher profitability could not offset the declining margins of the company's telecom side. OSD had recently introduced the remarkable office-productivity enhancer PhoneMail, but the product was not yet generating sufficient revenues to fuel growth. Major investments had been made in facility expansions. The ROCOs' overhead was higher than the competition's sales side. Taking a cue from the gorgeous Santa Clara facility, the ROCO offices were plusher than typical distributor sales offices, and ROLM's field employees had better personnel benefits. Expenditures were mounting.

ROLM was not yet reaping benefits from its investment in research and development. The sales ramp for some of the new products was long and gradual rather than steep and short. Margins were being compressed because of competition. Cost cuts and another hiring freeze were implemented.

ROLM needed cash to fund all the products that were in the hopper—CBX II, ROLM-phones, Cypress, Cedar, and Juniper—and to support the company until profitability rebounded. CBX II would be a short-term solution that would add several years of life to the CBX, but a new system was needed within four to five years, one that could take full advantage of new high-speed, high-bandwidth electronic components. Specs for the new system were already under way.

Ken's Oshman's leadership and confidence infused employees with a can-do attitude throughout ROLM's meteoric growth. Photo: Business-Week, November 19, 1984, p. 166.

In March 1983, ROLM placed another public offering of 3.85 million shares of common stock, which raised $172 million in cash. Ken Oshman, in his style of keeping all employees abreast of major corporate developments, sent a memo that said, "We should all be pleased that the stock market showed such interest in our stock." He went on to explain that ROLM invested more than its competitors in its employees ("the best in the world"), in customer support ("[we move] heaven and earth to satisfy our customers"), in technology ("clearly the industry leader"), and in marketing and distribution ("second to none in quality, tenacity, and effectiveness"). He then addressed financial resources: "All ROLM's primary competitors, as regulated utilities, de facto monopolies, or recipients of heavy foreign governmental subsidies, have substantially more financial resources than we do. AT&T just announced its intention to make its second equity offering of over a billion dollars this year." He ended with, "I expect that 1983 will be a pivotal year in our industry, with changes in technology, regulation, and hopefully the economy. We're ready and eager."

A few months later, fiscal year 1983 revenue reflected ROLM's ability to outperform and outlast its competitors. Sales grew 32 percent from 1982, to $503 million. Earnings were up 29 percent, at $35 million. The Mil-Spec Division's revenues were up 31 percent, a vast improvement over the previous year as the United States eased out of the recession. However, between 1979 and 1983, the company's overall net income had steadily slid from 9.6 percent of revenue to 7 percent, increasing pressure on management to find solutions that would not only prevent a further slide but also increase the profitability needed to fuel the investments in all facets of the organization that Oshman had outlined in the memo.

ROLM was simultaneously dealing with the ramifications of the AT&T divestiture, navigating the market shifts that merged voice and data—or threatened to, like the Mitel/IBM agreement—and supporting all that was going on internally even as profit margins declined. It was like "drinking from a fire hose," said Maxfield in an interview years later. "The pressure was getting pretty intense. And it was hard to foresee the situation rapidly improving under the current status quo." Something had to change—and it would.

CHAPTER 10

# A PIVOTAL YEAR

....................

Voice and data would be integrated—it seemed inevitable. ROLM's major competition in that potentially enormous market would be IBM and AT&T, both with far more corporate resources and in-house data expertise than ROLM had.

IBM already had the data side covered; its agreement with Mitel gave it the voice side. Even if Mitel failed to deliver what IBM needed in telecom, IBM could buy Mitel's PBX technology—or the entire company—and develop the voice/data integrated solutions itself. IBM, already selling an outdated PBX in Europe, was said to be developing a state-of-the-art PBX code-named Carnation in its La Gaude, France, development facility. Once IBM put all the pieces together, it would be a formidable competitor.

AT&T (including its subsidiary Western Electric) and the Baby Bells may have separated legally, but they were still one another's most loyal friends. Western Electric had been making computers and data communications equipment for AT&T's central offices for many years and more recently had been manufacturing the Dimension digital PBX. Adapting those systems to act as the hub of voice and data switching for the Baby Bells to sell to the Fortune 500 companies, all while entering the unregulated commercial computer market, seemed quite doable. The new AT&T extended family, with even greater resources than IBM, would make another formidable competitor to ROLM in the world of voice and data integration.

Suddenly ROLM faced the prospect of having to compete with not one but two giants, each with resources orders of magnitude larger than its own. With already shrinking margins due to price competition and a large plateful of product development efforts to be executed, it wasn't clear that ROLM could continue to go it alone.

## The Search for a Data Partner

In the fall of 1982, top management began quietly discussing the possibility of finding a partner to help counter the two behemoths—a partner that had a solid presence in the computer industry, that would lend credibility and access to the decision-makers on the data side of the customer corporation, and that would participate in shared development and marketing efforts.

ROLM was determined to be a major player when voice and data merged. The company held steadily to its Office of the Future strategy. The ROLMLink, under development, would provide the means of driving high-speed data and voice over the twisted-pair cable that already existed in all offices, and the CBX could provide the path for computers to communicate with desktops. The partners could share the development costs and jointly market integrated desktop devices, high-speed interfaces from the computer to the CBX, and advanced office automation applications such as electronic mail.

ROLM had several strategic-partner candidates in mind but no way to know for certain which partnership would work. The company's leaders had to do their due diligence—and then take a leap of faith.

At an off-site meeting in late 1982, management discussed possible partners. Three decades later Dick Moley recalled the reaction to someone's suggestion of partnering with IBM. "Big Blue"—the global company's nickname referring to its size, its blue logo, and its managers' penchant for wearing navy blue suits—had about 75 percent of the computer market. "Everyone laughed at the absurd notion that small, nimble ROLM would partner with the rigid behemoth," said Moley. Besides, IBM's agreement with Mitel seemed to take it off the table. The short-listed candidates were DEC, Data General, and HP, companies that had already endorsed connection with the CBX.

HP was the front-runner. ROLM knew its people from middle management to the top, it had a similar corporate culture, and it was headquartered in nearby Palo Alto. Oshman and Maxfield met with HP president Paul Ely, who expressed considerable interest. After a few weeks of discussions, HP presented a proposal—basically, Maxfield said, that ROLM would do half the work, and HP would take all the profit. Oshman refused to continue the discussion. "It's unfortunate that talks with HP fell flat," acknowledged Maxfield. "Things might have turned out very differently. They shared our vision and had a compatible culture."

$$\textbf{\Large \Phi}$$

## "It's unfortunate that talks with HP fell flat. Things might have turned out very differently."— Bob Maxfield

ROLM's top management regrouped at the Meadowood Resort in Napa in early 1983. This time, discussion about partnering with IBM turned serious. Everyone doubted Mitel's ability to deliver what IBM needed. Plus, ROLMLink would be available within months and would provide a very-high-speed data transport network to connect desktop personal computers, mini-computers, and mainframes—a link IBM wanted but did not have. It was obvious: ROLM had what IBM wanted—a voice/data transport system—and IBM had what ROLM wanted—a walloping presence in the data world, including $40 billion in revenue, 350,000 employees, and a long history of profitability.

Ken Oshman and IBM senior VP Jack Kuehler were well acquainted with each other from serving together on the board of the American

Electronics Association. Oshman called Kuehler and, in his casual, soft voice, said, "This probably doesn't make any sense, Jack, but in case your relationship with Mitel isn't going well, we'd be interested in talking with you about a partnership."

IBM's response was instantly positive. Oshman, Maxfield, and Moley flew to Armonk for a dinner with its top three executives: CEO John Opel, president John Akers, and executive vice president Paul Rizzo. The six men continued deeper discussions first thing the next morning in an elegantly appointed executive conference room at IBM headquarters.

Within two weeks, an IBM technical team arrived at ROLM to very discreetly kick the tires. A small group of ROLM managers gave presentation after presentation to the visitors. IBM seemed particularly impressed by ROLMLink, which would be announced within a month or two, and CBX II, which would be introduced later in the year. The IBMers were also impressed by ROLM's ROCOs, recognizing the same high quality of sales and service people that IBM comprised.

IBM top management indicated that the company would prefer to just buy ROLM outright, according to Maxfield. "But we wanted a partner, not an owner," he said, "and IBM accepted that." ROLM's CFO Bob Dahl and financial analyst Chris Stanfield hammered out the details, and within four weeks, in the spring of 1983, the two companies reached an agreement. "It was the perfect partnership—on paper," said Maxfield.

The public announcement was made on June 13, 1983. ROLM stock shot up to a peak of $80 during trading that day. IBM closed at $177.25, up $3. Both companies' stocks were on the most-active trading list of the New York Stock Exchange. The following day, IBM announced it had severed ties with Mitel. That relationship had never been sealed by a contract and was plagued by development delays. That left Mitel to "pursue alone complicated design work for the new voice and computer communications equipment," said the *Wall Street Journal*.[96] Mitel's stock dropped almost 25 percent.

Per the agreement IBM bought 15 percent of ROLM for $229 million in July 1983, at $59 a share. The deal nearly doubled ROLM's cash on hand after the successful stock offering just four months prior, and management breathed a collective sigh of relief at having ample funds to proceed with existing plans and nourish the vision for more. IBM had the right to acquire an additional 15 percent of ROLM on the open market during the next twenty years. IBM vice presidents Michael Armstrong and C. B. (Jack) Rogers joined the ROLM board of directors. *BusinessWeek* reported, "The deal will help both partners become more competitive in the information processing marketplace—especially against the newly unleashed American Telephone & Telegraph Co. . . . The investment gives IBM access to the advanced communications systems that will be the heart of the office of the future."[97]

"Ironically," said Maxfield much later, "AT&T's agreement with the Justice Department to split itself up in order to enter the computer market set the stage for the IBM-ROLM partnership. IBM felt pressured to come up with a viable path to voice and data integration." According to the *Wall Street Journal*, "The agreement, a coup for ROLM, creates a formidable partnership confronting competitors in the office-automation field, including AT&T."[98]

*Fortune* reported on the dual goals of the two cooperating companies: "to increase access to IBM computers through the digital telephone switching equipment ROLM sells to businesses and to integrate the transmission of voice and data." The article quoted Oshman, who said, "The IBM agreement should add increased momentum to the concept that the telephone system will be the hub of the office of the future."[99]

Ken Oshman sent a memo on June 17, 1983, to all employees, about the ramifications of the agreement with IBM. In his personal, frank tone, he wrote:

I believe our arrangement will bring considerable advantages to ROLM, but before going into that, I thought I would tell you what it will not do:

- Change the philosophy of ROLM
- Involve IBM in ROLM's day-to-day operations
- Allow us to be complacent

- "Sell out" ROLM—we'll remain independent
- Allow us to exceed current spending targets
- Affect our Mil-Spec Division
- End our cooperative arrangements with HP, Data General, or DEC

Oshman surely believed all these points to be true. Some of them, however, would not remain true for long.

## A Fortune 500 Start-up

Within a month, engineering and marketing executives from IBM and ROLM sat together to merge the two companies' development priorities. "We were pretty well synched," said Jim Kasson. The items that were high priority for both firms included network configuration and management systems, a computer host-to-CBX link, and a text mail system.

In a very rare appearance by an IBM executive on behalf of another company, IBM vice chairman Paul Rizzo opened ROLM's mega-teleconference in November 1983, introducing the CBX II and completing the public appearance of the ROLMphone family. Just prior to going "on air," all presenters gathered in the makeshift "green room." Rizzo, no doubt intending simply to be affable, turned to Kathie Hullmann, who would be the second presenter after him, and asked, "Are you the script girl?" To him, this must have seemed a more likely job for a young woman than being marketing manager of a major product line. Their conversation was quite short. On stage, Rizzo praised ROLM's strengths in telecommunications and set high expectations of joint efforts to come from the IBM/ROLM partnership.

IBM embraced ROLM openly at Telecom 83 in Geneva, Switzerland, in the fall of that year. *Think* magazine said, "ROLM shared the IBM logo as the two companies joined hands to underscore the importance of PBX systems that can integrate voice traffic with that of advanced data applications."[100]

Market research firm Dataquest had estimated the U.S. PBX market at $3 billion the previous year, in 1983.[101] AT&T had not completed its divestiture of the Baby Bells, and the portion that had not been divested accounted for 28 percent of total market sales. Northern Telecom and ROLM were neck and neck at 19 percent each, and a number of manufacturers and the already divested Baby Bells split the remaining one-third.

ROLM was also increasingly successful selling CBXs in international markets, thanks to the efforts of Wolfgang Schwartz and his team in the International Division. In the winter of 1984, it became the first firm to receive approval to sell PBXs in Japan, after submitting more than 3,000 pages of documentation, all translated into Japanese. *The New York Times* said, "This was no mean feat, and ROLM has done it with a combination of superior technology, patience, and money. Yet its experience shows just how hard it is for foreign companies, even industry leaders, to sell to the tightly knit Japanese corporate club."[102]

Canada's *Globe and Mail* praised ROLM for once again defeating international goliaths like Siemens: "The success of ROLM Corp. of Santa Clara shows the Japanese have opened their market for telecommunications equipment and establishes a precedent that Canadian companies could follow"[103]—hint, hint, Northern Telecom.

Bob Maxfield viewed the Japan approval as more of a public-relations win than anything. At the time, Fujitsu, NEC, and Hitachi were all selling PBXs in the United States, and yet no U.S. manufacturer could figure out how to sell in Japan. "It's not that Japan had heavy import tariffs," Maxfield explained later, "but they had many trade barriers that were far more subtle and quite effective." The U.S. government was pressing Japan to open its doors. AT&T and Northern Telecom wanted in, but Japan was leery of them, afraid it would be unable to control them once they had entered the market. "Japan saw ROLM and thought, 'Ah, here's a small company that won't be a threat. We'll allow them in,'" said Maxfield. ROLM sold approximately fifty systems in Japan—hardly a dent in the market. "But worth the PR nonetheless," he commented.

ROLM also sold hundreds of small and medium-size systems in Hong Kong and began making headway into China through that market. But foreign markets were experiencing even more severe price competition than the United States. Plus, information management was slower to catch hold there, so some of the CBX's benefits—such as improved cost control—were perhaps not as highly valued. "I doubt that international ever comprised more than 10 percent of CBX sales," said Maxfield. "But we saw international as having strong potential for expansion and never shied away from getting a toe in the door."

Sales hit an all-time high for the quarter ending December 1983, with orders up a whopping 52 percent from the previous year's same quarter. PhoneMail, ROLMphones, Cypress, and CBX II were on the market, stimulating sales and buzz. Cedar and Juniper were in the wings, almost ready to step forward.

Despite all this, ROLM's stock price was low in a generally weak stock market. In March 1984, with $420 million cash in the bank, the company bought back three million shares at $41 each. The board saw it as an attractive long-term return on investment given the sales performance expectations.

By mid-1984, 15,000 CBXs had been installed worldwide—25 percent more than the year before. Bank of America signed an agreement to replace all its systems with CBXs in more than 700 locations. By now, ROLM had sold systems to 92 of the top Fortune 100 firms.

Fiscal 1984 results popped ROLM onto the Fortune 500 list: Out of thousands of publicly held companies, it was number 454 of the 500 top corporate leaders in the United States. Revenue was just under $660 million (equivalent to almost $1.5 billion in 2013), up 31 percent. Orders grew steadily due to the improved state of the economy and increased technological differentiation of ROLM products. Within the company, the innovative, *whatever it takes* attitude remained pervasive, prompting John Mitcham—who'd taken over manufacturing when Wayne Mehl became GM of Telecommunications—to call ROLM "the Fortune 500 start-up." Mitcham knew of what he spoke, having recently arrived at ROLM from the more traditional environments of Memorex and Texas Instruments. That start-up attitude still stretched deep into field operations and throughout ROLM's manufacturing and development facilities.

## More Tales from the Field

ROLM's reputation for reliable products emanated from headquarters in Santa Clara. Service engineers joined the company's development teams early to continually prod them with questions regarding product reliability and serviceability. Development engineers infused these priorities into product designs.

The ROCOs had eighty direct sales offices in North America by 1984, and twelve independent distributors had fifty additional offices. More than half of ROLM's 9,000 employees were "in the field," in jobs that entailed daily contact with customers.

ROLM's field operations at the ROCOs and at independent distributors gained a reputation for above-and-beyond service—as Oshman had noted in a memo, they often "moved heaven and earth." When a customer received two bids that were comparable in price and function—particularly common when ROLM competed against Northern Telecom—ROLM's reputation for excellent service often swung the deal in its favor and resulted in increased customer satisfaction throughout the installation and life of the system.

Techs, sales reps, applications engineers, and customer service reps worked as hard and as long as employees at the Santa Clara headquarters, often seventy, even one hundred hours a week. Don Armstrong, based at ROLM's Technical Assistance Center (TAC) in Tyson's Corner, Virginia, routinely made road trips to support systems installations along the eastern seaboard. He would check into a hotel and then head right to the job site. "I often spent the first eighteen to thirty hours working before I got back to the hotel," he said. "My briefcase contained toothpaste, mouthwash, and clean socks."

One stop on this demanding schedule was the Bank of New England, called the BONE. Its complex VLCBX took two weeks, 24/7, to install. Sometimes techs would catch a nap in the service van parked on the street. One tech on the job found a big blue discarded bucket chair and placed it in a corner of the frame room, into which all the building's cables ran and were connected to the system. The chair was dubbed "the Bucket" and became the refuge for twenty-minute power naps. "Anyone in the Bucket was left alone, their much-needed downtime respected," said Armstrong. The chair remained in place for many years—an early version of Google's nap pods.

ROLM's Federal Systems Group, also in Tyson's Corner, sold multiple CBXs for installation on submarine tenders in 1982 and 1983. Armstrong described the troublesome install of a CBX on the Navy sub tender in a loch in Scotland:

> The Navy required that the tender be able to move within twenty-four hours, which meant we had to complete the install in less than that. But the CBX didn't fit in the ship's passageway to get it back to the system room. So we had to power it up on land, test it, then disassemble it so the parts could fit through and be reassembled. Plus, the system had to be welded to the deck because everything had to have a solid ground—the ship itself was the electrical ground. Because of that twenty-four-hour requirement, once we started coming through the doors, all this had to be done within twenty hours. Three of us hustled the entire time.

The CBX's capability of providing full data on all calls going in and out of the system—time and length of call, to and from whom—made ROLM New York very successful with large Manhattan law firms. Real hourly data, rather than lawyers' scribbled notes, was now the source for determining billable calls to clients. To save money installing a CBX system for a law firm on the twenty-fourth floor of a high rise in the Battery in about 1980, the firm's telecom manager contracted with electricians from the Jersey Teamsters Union to work the job site. Armstrong recalled the chaos that ensued:

> When the New York City teamsters who delivered the switch found out the Jersey Teamsters were working their area, they left the system out on the sidewalk in the rain. It got wrecked, of course, so another one had to be ordered.
>
> The replacement was delivered and installed. During testing, someone plugged 440 volts into the Direct Inward Dial cards and blew the motherboards right through the back of the switch. I got there and found the unmistakable stench of burnt electronics. I ordered a bunch of replacement parts for overnight delivery.
>
> To get things calmed down—there had been more trouble than just this incident—there was a meeting of the "families" that basically ran the unions. The agreement ended up that for every three Jersey electricians, we had to have one New York Master Local 3 electrician or equivalent. Plus, since we needed to catch up and get this CBX running, we had to have a New York City laborer and an electrician over the weekend, at double pay or more. The system cut happened within minutes of the committed hour, but I suspect the "cost-saving" measures ended up costing the firm a fortune.

ROLM took the committed cut time seriously, and support locations scattered around the United States and at Santa Clara jumped through hoops to make that happen. Saturday was the big sales day for Trafalgar Tours in Manhattan, the day when couples and families called to book vacations. Contractors ran all the cables. ROLM unpacked and cut over the system Friday evening. "Everything went perfectly," said Alex Gil, then a customer engineer with ROLM New York. Until the CBX failed at 9:00 p.m., thanks to a faulty T1 card.

> The customer's telecom manager, normally a calm, pleasant man, became frantic, foreseeing that he'd be responsible for lost revenue if the system weren't working by morning. I called Support. Intense searching failed to turn up an available T1 card on the entire East Coast. Support called Santa Clara and woke up someone from shipping, who agreed that a T1 card from a customer system not yet shipped could be pulled and sent to us, right away.
>
> Courier service Delta DASH picked up the package and rushed it to San Francisco International Airport. At 7:00 a.m. I picked it up at JFK Airport in New York, opened the package, and saw not one but two pristine T1 cards. I raced back to the site, popped one in, hit the power, and *voilà!* The thing hummed, just in time for the 800 number to start taking calls.

These tales of field experiences highlight ROLM's approach—how the company considered its commitments to and relationships with customers to be as important as the quality of its products. ROLM's customers received the kind of attention typical of a start-up eager to prove its value—even after ROLM became a Fortune 500 company. This reputation contributed to IBM's eagerness to partner with ROLM. It was the antithesis of the AT&T attitude—*We don't care, because we don't have to*—which had contributed to AT&T's stunning fall from towering heights.

# CHAPTER 11

# THINKING
# THE UNTHINKABLE

....................

The June 1983 announcement of the IBM-ROLM partnership had rattled both the computer and the telecommunications markets. The two companies had agreed to work toward enhancing interconnectability of their products and to explore joint venture opportunities for sales and service. Teams flew from coast to coast in a flurry of planning.

By late summer 1984, however, the agreement with IBM was fifteen months old, and there was nothing to show for it. Joint development proved frustrating. Looking back on the meeting just after the agreement was forged, when IBM and ROLM merged their development priorities, Kasson said, "We were feeling pretty heady with possibilities then. Little did we know that nothing would come of it."

## Frustration Mounts

ROLM's stock was starting to sag, down to $40 a share, after hitting $72 early in the year, though its PBX market share had increased to 23 percent. The financial press in general focused on ROLM's increasing revenues and had not yet picked up on declining margins. But it would soon. Fiscal 1984 net earnings of $37 million reflected an increase of only 6 percent, by far the smallest since the company's infancy. ROLM had never sustained a loss after its initial year, 1970—not even on a quarterly basis. With decreasing margins and no tangible results of the IBM partnership even on the horizon, the pressure was ratcheting up for ROLM's top management.

Joint marketing with IBM also had proved frustrating and problematic. Tony Carollo, then ROCO general manager, said in a 2013 phone interview that ROLM's few million dollars of sales to a major account like Texaco were minor in comparison to the tens of millions of dollars in computers that IBM was selling to the same account. "We just couldn't get the IBM Texaco account's attention," he said.

Coinciding with these concerns were a number of shifts within the management ranks. Wayne Mehl, VP and general manager of the Telecom Division, retired in 1984. VP Dennis Paboojian moved from being Mil-Spec's general manager to become Telecom's GM. Stan Tenold, who had headed up Mil-Spec engineering for a number of years, moved into the role of VP and general manager of that division.

ROLM's top management drilled down and found that concerns over antitrust issues were a major issue. IBM, the earliest computer manufacturer and marketer, had dominated the industry since the mid-1950s. It was sued for antitrust violations by the U.S. Justice Department, and the resulting 1956 Consent Decree required IBM to conduct its business in ways that made it clear that it was not acting in a monopolistic fashion. Hundreds, if not thousands, of IBM lawyers throughout the company saw to it that the government would have no reason to even contemplate bringing forth another antitrust action.

"These countless IBM lawyers persistently blocked joint development and sales efforts," said Maxfield. For example, IBM didn't manufacture some types of printers. But if an IBM computer customer asked the sales rep to recommend a printer that would interface to his computer, the rep had to mention all printer manufacturers so he didn't appear to favor one. "The easiest way to handle this was to stridently avoid any mention of non-IBM products," said Maxfield. It was almost humorous; the rep would have to say something like, "Printers? I have no idea. But they're out there." So when a joint ROLM-IBM sales call was scheduled at, say, Ford

Motor Company, an IBM lawyer insisted that a Northern Telecom rep be invited to the party.

Dick Moley echoed the frustration. "I spent a lot of time trying to get things going with IBM in product development and joint selling," he said, "but the lawyers always blocked it, claiming restraint of trade." According to Maxfield, if IBM implemented an interface to non-IBM products, the interface had to have an open architecture that all manufacturers could utilize. "When presented with plans to enable an IBM computer to talk with the CBX, an IBM lawyer insisted that the interface be published so other computers could also interface to the CBX," he explained, "which would nullify the advantage that was intended to be gained by the development in the first place."

Both Maxfield and Moley felt that this lack of cooperation must have surfaced in previous IBM partnerships and that IBM top management must have been well aware of this at the time of the partnership agreement. Nonetheless, IBM management had committed that its sales force would make joint sales calls and that its engineers would cooperate on joint development of products.

## "IBM's lawyers were the fatal flaw in the IBM partnership," said Maxfield.

Frustration mounted. "IBM's lawyers were the fatal flaw in the IBM partnership," said Maxfield in retrospect. Considerable discussion took place in Oshman's top management meetings about how to handle the situation, including the possibility of an amicable divorce.

If ROLM and IBM abandoned the joint marketing and development agreement, IBM would likely come out unscathed, because the agreement affected only a small segment of its total business. ROLM's credibility, on the other hand, could be so crucially damaged that future announcements of any kind would be met with distrust by customers and the press. There was no positive way in which ROLM could position a divorce. No matter what was said to the press by both sides, IBM carried such formidable clout that it would appear the company had lost confidence and divorced ROLM—not the other way around. ROLM's stock price would tank.

Lack of results from the IBM partnership was not the only complexity facing ROLM at the time. CBX margins continued to be under pressure. More and more system sales were being made on price rather than value as the Baby Bells—all of them now free of the mother ship, Ma Bell—flailed in the marketplace. The newly divested Baby Bells did not understand how to sell value and return on investment. Instead they relied on price reductions to make the sale. Plus, a strike by unionized Baby Bell employees delayed some ROLM installations, affecting the revenue stream. Even without a strike, ROLM still regularly struggled to obtain timely services from the Baby Bells to provide dial tone to newly installed CBXs.

Back in 1975, ROLM had assumed correctly that many companies would toss out their obsolete switches to attain the advantages of a computerized PBX. But that surge was now in the past; the normal growth of business would be new construction and attrition of old PBXs, a much smaller market. And now the Baby Bells were pushing Centrex, a monthly fee service offered by local phone companies, more than ever. Centrex first appeared in the 1960s and is still offered today. A giant PBX at the phone company's central office is partitioned so a company can rent a portion of the system and avoid the capital investment of purchasing a PBX, yet still have pared-down benefits of PBX capabilities. The Baby Bells pushed hard on renting Centrex service to customers rather than selling PBX systems, which meant that ROLM had to convince customers of the benefits of a large capital outlay. In the midst of a rapidly changing marketplace that had not yet settled on how voice and data would merge, some organizations compared this unfavorably to a monthly rental fee for Centrex, which allowed the customer to play the wait-and-see game.

ROLMphones' margin was on the upswing, as was penetration—the percentage of phones on a CBX that were ROLMphones rather than plain push-button phones. Cypress, however, was moving out the door at a slower rate than anticipated. ROLM was about to launch two new desktop terminals, Cedar and Juniper, but the forecasted ramp on those high-profit products was long, and their projected volumes were too low to affect overall corporate margins. Steady Mil-Spec was profitable, with high operating margins, but it now comprised only about one-tenth of the company revenues.

## The Deal Starts with a Seven

A meeting with IBM president John Akers was scheduled in Armonk in September 1984. On the way from the airport, Ken Oshman and Bob Maxfield chatted in the back of a sedan. Oshman, whom Maxfield had never seen pound a table, said that when they got into the meeting, he was going to pound the table and say, "By God, John, we entered into this agreement in good faith! You have to find a way to keep your damn lawyers from barring everything we do!"

To prepare for the assault, Oshman and Maxfield verbally reviewed the efforts that had been blocked or stalled. Then they sat silently for a while. About a half hour outside of Armonk, Maxfield uttered one of Dick Moley's favorite lines: "Maybe it's time to think the unthinkable."

Oshman drew on his cigar a time or two, then said, "Acquisition?"

Maxfield nodded.

After some time, Oshman asked, "You think we should bring that up at this meeting?"

Maxfield replied, "Seems to be the logical time." The stock was trading around $50, probably the highest it was going to be for the foreseeable future given that margins were under severe pressure. Years later, Maxfield said he was sure Oshman had been thinking the same thing: that ROLM's continued existence as an independent company was in doubt, and if acquisition was inevitable, there would be no better time in the future. "Right then represented the best negotiating stance we had," he recalled. "But in the car on the way to that meeting was the first time the topic was out in the open between us."

When they entered the IBM conference room, Oshman announced, "We have a new agenda for the meeting."

Big Blue lit up at the prospect of buying ROLM. After all, that's what it had really wanted to do back when the partnership agreement was reached. Within the fifteen months since, IBM had increased its ownership of ROLM from 15 percent to 23 percent, persistently moving toward the agreement cap of 30 percent. The two companies' customers were a perfect match. Both had achieved almost complete penetration of the Fortune 100 companies—IBM in data, ROLM in voice. Their products were a seamless overlap for the voice-data merger that was the technology hot button, still expected to be right around the corner.

When visitors from IBM's network group arrived within two weeks to check out this California company the data giant was thinking of buying, a small group of ROLM managers gave presentations. "There was a woman in the group who was not nearly as aggressive in her questioning as the others, so I didn't pay much attention to her," Jim Kasson recalled in 2013. That woman was Ellen Hancock. At dinner at the Lion and Compass that evening, she let Kasson know that in fact she was the decision maker, the head of the networking group. "I'd probably been politically incorrect, discounting her because she was a woman dealing with heavy technology issues," Kasson said. "I learned better. And later, at IBM, I learned to look at an org chart before going into a meeting, so I knew who was who."

Hancock knew that ROLM had a very good PBX. What concerned her, however, was the difference in how product upgrades were handled. "IBM's been around so long, it has customers who need to migrate as IBM products change," said Hancock. IBM has a very defined process for migration, often giving the customer a year's preparation or more. "We had phased switchovers, with multi-years and multi-releases going on. ROLM seemed to just put a new software update out there for all users to adopt right then. It's certainly easier, but IBM customers would not care for that."

Hancock detected another impediment to the deal: ROLM software code looked nothing like IBM code. At ROLM, the people who wrote the code were the ones who fixed the bugs after the product was out, so extensive explanation within the code was not necessary. At IBM, though, the service engineers fixed the bugs; they needed the aid of commentary to know how to proceed. "ROLM had executives who were brilliant and entrepreneurial," Hancock recalled. "I was very impressed with them. But IBM is process-driven rather than entrepreneurial. So at the end of the day, we recommended that IBM not buy ROLM."

Despite the review team's recommendation, IBM top management decided to go forward. Negotiations began for the purchase of ROLM.

Looking back, Maxfield tried to put himself in CEO John Opel's shoes. He explained, "IBM had had a PBX under development for ten years, to no avail. It had made a deal with Mitel, to no avail. Here come Opel's internal people saying, 'No, no, don't do this deal. We can do better on our own.' But all Opel had to do was look at the marketplace—the results were apparent. ROLM was the technology and market leader."

Besides, Maxfield reasoned, IBM was just as "pregnant" as ROLM was. Owning nearly 25 percent of ROLM stock gave Big Blue plenty of incentive to find a positive outcome. Dumping the stock and walking away would make it clear that IBM still lacked a voice/data integration solution. Opel could see that every joint project ROLM had tried with IBM had been blocked by lawyers. Something had to give. The status quo could not proceed. ROLM had expected more. IBM had expected more. The world had expected more. "And throw into this mix the fact that AT&T was attempting to blast its way into the computer market," Maxfield said, "trying to lock up all of voice and data communications in the Fortune 500s for them and their pals, the Baby Bells. IBM wanted the Fortune 500 to be 'blue' through and through."

Longtime counsel Larry Sonsini suspected that ROLM's start-up roots and GPW approach also had a lot to do with IBM's decision to buy. "[IBM

VP] Michael Armstrong had come to admire ROLM's nimble style during his time on the board," Sonsini said in 2013. "He probably hoped some of that style could be transferred to other IBM operations."

As negotiations began, Oshman headed for Scotland on a golf vacation that had long been on the calendar. Maxfield handled the negotiations, with Oshman calling him at the end of each day to give his input and wish him luck. Maxfield thought it was a savvy negotiating ploy, as if Oshman were saying to IBM, *This negotiation isn't important enough for me to interrupt my golf game. If you want my attention, you better make the offer worthwhile.* At one point in the negotiation, IBM told Maxfield, "There's no way the stock price of this deal is going to start with a seven."

By the end of the week, an agreement was struck: IBM would offer to buy all the remaining ROLM stock it did not own for $70 a share, for $1.25 billion, valuing the company at $1.8 billion—$3.9 billion in 2013 dollars. Again ROLM's Bob Dahl and Chris Stanfield hammered out the details. The next step was for the ROLM board of directors' vote of approval to put the offer in front of the company's shareholders.

In the midst of the negotiations in mid-September 1984, Cedar and Juniper launched. They were developed entirely independently of IBM, in ROLM Austin, and ROLM stated that repeatedly to the press. IBM had not contributed budget, people, or technology. Regardless, because the ROLM-IBM partnership had been in place for over a year, and because Juniper connected to IBM PCs, among others, the press assumed that Cedar and Juniper were joint developments between the two companies.

Oshman returned from Scotland and a board meeting was called. Michael Armstrong and C. B. Rogers, the two IBMers, abstained from voting, leaving the decision to seven directors. IBM's offer was accepted, pending shareholder approval.

## The Jittery Honeymoon

Oshman announced the proposed merger to the ROLM employees just before the press release hit the wires on September 26, 1984. It came as a complete surprise to most of them. In the two months between then and the shareholders meeting, ROLM's outgoing CEO wandered through the cafeteria often, answering questions, sitting for ten minutes at one table, for fifteen at another. "He understood how devoted our people were. He was very concerned about how they'd take this news," said Maxfield.

The proposed merger, the largest acquisition in IBM's history, hit the front page of the *New York Times:* "Freewheeling ROLM, started in a prune shed fifteen years ago, has been a haven for bright, independent people, mainly engineers, who helped push the company into a leading position in the telecommunications business. It now produces what many consider the industry's most sophisticated private business exchange."[104] The news took the top slot of the *Wall Street Journal's* front-page "What's News" column.[105]

*U.S. News and World Report* pointed out that the acquisition was IBM's first in twenty years, since it had bought tiny Scientific Research Associates in 1964—so it "was not on a buying binge by any means." IBM wanted "to play a significant role in the telecommunications market," the article asserted, and this move "put IBM right into AT&T's backyard."[106] The proposed merger also made the front pages of the *San Francisco Chronicle* and the *San Jose Mercury News* and was covered by *Time*, *USA Today*, *BusinessWeek*, and the computer, telecommunications, and international press.

Oshman provided the official word to the *New York Times,* saying, "We found ourselves paying less attention to the market and more to what IBM wanted ROLM to do and what ROLM wanted IBM to do . . . There was always something in the way of working together smoothly . . . Finally, we decided the best way to work together was to become part of IBM."[107] Frank as usual, he told the *Wall Street Journal*, "We're attractive to IBM because we've been successful in the way we do things. IBM is too smart to screw that up."[108]

Oshman, soon to be elected an IBM vice president, showed up at ROLM's annual Halloween party as Charlie Chaplin's Little Tramp character, which IBM had famously adopted in its long-running advertising campaign. With the cigar, derby hat, glued-on mustache, cane, black suit with oversized legs, and distinctive splayed-out walk, Oshman could have been Chaplin's clone. The Halloween levity boded well for the transition.

Maxfield later said that he suspected IBM knew an acquisition would be the ultimate result of the initial partnership with ROLM. "Top management must have known there'd be no way they'd be able to jointly develop and market new products given the legal constraints," he said. "They were probably thinking, 'We'll get them deep into this—then there's no backing out.'"

The Justice Department quickly approved the merger pending shareholder approval, with one startling proviso: IBM, one of the largest computer vendors to the U.S. military, had to sell the Mil-Spec Division within six months. The government claimed that the merger would result in reduced competition in that market.

The surprise ruling stunned ROLM's top management. "We thought it was ludicrous," said Maxfield, "to think that Mil-Spec's $81 million of revenue could swing IBM's multibillion-dollar government business toward a monopoly situation." The message ROLM had worked so diligently to pound into the government's head had taken hold—*monopolies stifle innovation*—but now it had been taken to a far-flung extreme.

Oshman informed all employees of the government's decision the following day, November 20, 1984, through a memo: "It is with deep regret that I make this announcement. As you all know, the mil-spec computer business was the original business of ROLM Corporation and it has a history of innovation and unbroken success."

"Frankly, around Mil-Spec," said customer service and support manager Nadine Grant, "the general reaction was relief that we weren't going to become a part of IBM." Stan Tenold, ROLM vice president and general manager of Mil-Spec, said, "We had always competed with IBM Federal Systems Division and really did not desire to be part of their operation." A petition was circulated and signed by the vast majority of Mil-Spec's 1,000 employees asking management to do a leveraged buyout so the division could become an independent company.

Less than eighteen months earlier, Oshman had written his memo stating what would not happen because of the IBM partnership. The two most alarming possibilities, loss of corporate independence and unity, had now come to pass, due to circumstances that he could not have foreseen: a partnership that would lead to repeated frustrations and no results.

## The End of Independence

A special shareholders meeting was called for 9:00 a.m. on November 21, 1984, to formally approve the merger. Larry Sonsini and his legal team had prepared all the needed documents. Sonsini had been a highly valued advisor and counselor since ROLM's early days. In 2006, *Fortune* reported, "Sonsini has been the most important lawyer in the most important industry for thirty years. He is the most influential and well-connected lawyer in the industry [and] an integral part of Silicon Valley's history and culture."[109] Sonsini recalled in 2013 that before the meeting, as he sat with Ken and Barbara Oshman and Bob Maxfield in Oshman's office, they all asked one another, "So, do we really want to do this?" It was a rhetorical question, of course—there was no turning back. The board had approved the merger, and it had to go to a shareholder vote. Those final few minutes before the meeting represented the last point in the fifteen-year process that had started in the prune shed. At last they solemnly rose and walked to the auditorium.

Ken Oshman's opening remarks included a lot of gracious acknowledgments:

> We are fortunate to have an outstanding board of directors: Leo Chamberlain, Jack Melchor, Les Hogan, Bob Maxfield, Bob Noyce, Ed van Bronkhorst, Michael Armstrong, and C. B. Rogers. They've been continuously dedicated to the success of ROLM, to our future. They've worked hard; they've been an enormous help. Two of those directors I'd like to mention specifically: Jack

Melchor, without whom ROLM wouldn't be in existence. He provided much of our early focus and continuing focus. And Bob Maxfield, we all know, is the single most significant contributor to the success of ROLM."[110]

Maxfield said later, "That was a very generous comment—so like Ken. But of course we all know that he was ROLM's most significant contributor."

Burt McMurtry said, "Ken and Jack and Bob all fall into the same class. They're about the smartest people you'll ever meet who have common sense and want to accomplish things. And not one of them wanted to be someone else." Remarkably, they simply wanted to see ROLM and its people succeed. Maintaining this as their priority undoubtedly had contributed to ROLM's stability and kept high-level politics at bay.

At the shareholders meeting, Oshman continued to comment on the Justice Department ruling that the Mil-Spec Division had to be spun out. "We in no way believe the Justice Department's position is correct." He promised that the divestiture would be done "with the employees' welfare most at heart."[111]

A slide show compared ROLM in 1969 to ROLM in 1984. Oshman reported that the company was currently operating at a $1 billion run rate and had almost 10,000 employees. He reviewed product history, saying, "As we added features and functions, we never obsoleted our customers. They were always able to grow with us."[112]

Mike Morris, ROLM's general counsel, conducted the vote. The merger was approved by 76 percent of shareholders. ROLM became a wholly owned subsidiary of IBM—not a division of IBM. After he announced the tally, Morris said, "You'll notice, my shirt is still not white," referring to IBM's undocumented dress code of a dark suit, club tie, and starched white shirt.[113]

*Forbes* said in 1985, "Of the 1,920 companies brought public at more than $1 a share in the past ten years, ROLM produced the biggest long-term relative gain over its offering price."[114] For the five original investors

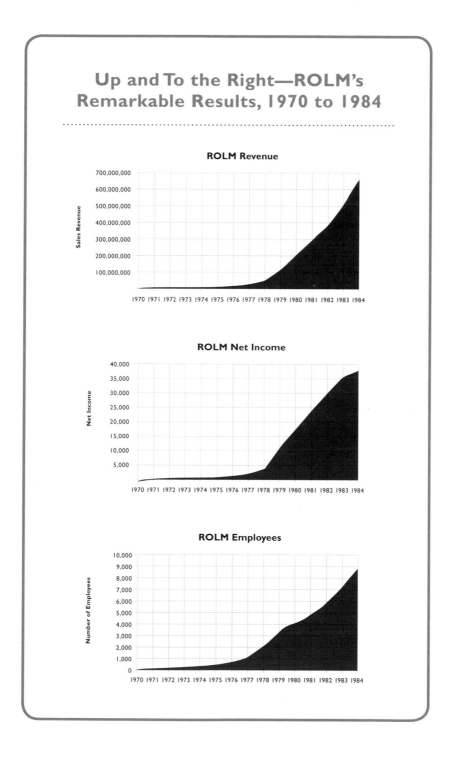

who each put in $15,000 in 1969—Richeson, Oshman, Loewenstern, Maxfield, and Melchor—the return on investment was 3,360-fold in sixteen years, with each original share having split into forty-eight shares. Patient investors at the 1976 IPO who held on until the 1984 merger saw a forty-fold return in eight years.

Silicon Valley had never witnessed such a remarkable merger and acquisition. Holiday parties of December 1984 toasted the Big Deal. The vast majority of employees held ROLM stock, and thousands of them became financially secure, a bittersweet feeling mixed with the knowledge that ROLM as they knew it had ceased to be.

The ROLM-IBM merger remained the benchmark of a "good deal" in Silicon Valley for many, many years. ROLM's sales and service organization was top-notch, matching IBM's reputation for putting the customer first. Maxfield suspected that the astonishing string of new products introduced during the years 1980 to 1984—PhoneMail; ROLMphones; the ROLM-Link; the CBXII; the VLCBX; the desktop devices Cypress, Cedar, and Juniper—deeply impressed IBM. Said Maxfield, "I was in the midst of all that development, and it still astounds me."

In hindsight, however, he found it interesting to think about whether ROLM could have made it without IBM:

After all, the pig in the belly of the snake was passing through—all that development expense was on the verge of turning into revenue. But succeeding without IBM's help would've been very problematic. The AT&T divestiture was wreaking havoc. The Baby Bells couldn't sell—all they could do was cut price or rent Centrex. And AT&T was poised to blast headfirst into computers and data communications. Who knew what would happen there. And it was clear IBM was going to get into the PBX market somehow. Moley kept saying, 'We have to go into this eyes wide open.' Could we succeed against both?

In early 1986, the six large wooden *ROLM* signs with the bold gold lettering that marked the entrances to the campus were replaced with signs that said *ROLM, an IBM Company.* The old signs were auctioned off to employees. The *San Jose Mercury News* reported that one buyer planned to make a table out of his.

This photo of employees at Halloween 1987 exaggerated the culture clash with Big Blue's button-down style—but the point was clear. Photo courtesy of M. Lee Epp.

## Mil-Spec Spins Out

Mil-Spec announced the Hawk/32 in the fall of 1984 in the midst of the merger, for shipment in 1985. It was the most technologically advanced engineering program undertaken by Mil-Spec, including new design methodologies and approaches. The effort was led by engineers Rex Cardinale, Jim McClure, and Kamron Malack. The Hawk/32 was the most powerful and most compact mil-spec 32-bit computer on the market. Target applications were command, control, communications, intelligence, signal processing, and weapons control. Mil-Spec's MAGNUM 4200 Disk Subsystem was also announced in 1984, designed for large online data storage of up to 280 megabytes in severe environments.

At the shareholders meeting that had approved the merger, Ken Oshman had pointed out the approach that had kept the MSC team on top of things: "Our success in Mil-Spec has always been based on our initial strategy: invest our own funds to design what we thought was right in the marketplace, provide the products based on that on an off-the-shelf basis, and provide a line of software and hardware tools to go along with it. And we've based that direction on a commercial architecture."[115] It had been a successful formula for fifteen years.

A leveraged buyout (LBO) for the division was explored. Nothing materialized. "These days, with Mil-Spec's profitability and competitive products," said Maxfield, "an LBO would be a no-brainer. But back then, there wasn't much of a structure out there for an LBO of a tech company."

IBM enlisted investment bank Salomon Brothers to seek a buyer. The January 1985 prospectus of the division's history, financials, and products showed annualized revenue rate for fiscal 1985 at $90 million, representing about one-tenth of ROLM's revenue and employees. During the previous five years, revenues had grown at a compound annual rate of 17 percent, with gross margins steady at around 60 percent and operating margins around 25 percent. The division was an attractive package for a company wanting to expand its defense offering.

Data General expressed interest. The size of the two companies and their corporate cultures were compatible. The best-selling, Pulitzer Prize–winning book *The Soul of a New Machine*—an inside look at DG's development of the Eclipse MV/8000 computer—illuminates a team endeavor and dedication similar to what could be found at ROLM. But DG was still shaky after stumbling financially in the early '80s and even liquidating the ROLM stock it had been granted back in 1969 to help keep the company afloat. No deal was struck.

William Lorenz and Leon Alpert had used a conjunction of their last names when they founded Loral Corporation in 1948. It was a small, publicly held defense contractor on the verge of bankruptcy when Bernard Schwartz bought it in 1972. Schwartz aggressively turned Loral into a major player in the global aerospace and defense industry. By 1984, its revenues were $3 billion. The company went on an acquisition binge in the 1980s, buying sixteen defense and aerospace businesses within a decade. One of them was ROLM's Mil-Spec Division.

ROLM's Chris Stanfield structured an agreement with Loral that encouraged retention of Mil-Spec employees through the creation of a fund paid by IBM that vested over four years. The benefits per employee grew as other former ROLMans departed. "This proved to be a good retention tool in the transition," Tenold commented later—though not for him personally.

A few weeks after the merger, Tenold picked up Loral's CEO Schwartz at the airport for his first visit as Mil-Spec's new owner. En route to the facility, Schwartz said, "You know, Stan, if things work out well, you could become a VP in two or three years."

Tenold took a moment to catch his breath before responding, "You know, Bernie, I am a VP at ROLM now."

Looking back, Tenold said, "Loral had a very different orientation from ROLM." After a few weeks of observing how Loral wanted the division to be managed, he decided it was time to move on.

Loral swallowed Mil-Spec whole. The Hawk/32 shipped under Loral's aegis. Mil-Spec's product lines gradually dispersed throughout the company—disk drives here, Eclipse products there. Because Loral continually bought and sold pieces and parts of companies, it is impossible to follow Mil-Spec's trail. But the end result is clear: In 1996, Loral sold its defense electronics and system integration businesses to Lockheed Martin for $9.1 billion.

## Are Suits and Saunas Compatible?

As soon as the agreement was announced, before the shareholders' approval, concerns surfaced that the merger between one of Silicon Valley's most fiercely independent companies and staid Big Blue would not go smoothly. Two months before the final vote, the *New York Times* ran a front-page article on the financial deal and an inside story about the potential culture clash: "In Santa Clara, the big question around the swimming pools, on the tennis courts, and in the Jacuzzis at the ROLM Corporation's headquarters today was whether ROLM's dream-come-true working conditions could long endure under the rule of the International Business Machines Corporation."[116]

*USA Today* ran a cover story comparing ROLM's tight-loose work mode with IBM's regimented, documented style. In it, Dick Moley said,

"There's no obvious formula to do this. But they are adjusting their culture to fuel entrepreneurship and creativity. That's very encouraging."[117]

A week after the shareholder vote, IBM vice chairman Paul Rizzo attempted to ease concern and avoid a mass exodus when he addressed the Santa Clara employees at an all-hands outdoor meeting. "We won't drain the swimming pool," he joked. "That he could even have such a thought sent chills down spines," said engineering manager Jeff Blohm years later. Questions swirled among the employees: Would navy blue suits, white shirts, and club ties become the de facto uniform? Would the saunas, pools, and gym be off-limits during work hours? Would specific work hours be imposed?

The meeting ended with the traditional beer bust. Rizzo, John Akers, and Ken Oshman opened things by toasting ROLM with cans of beer, despite IBM's strict rules against alcohol on site. A *San Jose Mercury News* reporter snapped a photo of the toast and raced to a phone to call in the story. Tony Seidel, then corporate communications manager, said, "I ran after him and, as he was dialing, pleaded with him not to print the photo in return for an exclusive interview with Ken later that day. He agreed." Many thought it was likely to be ROLM's last beer bust.

Many employees left ROLM soon after the merger. Bob Nugent resigned that day, saying he didn't "want to work for the post office." Gibson Anderson said, "I didn't want to help change a Great Place to Work into an IBM division." It was a somber day in early 1985 when ROLMans received letters notifying them that their employee number had been replaced with an IBM number. Maxfield, for example, went from #4 to #161138.

*BusinessWeek* captioned a photo of an outdoor lunch table at ROLM with a choice word from Oshman: "Speculation that the company's culture won't mesh with IBM's is 'bull.'"[118] Still, many employees feared that it would be the end of ROLM as a Great Place to Work, that Big Blue's bureaucratic style would swamp collegiality and teamwork. IBM had almost 400,000 employees worldwide in 1984, with almost $46 billion in revenue. Its average employee, who was ten to fifteen years older than ROLM's, expected lifetime employment with the company. Poor performers were shuffled into lesser roles or transferred to other sites. IBM had never had a layoff since its founding in 1911 (it would be rocked to the core by its first in 1993). Though ROLM had implemented hiring freezes, it had laid off only two people, back in its second year of existence. But ROLM fired workers when warranted. Spending a lifetime with one company was not within the mindscape of its young, ambitious workforce.

ROLM's upper management went to Armonk "for the lobotomy," said marketing manager Carol Wingard—to be trained on how to manage people and products IBM's way "We were all there in our navy blue suits and white shirts. Except Emil Wang," she recalled. He came in a pink shirt. "You'll get yourself fired," Wingard told him. But Wang, shaping a start-up in his mind, was not overly concerned. And he wasn't the only ROLMan whose entrepreneurial spirit would lead to new ventures. Many would go on to found or work for start-ups in the future.

## IBM Makes a Genuine Effort

According to Bob Maxfield, IBM respected the ROLM culture and tried hard to protect it from corporate bureaucracy. IBM had some twenty corporate staff departments—finance, HR, manufacturing technology, quality assurance, etc. The strategic and operating plans of every division had to be reviewed annually by every corporate staff department. Each division had an entire support staff just to interface with these corporate departments—to spend all their time giving or listening to presentations in special meetings that were dubbed "flipchart wars." Big Blue tried to spare ROLM this heavy bureaucratic burden. "One of the first edicts that went out from IBM headquarters was that only IBM's finance and human resources groups could deal directly with ROLM," Maxfield recalled—the former to roll up the financial results each quarter, the latter to figure out how to reconcile the differing personnel policies. "All the others were told to keep hands off unless they received special permission."

IBM offered ROLM six to eight senior-level IBM managers to act as liaisons, facilitating relationships and educating ROLM on how to do things IBM's way. It was an offer, however, not an edict. "That in itself was unique for them," said Maxfield. ROLM's top management interviewed liaison candidates and selected six, who moved to Silicon Valley. Still, Maxfield said, "We suspected these guys might really be moles who were supposed to secretly report flaws that IBM suspected we'd kept hidden during the merger. But we'd hidden nothing."

Dick Mattern was the first of these IBM liaisons to transfer to ROLM. Fawn Alvarez worked for him while she was on the crisis management team, solving acute customer problems. "Dick was perfect for the job of smoothing the transition," she said nearly three decades later. "He was very personable, with a great sense of humor. He was the only person who was ever the brunt of his own jokes."

"All the advisors fell in love with ROLM, with its casual yet intense style," Maxfield said, "and became ROLM advocates within IBM." Many IBMers contributed wholeheartedly to ROLM's efforts to bring good products into the marketplace as expediently as possible, including Paul Mugge, Glen Bacon, Woody Woodard, and Sam Kahn, all of them involved in product development.

Some things unique to ROLM had to change because they clashed with longstanding IBM practices. Sabbaticals were phased out. Beer busts became ice cream socials and occurred less often. Annual profit sharing, never an IBM perk, was eliminated. Stock options became scarce for anyone not in top management—IBM had the same number of option holders among almost 400,000 employees that ROLM had with its 10,000. However, IBM's excellent pension plan, something rarely seen in entrepreneurial Silicon Valley, became effective for all former ROLMans, starting with their original ROLM date of hire. It was tempting to think that the merger would turn out fine after all.

## Leadership Shifts

Ken Oshman remained CEO of IBM-ROLM, was named an IBM vice president, and joined the Corporate Management Board. He also joined an advisory committee for IBM business in Europe, the Middle East, and Africa (EMEA) to increase IBM's telecommunications presence in Europe. IBM had multiple telecom research and operations facilities in addition to ROLM: in Triangle Park, North Carolina; Yorktown Heights, New York; La Gaude, France; and Zurich, Switzerland. These facilities seemed to operate independently, and none had yet made an impact in telecommunications or presented a broad vision of integrating voice and data.

In the spring of 1985, Oshman and Moley went to Armonk to propose a radical new organization—IBM Telecommunications Division—that would unite the disparate telecom operations under Oshman. The mission would be to present a coordinated, unified approach with the objective of dominating the U.S. and European telecom markets. Maxfield explained, "Ken had run ROLM for almost twenty years and was ready to take on a larger challenge. He may have harbored thoughts that perhaps one day he could be a candidate to be CEO of IBM. He certainly had the ability to do it."

Oshman proposed that he would get an apartment in New York, for the sake of convenient access to the various telecom facilities, demonstrating his commitment to the plan. "He made this proposal out of loyalty to ROLM and its people," said Dick Moley. "It had become apparent that combining these various IBM telecom parts was the way to bring to fruition the full potential of the merger—that together ROLM and IBM would drive the integration of voice and data." But the idea was too radical—the IBMers in the meeting at Armonk headquarters controlled their voices, but they couldn't control their body language. "You could tell that what they really thought was, 'What would real IBMers think of reporting to these California cowboys?'," said Moley.

IBM declined the proposal. Oshman privately gave notice in July 1985 that he would leave the company in January 1986.

IBM's Jack Kuehler asked Bob Maxfield to succeed Oshman as president of IBM-ROLM. Maxfield's focus, however, had shifted to an urgent family crisis: Shortly after the merger, his younger daughter had been diagnosed with leukemia. Knowing of the personal complication, Kuehler quickly added, "Before you say no, please meet me halfway for breakfast."

An IBM Learjet picked up Maxfield in San Jose at 6:00 one morning in the fall of 1985 and flew him two hours to Omaha, Nebraska. Kuehler flew in from the East Coast. They discussed the offer over breakfast at the airport restaurant. After it became clear that Maxfield would not accept the job, Kuehler asked for his recommendation. Maxfield named Dennis Paboojian. Although Paboojian lacked sales and marketing experience, he had a strong grasp of development and manufacturing.

At noon on his final day at ROLM in mid-January 1986, Oshman took to the podium for the last time. He eschewed the auditorium and, once again, went instead to the cafeteria. As he stepped onto a lunch table, the room went silent. He said that his time at ROLM had been a happy time and that he was very proud to have been the leader of such a fine company. He didn't know what he would do next, but he "wouldn't be sitting in front of the TV drinking a beer." He saluted the employees. Tears rolled as he stepped off the table. He stayed for a while to mingle and shake hands.

Oshman told the *New York Times* the next day, "It's definitely related to the merger . . . If things weren't going well, I wouldn't leave. But things are going well, and it's time."[119] IBM threw a lavish dinner for the *O* in ROLM, the only president the company had had in its fifteen years of independence.

Ten years later, Oshman said in a taped interview, "I estimated that we could maybe be a $40 million company in the PBX business, for a total of $50 million. But the [mil-spec] computer business had grown to be $100 million, and PBX was at $700 to $800 million when IBM bought us. It's good to be lucky rather than right."[120]

Dennis Paboojian, age forty-two, took over the helm, reporting to IBM's Mitchell Watson. Maxfield, whose daughter died in January 1986, reduced his workload to half time, acting primarily as Paboojian's advisor. Maxfield remained a symbol of ROLM's unbureaucratic, collegial culture. His quiet, always pleasant presence indicated that the ROLM Philosophy just might survive. In the spring of 1986, he went to Austin to attend an all-employee meeting. "When I entered," he said, "everyone stood and applauded. I was flabbergasted and hugely honored—a standing ovation! It brought tears to my eyes."

This dedication and support seemed a mark of ROLMans' attitude toward the company's irreplaceable founders. As Bob Nugent observed, "The devotion Oshman had from his staff was amazing. All of them thought he was the smartest guy on the planet." A number of key executives and managers left soon after Oshman, among them Dick Moley, the marketing and sales leader who had put ROLM into the CBX business. Tony Carollo, head of the ROCO Division, told *BusinessWeek*, "When Ken left, it took a lot of spirit out of people." Bob Finocchio, head of ROLM Service, commented in the same article, "How full was the ROLM parking lot at six o'clock Friday night, or on Saturday? Big difference."[121]

The fire in the belly of ROLM was out.

# CHAPTER 12

# DANCING WITH THE GORILLA

......................

"IBM got tougher with ROLM by the month," said Dick Moley, speaking of 1986, after Ken Oshman left. It rejected more than half of the stock-option proposals ROLM asked for. Without the lure of stock options, ROLM could not effectively compete in hiring from within Silicon Valley's talent pool. By that time only a few hundred acres of "heritage" orchards were left, replaced by new construction to house technology companies. Start-ups for software, peripherals, computers, and components were ubiquitous. Talent was everywhere—and yet with very few exceptions, ROLM could hire only the IBMers offered to them by the corporate machine. The full meaning of the phrase *wholly owned* before *subsidiary* was becoming increasingly clear. As IBM executive Ellen Hancock explained in 2013, "In IBM terms, if you buy it, you manage it."

## Separation of Field and Home

Shortly after the merger, IBM had begun telling Oshman that it wanted to fold ROLM's sales and service organization into its own, which had a reputation for astute salespeople who put the customer first. Oshman fought vigorously against this separation within the ROLM structure, as did Paboojian after him. By March 1987, however, the battle was lost. The "field" and the development and manufacturing side now reported in parallel to Mitchell Watson, along with a handful of other IBM divisions. The tight feedback loop that Oshman had fostered between the customer and the development team was severed.

Bob Finocchio, then VP ROLM Service, said the announcement "seemed like an act of treason." It was the exit bell for more key ROLM executives, managers, engineers, and salespeople, including Tony Carollo. Finocchio stayed until his stock options vested a year later, even though IBM kept saying, in effect, *Oh, you have to do it this way*, and then, *You have to do something else that way*. "It was always IBM's way, bit by bit," Finocchio said. "That year was death by a thousand cuts."

Salespeople and service workers began taking orders directly from IBM heads in New York rather than ROLM executives in Silicon Valley. All pricing proposals on major systems had to be reviewed by IBM staff, sometimes delaying a deal for weeks—an eternity in the fast-moving PBX market. "It was painstakingly slow to get things done," Finocchio told *BusinessWeek*.[122] Nonetheless, this was how things were to be accomplished going forward. *Electronic News* wrote, "Now no one can deny it; IBM has conquered the ROLMan empire . . . For ROLM's founders, IBM's decision to merge its sales and service organization . . . was hard to swallow."[123]

## Products Keep Coming—or Not

The integrated voice/data terminal (IVDT) market that had been the industry's hot-button issue in 1983 had turned out to be all talk and no sales. Start-ups that had entered the IVDT craze quickly folded. Cypress, Cedar, and Juniper all had single-window operation and were hobbled as multi-window personal computer systems emerged from IBM and Apple in the mid-1980s, and development costs for new versions were not affordable. Only 3,000 of the "forest family" had sold by 1986.[124]

Companies within the industry were finding that the speed of change in personal computers was very rapid. "We hoped that with IBM's support, we could track the changes in our integrated desktop devices," said

Maxfield. This did not happen, however. The IBM PC division in Florida was "too busy" to work with the ROLM division, and the network division in Raleigh was promoting an ill-fated and expensive local area network, the IBM Token Ring, as the way to connect desktop data devices; they seemed to view ROLMLink as a competitor. "Had we been able to work together," Maxfield lamented, "I believe we could have had a very successful line of integrated desktop devices and could have evolved ROLMLink to accommodate the successful switched-Ethernet local area network that later became the industry standard." Perhaps if AT&T had been able to mount a serious threat to IBM's mainframe business and had promoted integrated voice and data at the desktop, Maxfield suggested, IBM's marketing folks would have forced cooperation in product development. "Things might have turned out very differently," he said.

The CBX II announcement in late 1983 had laid out a road map of new capabilities that ROLM would implement over a period of a few years, which meant avoiding obsolescence of installed systems. At the time, the software base for CBX systems using the Nova-compatible 16-bit 8000 processor was clearly near the end of its useful life as capabilities had been added far beyond its inherent capacity. Ron Raffensperger said, "That 16-bit processor was like the little engine that could. As more capability was added, it became the epitome of what's called 'spaghetti code'—a jumble of software. Without a team of software heroes, it could not have held together."

One solution pondered would be to use the VI's 32-bit 9000 processor and software for the single-node systems, but that system was too expensive in a smaller configuration, and it was very difficult to develop new features using ROLM's homegrown programming language.

The decision was made to bite the bullet: The team would undertake a major CPU hardware-software project to insert up-to-date technology, by moving to one of the powerful new single-chip, 32-bit microprocessors that had far more performance than the old VLCBX CPU. The software engineers had to port the VLCBX software by rewriting it in a modern high-level language, called C. After this, the new software and hardware would replace both the old 8000 and the 9000 CPUs, and the entire product line (from forty to 10,000 lines) would finally use a common low-cost CPU and a common code base that would dramatically reduce the effort needed to introduce new features over time.

The enormous, lengthy development project kicked off in 1984. The new Motorola 68020 was selected as the heart of the system. That one chip the size of a quarter accomplished what had taken several boards, each chockablock with chips, to accomplish in the VLCBX.

The CBX II 9000 software was ported over and rewritten in C, overseen by Mike Gilbert, who had formerly headed up Mil-Spec software, with the help of a team of engineers that included Bob Dolin. IBM provided marketing input on the specifications of the systems, with coordination from product manager Mark Housley.

When the project was completed in 1987, the decision was made to position the system as an entirely new product line: the IBM 9751 CBX. The cabinets were cost-reduced, given a new look, and painted IBM beige—no more ROLM orange. In theory, any existing CBX system could still be upgraded to new features by changing out the CPU, but no customer demand existed for this, since it took another eighteen months before all the existing CBX II software features were available on the 9751. The project illustrated an important point for Ron Raffensperger: "You can always add new features to an old software base faster than you can create a new 'port.' Of course, the features were much better, but it was really hard to catch up."

Plus, there were some unforeseen ramifications of changing software languages. One of the initial assumptions Raffensperger and the product team made in moving from a low-level language on the 8000 to a high-level language like C was that they could then use "normal" programmers instead of "rock stars" and still get features out faster. This turned out not to be true. "There's just no substitute for having a team full of Steve Plants and Dave Ladds," Raffensperger quipped.

Several months before the new CBX product was due to ship in late 1987, IBM reviewed the project with a fine-toothed comb. Only one change was needed, according to Ken Lavezzo, the project's program manager: IBM corporate was worried about service workers in the telephone unions gaining access to the inside of the CBX cabinet. "They feared that if the unions were allowed to open the cabinet rear doors to install cable," said Lavezzo, "the unions would then argue that they should be given overall responsibility for maintaining the switch." No way was IBM going to allow that—in fact, Big Blue wanted to avoid entirely the possibility of even having that discussion.

"The redesign of the backdoor access put us under a lot of last-minute pressure," Lavezzo admitted. "Woody Woodard, an IBM engineer who ran the mechanical group, saved our behind." Woodard was in his early

Nameplates on CBX cabinets identified the size of the system, very small through very large. The 9751, a joint effort with IBM, spanned all sizes and was a very successful product for many years. Photo courtesy of Vito A. Denaro.

sixties and nearing the end of his career, but he remained committed to making the revision happen without delaying the first shipment. Said Lavezzo, "He worked as hard as anyone I had ever worked with in Silicon Valley."

The new IBM 9751 shipped in late 1987, replacing the CBX II 8000 and 9000. It introduced a new compact, sleek attendants' console. The console project was headed by former ROLMphones engineer Pete Bonee, with Ben Yamada doing the design. The previous one, introduced with the original CBX, had had a twelve-year run.

An international version of the CBX II 8000 was also due to come out, in 1988. Called the 8750, the project had been initiated in 1984, intended primarily for the European market. The system was designed to more easily implement each country's PBX specifications. This large, lengthy project had met with significant development delays and complications, almost all of them due to software problems. Because of time-to-market pressures, the software was built on the old CBX 8000 software base rather than the new software base announced with the 9751.

The project had been under way for two years when IBM called for an extensive review. Ron Raffensperger said, "The project had gone off in the wrong direction technologically and marketwise." IBMer Paul Mugge made the decision to cancel it in 1987. Many of the engineers working on the 8750 were demoralized and left the company. IBM in Europe had its 1750, 2750, and 3750 PBXs that had been developed in its facility in La Gaude, France. But these were outdated switches, and the cancellation of the 8750 left IBM without a contemporary product for the European market.

For several years, ROLM's sales force's wish list had included a small ROLM system that could cost-effectively handle fewer than forty lines. Such small office systems were typically handled by bare-bones, inexpensive "key systems" made by other manufacturers and sold through interconnect distributors. The field reps claimed that their large customers did not want to resort to inferior products in their small, outlying offices. They wanted to be ROLM through and through.

Redwood, the fourth "forest product," had been launched in summer 1986 into a fray of new low-end competitors, for sites that needed just a few lines (no more than forty): Siemens Saturn, ATT System 25, and Mitel's digital version of its SX 200.[125] Redwood functioned well, worked only with ROLMphones, and was highly reliable. But it did not sell well. Maxfield said, "We, or rather IBM, should have put the Redwood into interconnect distribution channels rather than solely with the IBM-ROLM sales force. But it was probably too minor an issue to garner enough attention at corporate to study the options, especially given all that was going on at the time with the merger."

A stand-alone version of PhoneMail was launched in February 1987, initially for adding on to Centrex, but soon it also supported Northern

Telecom SL-1, ATT Systems 75 and 85, and NEC NEAX 2400. It was primarily successful with national accounts that did not have CBXs at all locations, enabling them to standardize on their voice message procedures.

In early 1985, a team of engineers led by Jim Kasson proposed a clean-sheet hardware redesign driven by a new version of the 9000 software. The elegant concept involved a packet-switching fabric based on technology developed at IBM's research lab in Zurich. All communications, whether voice, data, or control, would flow through the packet switch. The control computer, typically the logical center of the CBX, would connect to the switch like an ordinary line interface. No longer would packet data ride on circuits; now virtual circuits would be built out of packets. The concept was too radical and too expensive to develop, and was rejected. Decades later, it would find marketplace success in the Voice over Internet Protocol (VoIP).

Kasson had dotted-line responsibility for overseeing IBM's various telecommunications research operations. "It was a fool's errand from the beginning," Kasson said in 2013, "and in retrospect I was silly to even try. The objective was to integrate the technology of many different telecommunications products under development within IBM. But the product developers resisted that (putting it mildly) because it made them dependent on work done in other organizations." Kasson eventually got fed up, turned away from trying to make a difference in telecommunications, and moved into basic research, working on translating colors into software (color rendering) at IBM's Almaden Research Center.

Shortly after the merger, Oshman and Maxfield had quietly petitioned that Jim Kasson be named an IBM Fellow, the highest honor an IBM scientist, engineer, or programmer can achieve. They felt it was important that ROLM be recognized and respected within IBM for its technological achievement, and Kasson represented that achievement. The award was bestowed at the annual IBM Fellow's dinner in the spring of 1986.

IBM counted the date Kasson joined ROLM in 1973 as his date of hire at IBM, as it did for all ROLM employees, per the merger agreement. He

## Not a "Clapper" After All—Jim Kasson

I wasn't aware that I'd been nominated to be an IBM Fellow. When I was invited to attend the annual Fellows event in spring 1986, I assumed I'd be what IBM called a "clapper"—a warm body to congratulate the winners. I was stunned to be named an IBM Fellow.

My wife, Betty, and I were seated on either side of IBM's new CEO, John Akers, at a table for twelve. About halfway through dinner, Betty addressed the table, saying, "We've monopolized your chief. Let's move around so others can talk with him." Everyone gladly shuffled. Afterwards, the event protocol officer—there actually was one—came up to her and said, "That was very generous of you. Don't ever do it again." Between that and the earlier miscalculation about Ellen Hancock's leadership position, the message was clear: I'd better stay "in the box" if I intended to stay at all.

retired in 1998 with a twenty-five-year pin, an IBM pension, and lifetime health insurance benefits—possibly the only ROLMan to do so.

## At a Loss

In winter 1987, Dennis Paboojian, president of ROLM-IBM, presented a status review to the IBM executive committee in Armonk, headed by CEO John Akers. Ellen Hancock, whose networking group's report was slotted for the same time, was at that presentation. When Paboojian presented the operating results and budgets, Akers blanched. ROLM was now operating at a loss. "There was stony silence," said Hancock years later. "Akers had to be wondering, 'How could this happen, when we'd just bought a profitable company only two years prior?' IBM divisions were not supposed to lose money."

How could this happen? It came down to a confluence of factors: ROLM's highly profitable Mil-Spec Division had been sold. Management had resigned by the dozens. The CBX sales pipeline was disrupted by wariness and by IBM's slow review process for large system proposals. Prices, and therefore margins, were under pressure.

Dennis Paboojian left the company two months after the division review presentation at Armonk, after fourteen months on the job and one week after the announcement that ROLM's sales force would be merged into IBM's sales force. "Splitting off sales and service was the last straw for him," said Maxfield, "but I can also imagine that it became clear to both him and Armonk that he would only reluctantly jump through IBM's hoops."

Ray AbuZayyad, a career IBMer who headed its disk drives division in San Jose, became president of ROLM-IBM, reporting to Mitchell Watson. Bob Maxfield remained a part-time advisor, on call as AbuZayyad needed.

By the end of 1987, ROLM's development and manufacturing side was shifted laterally away from Watson and put in Ellen Hancock's networks group. "It was thought that perhaps I could do something with it," she said, pointing out that while the new CEO was a very good engineer, someone from hardware might not be the ideal choice to run a sophisticated systems group. "He was chosen because he lived in Silicon Valley and presumably understood its ways and culture."

In the new role, Hancock visited Santa Clara regularly. "I loved going to ROLM," she said. "It was a great development organization. I loved meeting with all those bright MBAs and smart engineers. And the pool! No other IBM facility had a pool." Still, Hancock felt that all that stuff—the big gym, the beer busts—was little more than Silicon Valley hoopla.

In fact, from her perspective it obscured the really important things that ROLM and IBM had in common: a similar work ethic and discipline. "I had a fond hope that the networking division would understand what ROLM was doing and why it was important," she said, "and that there was synergistic energy."

In the spring of 1987, Fawn Alvarez returned from a vacation to a recording on her home phone that said she had been selected to be an assistant to Ray AbuZayyad and was to report to his office first thing the next morning. "I hadn't even applied for the job," she said in 2013. She'd been working within ROLM's crisis management team, solving acute customer problems, a group that reported to IBMer Dick Mattern, who had recommended her to AbuZayyad.

"Ray was good-natured and cooperative," said Alvarez. "He would never be rude to anyone, never cut them off with impatience. He was willing to soothe upset customers, to go out to customer dinners. But he was all work." According to Alvarez, AbuZayyad was in nonstop meetings and worked 6:00 a.m. to 6:00 p.m. weekdays and 6:00 a.m. to 3:00 p.m. on Saturdays. Her job was to record and follow up on every "handshake." Whenever the new president committed to do something for someone—or vice versa—her job was to record that agreement and see that it was met. This meant coordinating with a lot of people in various aspects of IBM and ROLM. "Above all," she said, "I considered myself a liaison between the two cultures."

The mood and style shifted significantly once an IBMer was fully in charge. Ken Lavezzo, a member of AbuZayyad's executive staff, said that the new president was a quiet guy who managed the business from his office in Building 1. Dick Mattern, an IBMer, handled many of the administrative duties; another IBMer, Paul Mugge, took the lead on technology issues. "AbuZayyad was never seen out and about, and because of that the employees felt he was not very engaged in ROLM."

As head of ROLM sales and service, Bob Finocchio participated in a product meeting in White Plains, New York—what he thought would be a "freewheeling product strategy meeting" typical of those experienced at ROLM. He was the lowest-ranking person in the room of about twelve IBM executives representing three or four product areas. Some of the execs had administrative assistants (AAs) who would now and then hand over a note they'd just written on a 3-x-5 index card. When one exec said something that Finocchio knew was impracticable, he blurted out, "That's a stupid idea. It won't work."

Stunned silence stopped everything cold. Too late, Finocchio realized that he should have chosen his words more carefully. But he knew he was right—surely the others would recognize this.

Several moments passed. Then the meeting started up again as if he had said nothing.

Afterward, an IBMer took Finocchio aside and said, "Never, ever, ever disagree with an IBM executive in a meeting." He said that if Finocchio felt strongly enough, he should push the issue with his boss's AA. If the AA agreed with him, that person would work it through with the other executives' AAs.

"That's when I realized that all meetings like this were theater," Finocchio said, looking back. Everything had been worked out at the AA level beforehand. These meetings were just formalities that put the plan in motion. "The AAs were there with their index cards to tell the exec who was who and what to say next. That's also when I realized I wasn't a player and wasn't going to be one." He explained the disparate environments in no uncertain terms:

> IBM was a closed ecosystem breathing its own air. ROLM was an open system through which fresh air constantly blew. ROLM bet on people: If you had a good idea, you just might be given the chance to run with it. That's how I succeeded at ROLM. To succeed at IBM, you had to know how to maneuver through the hierarchy. You had to shadow someone, then shadow someone a bit more powerful, over and over again, on up the ladder.

Many IBM execs knew little about the computer business or telecom or disk drives. But they knew very well how to play within IBM's protocol.

## "IBM was a closed ecosystem breathing its own air. ROLM was an open system through which fresh air constantly blew." — Bob Finocchio

Within a year after Paboojian's pivotal presentation at Armonk, all IBM operations were being closely examined in light of IBM's severe financial pressures. In early 1988, Hancock, AbuZayyad's boss, had him crunch the numbers for ROLM. The results were dismal: ROLM's revenues had dropped 20 percent since the merger. The division had shown three years of annual deficits, according to *BusinessWeek*.[126] The PBX business was now a commodity market with cutthroat pricing, with all systems offering many of the once-innovative capabilities for which the CBX had been known. Few, if any, products were accelerating the convergence of voice and data.

IBM top executives toured the Santa Clara facility to get a look at the problems firsthand. Lavezzo, who did not know the purpose of the visit, said, "The visit plan was established weeks in advance, including their route through the buildings and . . . the hallways through which they would walk. Those halls were freshly painted, and fresh plants were put in before they arrived. These were top-level executives, and even they had no flexibility to amend the visit on the spur of the moment." Like the "theater"-style meeting Finocchio had experienced, this tour was staged and scripted.

Shortly afterward, probably in early summer of 1988, Hancock, according to *BusinessWeek*, recommended to John Akers that IBM pull the plug on ROLM.[127] However, Hancock said, "I was on vacation when I got the call that management had decided to sell ROLM." She was not involved in the final decision—but she was among those who would have to implement it.

# CHAPTER 13

# BLINDSIDED

.....................

In highly guarded secrecy, IBM sought a buyer for its ROLM telecom business. A key player in the next move, according to both Maxfield and Hancock, was probably IBM's Michael Armstrong, the former ROLM board member who had become head of IBM Europe. IBM was still offering old-school telecom products in Europe and was in need of something that could address contemporary telecommunications demands. So the company approached Siemens, the 150-year-old, $33 billion German electronics conglomerate that had a significant telecommunications presence in Europe.

## The Not-So-Smooth Handoff

"It was likely that Armstrong foresaw IBM being able to market the Siemens PBX in Europe," said Bob Maxfield in a 2012 interview, "and in turn IBM could sell a lot more computers to Siemens." As a bonus Siemens, an insignificant player within the United States at the time, would get ROLM's products for the U.S. market.

Ellen Hancock concurred. "Siemens had almost no PBX presence in the United States. IBM wanted to be sure it stayed in the telecom game in Europe—that was important to its European strategy."

Fawn Alvarez accompanied AbuZayyad to many of the negotiation discussions in Santa Clara and Boca Raton, Florida. Peter Pribilla, the head of

Siemens Telecommunications in the United States, was the key person on Siemens's side. "He always came with an entourage," said Alvarez. "When Siemens came to Santa Clara, they had to stay away from the campus because they were so clearly a crowd of Germans, their presence would have alerted the entire campus that something big was up with Siemens."

Hancock was responsible for negotiating the sale of ROLM's manufacturing and development side to Siemens. Mitchell Watson, Hancock's peer, was responsible for negotiating the sales and service side. "My job was to protect all the assets relative to ROLM and IBM," Hancock said. "Siemens was practically the bank of the world, they had so much cash. But when it came to negotiating, they took a hard look at every penny. We spent way too much time talking about the condition of the roofs of the Santa Clara facility." Hancock said she tried hard in the negotiations to keep PhoneMail for IBM, but Siemens would not permit it.

Rumors about a sale circulated in the fall of 1988. In a staff meeting in November, AbuZayyad was asked if the rumors were true. He said absolutely not, according to Lavezzo. About three weeks later, however, he told his staff that the rumors were indeed true, but he wouldn't name the buyer or the time frame. And staffers were implored to keep it secret—even from their spouses. "That was one thing about IBM," said Lavezzo. "The company thought it came above spouses, friends, or anything else in your life."

AbuZayyad called Maxfield at home the evening of December 12, 1988, and asked to meet with him first thing in the morning in what once had been Ken Oshman's office. There, AbuZayyad closed the door and told Maxfield that IBM had sold ROLM's manufacturing and development to Siemens. The sales and service side would be a 50/50 joint venture between IBM and Siemens. The press release was going out as they spoke. Simultaneously, Jack Kuehler, in Armonk, was informing Ken Oshman by phone. AbuZayyad would later drive up the peninsula to meet with Oshman in his home.

Maxfield sat stunned for a while. Then he said, "So you didn't want my opinion in all this?"

"We had to keep it very quiet."

Maxfield responded, "So you didn't feel you could trust me." He got up, went to his office, penned a two-line letter of resignation on a yellow pad, and dropped it on AbuZayyad's desk on his way out.

Decades later, Maxfield recalled that rumors had circulated about IBM being unhappy with ROLM. Employees occasionally asked him whether a sale was in the works. "Even if I'd known there was, I'd have said, 'Not that I know of,' if I'd been told to keep it quiet," he explained in 2012. "I guess they needed me to say that with full honesty. But I felt sure I'd have been told if there was anything in the works. Guess I was wrong on that one." Whenever asked why he left at that point in time, Maxfield always answered, "I spent a couple of years trying to educate the first buyer in ROLM ways. I wasn't about to do it a second time."

The *New York Times* called Oshman as soon as the press release came across the newswire. The next day it reported the sale of ROLM to Siemens as IBM's "tacit admission that its $1.5 billion thrust into the telecommunications industry had stalled."[128] Analysts estimated that ROLM had lost more than $100 million in each of the last two years, even though it had gained market share during those years.

The *New York Times* quoted Oshman as saying, "IBM failed to grasp the vision [of the ROLM CBX being the hub of the Office of the Future]." He acknowledged that the merger of voice and data "didn't happen . . . It required a leader. Our vision was that IBM would be the leader.'"[129]

Jack Kuehler, by this time IBM executive vice president, called Oshman that evening. Judging from a letter Oshman wrote to Kuehler four days later, Kuehler had seemed quite angry about Oshman's comments to the *Times*. Apparently Kuehler had gone so far as to suggest that Oshman had been well compensated and thus had no right to complain.

Oshman likely rewrote his letter several times before mailing it early the following week. He stated that the cutthroat pricing of the current PBX market made it impossible for any PBX manufacturer to make money. The way out of that was to differentiate the ROLM PBX as the hub of office

# Ken Oshman's Letter to Jack Kuehler, December 18, 1988

Dear Jack,

You were clearly upset when you called me Wednesday night after reading the *New York Times* quote from me following your announcement that you were selling ROLM. No one was more upset than I that evening. The announcement signaled the very sad ending of a merger for which I had great hopes and expectations. The announcement signaled the end of a proud, entrepreneurial company that I had spent most of my creative energy building. The failure of IBM was no less a failure for me. I get the impression that you feel that I was well paid for ROLM and should have quit caring. I cared deeply and felt helpless. If anyone should be upset, it should be me.

I was quoted out of context but I do believe what I said. I did not receive any hard information about the transaction other than during a thirty-minute visit from Ray AbuZayyad. He had very little to tell me other than the structure of the new entities. There was certainly no information about the intentions of Siemens, which I read as a lack of his or IBM's desire to know or as his naiveté.

When reporters asked why the merger had not worked as IBM had wanted it to, I suggested that question should be answered by you. I did respond with the two reasons it did not work as I had hoped:

1. The market price made it impossible for anyone to make money in the PBX business. AT&T had decided

to lose as much as necessary to gain market share and drive out the marginal players. The RBOCs [Regional Bell Operating Companies] priced Centrex well below its cost to protect their installed base. I believe that AT&T is losing close to $1B a year in the PBX and key [under twenty lines] systems business. I have no idea how much Centrex is costing the RBOCs, but it must be enormous.

2. In the face of intense price competition, product differentiation using the PBX as the hub for much of the voice and data communications in the office could provide a cushion on margins and a whole new market opportunity for IBM data products. This was my vision even without the intense price war. This was a difficult technical problem that could be solved. More importantly, it required leadership by IBM to affirm that indeed it was committed to this direction in order to set this standard. That required that IBM change. It did not change (especially in CPD [Communications Products Division]). Instead, ROLM changed to being a commodity supplier against monopolists [sic]. It is very possible data communication via the PBX would never prove effective in the office. On the other hand, to the best of my knowledge, it was never really tried.

I was also asked about the future. I have no reason to believe that Siemens will do other than try to establish a U.S. distribution channel for its existing product line. I therefore see very little future for the concentrated efforts of the past, and

*continued on next page*

I expect the ROLM product line will cease to be developed aggressively in the future. That makes me very sad for ROLM employees who stayed and tried to make a success of the merger. It also makes me sad for the IBM employees who transferred to ROLM and now find their future in the hands of Siemens.

I am offended by your implication that I had done a dirty deed to talk to the press after IBM had been so good to me. I think I responded honestly and, as is my nature, candidly without airing dirty linen. I felt a responsibility to answer the questions and try to correct the misconceptions. I do not believe the failure of the merger was due to bungling by IBM as the press would like to characterize it. Under the best of circumstances a merger is difficult. This merger faced a difficult sea change in its market. Additionally you were trying to accomplish a difficult task without the management that could understand the business and the strategic levers to success for both ROLM and the other businesses of IBM. In fact, you had IBM management actively fighting the concept. You also were constrained in hiring and keeping good development people.

If there was additional information that I should have known that would have changed my perspective, I would have been pleased to hear from you or John [Akers]. No one is more unhappy about the outcome of the once glorious promise of the IBM acquisition of ROLM than I.

Sincerely, M. Kenneth Oshman
cc: John Akers[130]

voice and data communications. He said IBM never got behind that vision, never provided the leadership to make it happen, so the PBX as a hub "was never really tried."

Oshman wrote that he was upset both by the announcement and by Kuehler's call: "I was offended by the implication that I had done a dirty deed to talk to the press after IBM had been so good to me. I think I responded honestly and, as is my nature, candidly without airing dirty linen. I felt a responsibility to answer the questions and try to correct the misconceptions."

Maxfield also felt upset by this, even years later. "How outrageous for Kuehler to suggest that Ken had been well compensated and should keep his opinions to himself!" he exclaimed. Besides being extremely disappointed that things had not worked out as envisioned with IBM, both Maxfield and Oshman were disgusted by the cloak of secrecy that surrounded the search for a buyer. "It points to the IBM corporate philosophy that you're either an insider or you're an outsider. We were never going to be insiders."

Regardless, Oshman's ability to see the big picture had not failed. "Ken's assessment of the market, his 40,000-foot view, is spot on," Maxfield said. "ROLM had determined in 1979 that we needed to move in the direction of making the CBX the hub of all office communications—voice and data. That's what OSD and so many of our products were all about. That forward-going vision ceased after IBM took over."

Ellen Hancock developed a diplomatic explanation for how things turned out. "IBM was very much a data company with some networking," she said. "Buying ROLM was the first time it went into telecom. Siemens loved telecom. IBM may not have loved ROLM, but it really wanted it to succeed. Everyone predicted an evolution that never occurred."

"We gave it a good try," said Dick Moley. "We tried everything we could think of to make the merger a success."

The *San Jose Mercury News* reported many years later its own views on IBM's failure in regards to ROLM: "Deregulation brought new players

# He Said, She Said

Ellen Hancock recalled in 2012 how upset Jack Kuehler and other IBM executives were when they saw Ken Oshman's remarks in the *New York Times*. She said, "Jack knew it would be painful for Ken, that there would be a lot of emotion involved." Hancock understood that Kap Cassani, head of IBM's European PBX operation, had a good relationship with Oshman and was asked to call him several days prior to the announcement of the sale to Siemens. She presumed this was intended to prepare him and to ask him to support IBM on this. "IBM didn't want to get kicked in the press," she said. "We all understood that Kap made that call. I, of course, don't know whether or not Ken agreed to cooperate."

If Oshman had said, "Sorry, I can't go along with that," she claimed, IBM would have come up with a backup plan. "IBM's

to the arena, reducing prices and shrinking profits. The convergence of telecom and computers occurred more slowly and in different ways than IBM had anticipated. And IBM had no idea how to manage a company as resilient, energetic, and unbureaucratic as ROLM."[131]

Maxfield provided further perspective: "The merger failed largely because of IBM's broad financial problems at the time, the most critical time in their history up till then. They had to cut everywhere, and ROLM was no exception." In addition, he pointed out, IBM's original motivation for the merger was strategic—but the need to counter the AT&T threat had evaporated. "AT&T was a complete failure in the computer market, with no success in the complex integration of voice and data in the PBX the sort of company that when we ask, unless told otherwise, we pretty much assume it'll be done. So when the *Times* came out, IBM was stunned to read Ken's comments."

Neither Bob Maxfield nor Barbara Oshman remembered Oshman mentioning a call from Cassani, and Maxfield in particular felt sure it was something he would not have forgotten. Both responded with almost identical words to the possibility that there was such a phone call: "No way would Ken have agreed to side with IBM," said Maxfield. "He could not have been swayed in that way. He would always speak his thoughts. And if he had agreed, by some wild change of personality, no way would he ever go against an agreement he had made." And Barbara Oshman said, "Ken was not the kind of person to not mention a call of this sort to anyone, and he certainly wouldn't have made an agreement like that and kept it to himself. He simply wouldn't have done it."

market," said Maxfield. "Otherwise, IBM might have had the patience to see ROLM through. Perhaps with that patience, the PBX as the voice/data hub might have happened."

But it didn't. And except for products creating a link between computers, such as modems and Internet interfaces, IBM never again attempted to enter the telecommunications market.

## Siemens Takes Over

The *San Jose Mercury News* said only that the sale was "for about a third of a billion dollars."[132] The contract almost surely required nondisclosure by both parties, as the relatively low selling price was likely an embarrassment to IBM, which just three years earlier had paid a premium price for a company that it felt sure would be its path to domination in the combined voice/data market.

The sale to Siemens was announced to the employees the same day the press release went out. They were told that full details would be provided at a corporate-wide meeting the next day, in a ballroom at the San Jose Convention Center. Given the venue and build-up, the expectation was that something exciting was about to unfold—perhaps Siemens would make ROLM an autonomous division and restore its culture.

Santa Clara's 2,800 employees were given a free ride on the San Jose Light Rail. Guarded excitement prevailed as they lined up at the terminal a few miles from Old Ironsides Drive to be transported to downtown San Jose, about seven miles away.

AbuZayyad introduced the new boss, Peter Pribilla, CEO and president of ROLM Systems. At least Siemens was not imposing its own name on the organization—yet. Pribilla showed slides of Siemens's vast array of products and how the ROLM cog fit into the giant wheel. ROLM's employees were lavished with great praise. IBM executive Terry Lautenbach said, "You are among the best in the world at what you do. In simpler, less demanding times, we might have stayed where we were . . . and hoped for the best. But not today."[133]

Jeff Blohm, an engineering manager in the PhoneMail group at the time, said, "It seemed like at the end of the event, Pribilla and AbuZayyad expected a round of applause, but we just sat there in silence. It was rather awkward." When those two executives left the stage, the employees quietly filed out, got on the Light Rail, and went back to work. "It was a nonevent," said Blohm. "The general consensus was that a buttoned-up German culture couldn't be any worse than IBM's white shirts and club ties."

Fawn Alvarez became Peter Pribilla's assistant. On her first day with him, he asked her to read a brief employment contract while he stood behind her. After she signed it, he picked it up and put it in the shredder.

"I saw him do that many times," she revealed. "He left no paper trail." Pribilla held different hours than she was accustomed to, coming in at 7:00 a.m. in order to call Germany and leaving work every day at 5:00 p.m. When Alvarez explained that his presence had been requested at a customer dinner, he would say, "Why would I do that? I have dinner with my wife." In fact, Alvarez explained, he attended no meetings, instead asking people to his office to provide a three-minute update. "I'd prep them beforehand that he literally meant three minutes and would chop the discussion off at that point," she said. "He got to the nut of the problem very quickly that way." Alvarez remained Pribilla's assistant for eighteen "difficult" months before moving to head up employee communications in marketing. She left Siemens in 1997.

Ellen Hancock joined the Siemens/ROLM board. She said, "Peter Pribilla was one of the best executives I ever met in terms of taking care of the business he was responsible for. He understood the PBX business, the products, the branding." Having a top executive who grasped these broad market issues must have been a relief to the ROLMans who remained in place.

IBMers who had transferred to ROLM had to wait two years before they could reapply for openings at IBM. Most executives, except Dick Mattern, returned to IBM jobs. Below the executive level, a fair number chose to remain at the new ROLM. The work was more interesting, and work options were abundant in Silicon Valley in general. What remained of the ROLM culture was still appealing, and after all, it was sunny California, with mountains four hours away and the ocean less than an hour. The retirement and benefits packages became complex, depending on the originating company, with employees labeled as *ROLM Legacy* or *IBM Legacy* from an HR perspective.

Dress-down days and Friday beer busts were restored at "ROLM headquarters," where new signs now read *ROLM Systems, a Siemens Company* in startling "Siemens blue." Employees found Siemens's management more accessible than IBM's. Blohm felt that the mood in general gradually picked up.

Siemens, like IBM before it, commenced in-depth product reviews. The 9751 model of the CBX had been on the market in the United States for about a year and was doing well; a new release of software features was being planned. Siemens also had a new PBX in test trials in Europe. Like ROLM's 8750 that had been killed, it was defined to be a flexible, universal system that would make country-related specifications relatively easy to handle. Significant modifications would have to be made before the product could be sold in the United States. The American marketplace required the CBX to provide far more capability than European customers demanded. U.S. PBXs' feature-rich, sophisticated applications included Automatic Call Distribution (ACD) and Centralized Attendant Service (CAS). Considerably more development work would be needed for the new Siemens system to be feasible in the United States.

"It was a 'bake-off' between the two switches for the American market," said Lavezzo. "Only one would survive." Ron Raffensperger made the presentation—two days of comparison between the two systems—as Siemens debated which system to kill. "Ours was far superior to theirs, and Ron made no bones about it. He left blood on the floor when discussing the Siemens switch."

*"It was like . . . I told them that their baby was ugly. They said, 'No, no, it's not. Go take a second look.' So I took a second look and came back and said, 'You're right. The baby's not only ugly, it's stupid, too.'"*
**—Ron Raffensperger**

Raffensperger is more graphic in describing his assessment. "It was like on day one I told them that their baby was ugly. They said, 'No, no, it's not.

Go take a second look.' So I took a second look and came back and said, 'You're right. The baby's not only ugly, it's stupid, too.'"

After the presentation, according to Lavezzo, a Siemens executive demanded that Raffensperger's boss, former IBM man Paul Mugge, fire him. "Paul had stayed on a while to help with the transition," explained Lavezzo. "To his credit, he said, 'You'll have to fire me first.'"

Instead of getting fired, Raffensperger got transferred to a Siemens division in Kansas City—thanks to some friendly interference by a fellow ROLMan. "Fawn Alvarez saved me from being sent to Siemens's Greenland Division," he joked. "I eventually got along okay with the German development VP." He had joined ROLM in 1976 and had served as product manager for the CBX, ETS, numerous applications, and projects. He stayed with Siemens for ten years.

The 9751 won the bake-off. Siemens sold the 9751 Models 10, 20, 30, and 40 for many years. It was a sophisticated system that performed well and was very reliable—probably the most successful result of the IBM-ROLM years.

The small Redwood system lost its bake-off, which was decided in favor of Siemens's Saturn line. Saturn was sold by distributors rather than by the company's systems sales force. Redwood production was shut down in mid-1989. Maxfield had installed a Redwood in his private office in 1987. In twenty-five years of operation, it never once required service. It was retired to storage as a memento when Maxfield closed his office in 2012.

IBM gained rights to distribute the Siemens PBX in Europe. U.S. marketing and sales became the responsibility of a 50/50 IBM-Siemens joint venture with the straightforward name ROLM—an IBM and Siemens Company. But the PBX market slumped. *BusinessWeek*, in an article titled "For PBX Makers, the Future Is Later," reported that losses for the IBM-Siemens sales venture amounted to $100 million in 1989, half that in 1990.[134] Siemens bought IBM's half of the marketing and sales side in 1992. Perhaps it too had become frustrated by the same difficulty of working effectively with IBM's sales and service organization that ROLM had encountered. That same year, Siemens completed a 190,000-square-foot facility in Austin that consolidated all of its telecommunications manufacturing and development. It had the capacity to build one million telephones a year. The Colorado Springs facility was phased out.

Dedication to reliable ROLM products and responsive service remained undaunted on many levels. One example is the installation at BP Exploration, at Prudhoe Bay on the edge of the Arctic Circle, in the winter of 1992. Longtime ROLM distributor Comtec installed cable in permafrost to connect a new ROLM hub, four new ROLM remotes, four existing ROLM CBXs, three other PBXs, and Arco's ten ROLM 9000s (VLs). The installation of the five new systems took two months, with an average temperature of –65 degrees F (–54 degrees C) and winds of 30 mph, not to mention four days of a Phase 3 blizzard. The cutover took twenty-eight hours. "It was an amazing feat by many good ROLM, Comtec, and BP employees who really busted their butts," said the project's manager, Duane Nelson, who started at ROLM Dallas and ended up staying in Alaska another twenty years.

Customer preference for, and loyalty to, ROLM products continued despite the turmoil that had started with the IBM merger in 1985 and continued until the ramifications of the Siemens buyout settled down in 1990. Jeff Blohm stayed until Siemens shut down the development segment of its San Jose office in 2009. He had joined ROLM in 1981, right out of the Stanford master's in engineering program, so he saw all the changes. According to Blohm, the PhoneMail development team remained fairly intact and took on numerous advanced product development projects for Siemens over the next decade and a half. "It was a different kind of organization," he explained, "with multiple—and sometimes competing—development groups spread around the world. We had a lot of good projects to work on. We kept the ROLM spirit alive for probably fifteen years, until about 2004, when we were all dispersed within different groups."

## All in a Name

Siemens's presence in the U.S. PBX market was far weaker than it was in Europe at the time of the buyout. By retaining the ROLM name, synonymous with robust, reliable products, and responsive service, Siemens advanced its U.S. credibility. The ROLM label, which stood for unswerving dependability and performance was even applied to Siemens telecom products that ROLM never had a hand in designing.

When Siemens bought out IBM's half of the marketing and sales side in 1992, manufacturing, development, sales, and service were united under one organization again—Siemens ROLM Communications, under Pribilla. The 9751, ROLMphones, and PhoneMail continued to sell and perform well. PhoneMail support was eventually outsourced to a firm in Brazil. Siemens brought out many iterations of ROLMphones over the years, including the 300 and 600 series.

## *"ROLM . . . was a leading cultural icon of Silicon Valley, a company that was admired and imitated."*— San Jose Mercury News

In 1996, Siemens must have felt that it had earned its chops in the U.S. market and no longer needed the cachet of the ROLM label. It announced that the name would be phased out from products, logos, signs, and all communications materials over the next two years—the thirtieth anniversary of the founding of ROLM. The *San Jose Mercury News* ran a major retrospective at the time of the announcement:

It's a poignant moment for Silicon Valley because ROLM, in its prime, was called a Great Place to Work and epitomized how successful an agile, well-managed start-up could be in a world dominated by giants . . . From the mid-'70s until IBM bought it, ROLM was a leading cultural icon of Silicon Valley, a company that was admired and imitated.[135] [Used with permission of *San Jose Mercury News.* Copyright © 2013.]

In 2001, Siemens vacated ROLM's former headquarters on Old Ironsides Drive. Reluctant to abandon the bronze alligator, a few ex-ROLMans relocated it to beneath the shrubs at Siemens Communications at Skyport, an office complex near the San Jose Airport. "ROLMy" was put up for grabs in an employee lottery when Siemens closed that facility in 2009. He resides in the winner's verdant backyard garden.

One River Oaks, Mil-Spec's former home, is now the address of new low-rise apartments and townhomes amid broad boulevards lined with recently planted trees. The North San Jose area is a dense mix of housing, major corporations like Cisco, and start-ups. Many tens of thousands of workers live within bike-riding distance of their jobs.

The next major use of the land at 4900 Old Ironsides Drive remains undetermined at this time. During years of vacancy after 2001, the wooden bridges over the brook, the many vine-covered trellises, and all the buildings deteriorated. The tranquil pond and stream dried up. After vandalism began, the structures were demolished, the materials hauled off, and a surrounding chain-link fence erected. Weeds penetrate the asphalt of the perimeter parking lots, and wild vines creep up the light poles.

Yahoo, the site's current owner, is not likely to develop the property while it struggles with financial health. The new San Francisco 49ers stadium is only a few blocks away, however. Planned near that are an upscale shopping/dining/living complex and a resort hotel—perhaps foretelling a very different future for the site that was once the home of a great place to work: ROLM, a company that played a key role in starting up Silicon Valley.

# ROLM'S LEGACY

....................

ROLM's reach extends even today. Many ROLM employees went on to found start-ups or to work for start-ups. Having ROLM on one's resume was an excellent reference in itself, so many employees went to existing tech companies, often in middle or top management, where they could influence the culture. These ROLMans took the "Great Place to Work" philosophy and attributes with them, infusing those companies with the rewarding and fun work style exemplified by ROLM.

By the time Siemens discontinued the use of the ROLM name on products in 1996, tens of millions of people in the United States and around the world had seen that name on their desks at work every day—on their phones. Many companies across the United States still use CBXs, ROLM-phones, and PhoneMail that continue to provide excellent telecommunications service. These systems are serviced by companies that often have ROLM roots—with the founder or technicians having worked for ROLM.

ROLM proved that mixing fun with work and providing a pleasant place in which to work resulted in success in hiring and retaining exceptional people. That success was noted by other companies trying to hire similar types of people, and it continues to influence the unusual work style that today remains a hallmark of Silicon Valley, which employs some of the world's brightest and most innovative workers.

# ROLM CBXs Still in Use

ROLM CBX systems, some with ROLMphones and Phone-Mail, continue to provide companies all over the United States with excellent telecommunications service, including the following (as of summer 2013):

- Sears (across the U.S.)
- Macy's (across the U.S).
- Bloomingdale's (across the U.S.)
- Boscov's Department Stores (mid-Atlantic states)
- Fred Meyer (Pacific Northwest)
- Broadmoor Hotel (Colorado Springs, Colorado)
- Blue Cross/Blue Shield (New York)
- Many Veterans Health Administration Medical Centers (across the U.S.)
- Kaiser Permanente Hospitals (Northern California)
- Siemens Medical (Malvern, Pennsylvania)
- Columbia University (New York, New York)
- Lawrence Livermore National Laboratory (Livermore, California)
- Virginia Tech (Virginia Polytechnic Institute and State University, Blacksburg, Virginia)
- IBM Silicon Valley Laboratory (San Jose, California)
- IBM facility (Boulder, Colorado)

# Spreading the ROLM Culture

The IBM merger was prime time for headhunters—recruiters—eager to get hold of ROLM's greatest asset: its people. The ROLM Philosophy diffused throughout Silicon Valley as ROLMans moved to existing companies and start-ups. Some employees went on to participate in successful IPOs or stock-growth situations, so the gains they earned at ROLM were repeated several times over.

Many employees left to go find a more entrepreneurial environment than the one they foresaw coming under IBM. Some started companies, opting for the ultimate entrepreneurial experience. Ken Oshman and Bob Maxfield often talked about the success of former ROLM employees. Maxfield said, "We were proud that ROLM had the quality of people who could take the giant step to start a new company, to do the hard work it takes to turn the concept of a product or technology into reality."

The USCBX group that departed after ROLM cancelled the project floundered with their first venture, Sydis, but some of them, like Bill Stensrud and Gaymond Schultz, eventually found firm footing when they started Stratacom, which produced the first commercial cell switch. Stratacom nabbed Dick Moley as CEO. Cisco bought the company for $4 billion in 1997, setting another Silicon Valley benchmark for "the good deal."

Pete Slosberg, in telecom marketing, used to brew beer in his bathtub and bring in small batches to sample at Friday beer busts. He welcomed feedback, especially from Oshman, a beer aficionado. Slosberg left ROLM in 1986 to start Pete's Wicked Ale, which was sold to the Gambrinus Company in 1998. Cocoa Pete's Chocolate Adventures appeared a few years later.

Dave Ladd, Dave Sant, and other engineers formed Optimum Communications (Opcom), a voice-messaging company, which later merged with VMX. It then became part of Octel Communications, the company that made voicemail ubiquitous. CBX engineers Bob Lundy and Ann Stevens founded Opthos, a provider of IP-managed solutions for metropolitan core networks. Engineering manager Pete Bonee founded Sylantro, which enabled the delivery of enhanced telephony services over broadband networks.

Emil Wang, PhoneMail's marketing manager, founded Latitude, which established e-conferencing. Janet Gregory, from sales and marketing, was a member of the founding executive team at Latitude and later cofounded Kickstartalliance.com, a virtual team of marketing and sales executives. Jeff Crowe, another OSD marketing manager, founded Edify, an early player in voice and Internet e-commerce platforms and applications. Keith Raffel, now a successful crime novelist, founded Upshot, a pioneer in cloud computing and the first online sales-force automation service. Cheryl Breetwor, manager of ROLM investor relations, cofounded ShareData, a stock equity management system that was acquired by E*Trade in 1998.

Dan Smith of ROLM New York cofounded Sycamore Networks, a $45 billion leader in multi-service networking solutions. Joey Harris founded Comtura, an information technology provider. Dick Hermann of ROLM Houston founded Ti3, which automated temporary timesheets and approval processes for the staffing industry. Bill Friedman, ROLM's general counsel and head of the ROCO Western Region, cofounded Allergene, which specialized in treatments for immune-system diseases.

Undoubtedly many other ROLMans also became entrepreneurs, having gained the skill and courage to start new companies, not to mention an understanding of how to infuse employees with the will to give it their best each day.

## ROLM Products: Built to Last

Many CBX systems are still in operation, providing sophisticated features and reliability. Support and replacement parts for these systems come from companies like T&T Communications in Atlanta. John Litland, a T&T sales rep who joined ROLM Southeast as a rep in 1983, still uses a Cypress. He said, "It's the world's best Rolodex™."

According to its website, Black Box Communications, headquartered in Pennsylvania, is a "leading integrator dedicated to designing, sourcing, implementing, and maintaining today's complex communications systems"—the very complexity that ROLM launched in 1975. For those who were present when the impacts of the Carterfone decision were still being felt, the name Black Box conjures up the sham "protector" that had to be attached to every piece of non-AT&T telecom equipment lest it torch the network. But the company Black Box provides excellent service to systems of all kinds, most of which still come in black or gray cabinets or casings. The company maintains many CBX systems throughout the U.S., particularly in the East and the Midwest. Black Box Resale handles ROLMphones and some ROLM systems.

Comtura Networks "provides world-class communications solutions to organizations that value support," said its website. In addition to selling and supporting very complex contemporary products, the company supports more than 10,000 CBX lines in the Georgia and South Carolina area. Joey Harris, originally with ROLM in Atlanta, founded Comtura. He said, "Although my company has evolved into an IT provider, I still owe everything we have accomplished to what ROLM started so long ago. I would never have gone into business had it not been for the ROLM CBX."

Mark Daley started with IBM-ROLM in Atlanta in 1986 and ran Siemens's ROLM Resale unit from 2002 to 2007. IBM was its largest customer. He said that ROLMphones were so reliable and well liked that companies did not want to get rid of them. After twenty years of usage, however, their outer casings "get to looking pretty grungy." ROLM Resale acquired the original ROLMphone injection molds designed by Ben Yamada. "IBM and many other companies sent pallets full of well-used, working ROLMphones to our warehouse," said Daley. "We'd open the phones up, throw away the outer shells, blow out the insides with an air gun, lubricate the few movable parts, and put on new shells made from those molds. Users were thrilled to get "new" ROLMphones back, with a two-year warranty.

"The problem with ROLMphones," Daley said, "and the CBX too, was that they were practically bulletproof. They worked so well that no one wanted to get rid of them." Ken Lavezzo imagined that Ken Oshman might jokingly comment, "If we hadn't designed them to last so long, our margins might have been better."

In the mid-2000s, long before it had a buyer in place, Siemens announced the intent to sell its Enterprise group, which was once ROLM. Competitive PBX manufacturers descended on customers still using a CBX and warned them that they better replace their systems promptly, that support was going to evaporate. Compounding that, Siemens made headline news over international bribery issues. Mark Daley took matters into his own hands in the face of this abysmal environment for a company supporting ROLM products. "To quell the riot," he said, "I posted an anonymous rumor on Yahoo Finance that the four original founders of ROLM were in Germany, studying the possibility of buying back Siemens's telecommunications business. If they succeeded, they would once again change the paradigm of the industry." Daley fed this Yahoo "news" to his staff and customers in order to calm them down. "It was met with great excitement from those who had known the success of ROLM," he said. "It just about got me fired, however."

The National ROLM Users Group (NRUG) was renamed in the early 2000s to JUST-US—Joint Users of Siemens Technologies, United States. Members were typically large Siemens customers with hundreds of locations, and many still had ROLM products within their networks. According to Daley, this consortium of ROLM customers remained dedicated throughout the IBM and Siemens phases.

"The sales and service delivery group that ROLM started was very much responsible for keeping ROLM products in the marketplace long afterward," said Daley. "Affection for ROLM's products, services, and culture was due in large part to ROLM's original field employees, many of whom are still in the field today. They retain the ROLM spirit of taking care of the customer—while having fun too, just at a slower pace."

The ROLM name lives on in an unlikely location—as a rentable banquet room in a Dallas hotel. ROLM Dallas held so many sales and service training sessions that the contract hotel at Dallas Love Field provided a break room for ROLM employees to gather. A scribbled *ROLM Lounge* sign was stuck on the door—a bit of a joke for a basement room that was barely the size of a broom closet. Ex-ROLMan Laura Kolbe Nelson was amazed to attend a wedding dinner in 2005 in the Sheraton ROLM Lounge, enlarged and upscaled. The hotel, now a Radisson, still has the ROLM Lounge. "We left a mark!" said Nelson.

## ROLM's Long-Lasting Impact

ROLM made a significant impact well beyond Silicon Valley. The young company taught the military back in the early 1970s that it could have affordable, readily available, state-of-the-art computers, without lengthy, expensive custom developments. And ROLM computers could function perfectly well on helicopters, in submarines, on jeeps, in test aircraft— wherever the military wished to take them. ROLM Mil-Spec consistently updated its defense products to stay abreast of the latest capability. It did this reliably and profitably until the division was sold to Loral in 1985.

In the mid-1970s, ROLM brought disruptive technology to corporate telecommunications and brought the field out of the dark ages and into the light of digital technology. It was one of the first companies, perhaps the first, to enable companies to use information technology to control one of their largest expenses—their telephone bills. ROLM's computer-based CBX brought newfound flexibility so phones could be added, deleted, or moved by a "mere software command"—a phrase that software engineers detest, because it is "mere" only after they've applied their very hard, smart work to solving truly complex programming problems. Telecommunications management was introduced to the world of IT—information technology—through the CBX. For the first time, companies could run reports to find out where their telephone costs were actually going—who was calling where and talking for how long at what cost via which network. Trunks could be added or deleted to expand or reduce call capacity.

SPEED
OF
NEWS

"Historians will ... marvel at the power of instant communications
to spread the truth, the news and courage across borders."
—George W. Bush, 43rd U.S. president, 2003

Speed has always been a primary concern in the gathering and telling of news. The substance of news has changed little over time. What has changed has been the speed at which news travels. Early telephones required an operator's assistance; rotary dial and touch-tone telephones allowed direct and ever faster connections. Modern cell phones gave reporters greater mobility. News travels as rapidly as technology allows. ∎

This permanent display at The Newseum, the museum of news in Washington, D.C., highlights the progression of technology and its impact on spreading news quickly. A ROLMphone 120 proudly represents the industry's advancement into the digital age. 2013 photo courtesy of James Buchholz.

The total amount of wiring needed in a building to support a phone system was often cut by half, an enormous savings of labor and material in the construction of a new facility.

ROLM brought integrated PhoneMail to the corporate world, practically eliminating pink message pads and content-free "telephone tag." Users loved the whole family of ROLMphones because the phones accessed CBX features at the touch of a button, displayed the name of the person calling as well as other information, had a speakerphone, had PhoneMail, and, on top of all that, looked good on the desk.

The strategy adopted by ROLM management prepared the company to be an active, perhaps even dominant, player in the integration of voice and data. "Technologically," pointed out Bob Maxfield, "ROLM could have accomplished everything under the skins of the CBX, including the emerging LAN technology. We were correct in the assumption that voice and data would be combined. IBM top management fully grasped the vision but that vision never permeated through the many IBM product development organizations or sales force." In Silicon Valley, that risk is called being on the "bleeding edge": When a company or product is ahead of its time, the result can be financially painful, even catastrophic. But someone has to be there first. Maybe that company will dominate, or maybe it will light the path a bit, showing followers what to do or not do. The path to telephone-computer integration was far longer than anyone could have predicted. Apple's elegant iPhone, inspired by Steve Jobs and launched in 2007, combined voice and data for consumers. Yet despite the rise of VoIP, voice and data still haven't merged on the corporate desk, where large volumes of data are regularly processed on a laptop sitting next to a cell phone sitting next to the corporate phone.

ROLM's position among the founding companies of Silicon Valley was recognized in 1991 when *Stanford Magazine* published its centennial issue, which included a full-color centerfold "board game" titled The Valley of Heart's Delight. The player rolled the dice and moved to squares that meandered through Silicon Valley. Each square represented a company founded by Stanford graduates who had built the Valley, such as David Packard and Bill Hewlett, and Sandy Kurtzig, founder of ASK Computer Systems. (Kurtzig, now founder of Kenandy, providing cloud-based enterprise resource planning solutions, said in 2013 that back at ASK, "We tried very hard to emulate ROLM's culture and ideals.") Step 24 of the board game was ROLM. The finish-line congratulations read, "End of game. You have attained your heart's desire. Move to Bora Bora and take up painting at age forty-five."[136] Besides commemorating Stanford's impact in starting up Silicon Valley, the game expressed the Silicon Valley dream. The truth is, however, that true entrepreneurs seldom retire to Bora Bora after achieving success in one venture. Most dig into something new with the same intensity that made them successful in the first place.

ROLM shared its good fortune with its dedicated employees all along the way, with generous stock options throughout the ranks, profit sharing, and a stock purchase plan. The sale of ROLM to IBM occurred at the most opportune time for ROLM shareholders, including most of the company's employees. IBM paid the highest price per share that ROLM could possibly have garnered at the time or in the foreseeable future.

ROLM set an example for how a start-up—or any company, for that matter—could treat its employees to the mutual benefit of the individual and the company. As such, ROLM left an indelible mark on the culture of Silicon Valley. The synergy between the idyllic Santa Clara campus—with its gym, bubbling brook, and wooden footbridges—and the ROLM

Philosophy that codified the two-way respect between company and employee made ROLM *the* Great Place to Work. Informality and the merging of work and play epitomized a management style that distinguished ROLM, and eventually Silicon Valley, from the rest of corporate America. ROLM set a very high bar for what companies had to do to get and keep smart workers in a competitive hiring environment. Google, Apple, Facebook, and other contemporary Silicon Valley firms in the new millennium have campuses that resemble ROLM's dozens of lush acres in the 1970s, though now their security might rival the Pentagon's. Organizations today that need the best and brightest workers have gourmet cafeterias and amenities such as haircuts, dry cleaning services, and sports facilities that make it easy for employees to remain on-site and still take care of themselves. Some have "nap pods" (sophisticated versions of the blue Bucket chair) and welcome well-behaved pets (not a perk that ROLM ever offered). Many display remarkable outdoor sculptures, providing artistic inspiration for employees who are feverishly working to implement creative technological solutions. All these factors, intended to attract and retain the best workers possible, are extensions of ROLM's innovations decades ago.

The three simple documents that together accurately portray why ROLM was such a great place to work—ROLM Philosophy, Attributes of All ROLM People, and Attributes of ROLM Managers—are applicable to all kinds of companies and organizations today. Nonprofits can use these guidelines by replacing the ROLM Philosophy profit motive with *Maintain a balanced budget* to help establish an appealing, collegial work environment. Any manager who wants to understand how to motivate employees might study ROLM's example of giving smart workers freedom to do their best and rewarding them for their contributions to the organization's success.

Larry Sonsini said, "To me, ROLM was one of the first great Silicon Valley companies, one of the first great ventures, with a great culture and style. Even its building was a landmark, with its elegant design, the cafeteria, and gorgeous grounds. ROLM was a pioneer in many ways."

"When I think about all the years I worked," Ben Yamada said, "ROLM was the best by far." Many former ROLMans—whether they were engineers, field technicians, salespeople, or in manufacturing, administration, or management—have a similar reaction. A tone of nostalgia, sadness, even longing can often be heard in those words whenever ROLMans get together. Working very hard and very smart, tackling tough challenges, making a difference, and being rewarded are a career combination that many people never experience. Most ROLMans consider themselves lucky to have been in the right place at the right time, and most wish the time had not stopped. Some have worked more than thirty years since the acquisition, without again experiencing the mental stimulation, energy, camaraderie, and sense of accomplishment that permeated ROLM. Even though employees were almost surely better off financially than if the acquisition had not occurred, there remains a sense of longing for the day-to-day joy and thrill of working so hard and so well.

John Litland puts it this way: "ROLM was the most fabulous place to work. You could tell that people really wanted to excel. I felt like an important part of the company, not just a number."

The Computer History Museum (CHM) hosted an event in 2004 that put the *R, O, L,* and *M* of ROLM on a panel moderated by Leo Chamberlain. It drew the largest audience CHM had ever had, and the first time the four founders had been together in many years. Each was asked why ROLM succeeded. Maxfield said that Rice University, from which they'd all graduated, had prepared them. "At Rice you worked your butt off, you learned to focus, to manage your time. Doing a start-up was like being back at Rice." Oshman agreed with Chamberlain that ROLM's success came from the employees and added, "Luck. We were in the right place at the right time. Silicon Valley was the only place where this could have been done at that time."[137]

In 1969, Bob Maxfield told Jack Melchor that he just wanted to help build a successful company. "Back then," he said more than four decades later, "I couldn't have imagined that so many thousands of people would help work toward that goal." For Maxfield and the other founders, long after the company's history unfolded, satisfaction came from seeing the impact of their ideas on Silicon Valley and on individuals. ROLM not only put great products out into the world during its time, it also provided a life-enriching work experience for thousands of ROLMans and a lasting legacy for millions who, since then, have experienced some aspect of ROLM's Great Place to Work philosophy.

# UPDATES ON
# THE FOUNDERS

.....................

## The R in ROLM

Gene Richeson grew up in a tiny oil town in east Texas. He and his wife, Donna Seghi, a native of Sunnyvale, California, met at Sylvania. They had two sons during the early days of ROLM. They now have five grandchildren who love being with them on their ranch in Northern California.

After Gene left ROLM for the second time in the summer of 1977, the Richesons paid off their home mortgage, put money aside for their sons' education, and invested the rest in secure government bonds. They devoted their time and effort to Creative Initiative, working toward the cooperation of nations, races, and religions of the world, until after the Berlin Wall fell in 1989.

2004 photo courtesy of the Computer History Museum.

Gene and Donna live in a modest cottage on their ranch near the coast, which they bought "to get the intensity out of our lives." They have no television but do have an off-and-on Internet connection. Gene flew his own helicopter for years and had a landing pad on the ranch. They raise much of what they eat and are active members of the local ranching and farming community, often hosting communal dinners in the barn loft, which is many times larger than their home and tall enough to hold a full-size teepee. Gene said, "Now we work toward understanding sustainability."

## The O in ROLM

Ken Oshman was raised by adoptive parents in Rosenberg, Texas, near Houston. He married his high school sweetheart, Barbara Daily, the year before he graduated from Rice University. During the frantic early years of ROLM, they had two sons. Ken's four grandchildren were his greatest thrill. He took the oldest out every Sunday morning for doughnuts.

2004 photo courtesy of the Computer History Museum.

Ken died on August 6, 2011, at age seventy-one, from complications from lung cancer. The obituary released by his family noted certain highlights and accomplishments:

> He was a past President of the Board of Stanford Alumni Association and a past member of the Advisory Council of the Stanford Graduate School of Business, of Stanford Associates, and of the Board of Directors of the Community Foundation of Santa Clara County. He was an American Electronics Association director for five years serving as the chairman in 1977, a former director and chairman of the Santa Clara County Manufacturing Group,

and a member of President Reagan's Economic Policy Planning Committee and the Committee to Advise the President on High Temperature Superconductivity. Ken was a recipient of the Distinguished Alumnus Award from Rice University and a member of the National Academy of Engineering. He was a member of Phi Beta Kappa, Tau Beta Pi, Sigma Xi, Sigma Tau, and IEEE. Ken was an incredibly gifted businessman and lent his expertise on the boards of Sun Microsystems, Knight Ridder, ASK Computer Systems, Stratacom, and Charles Schwab Corporation, among others. Ken enjoyed playing golf with friends, opera, and spending time in Hawaii.

Since 1989, Ken had been CEO of Echelon Corporation, a major player in the smart-grid and the "Internet of things" markets.

Ken and Barbara gave generously of their time and financial support to their community—Barbara still does—with special focus on the Oshman Family Jewish Community Center of Palo Alto, the San Jose Museum of Art, the San Francisco Opera, and many other nonprofits. The Oshman Engineering Design Kitchen at Rice University provides a space for engineering students to design, prototype, and deploy solutions to real-world engineering challenges. The Oshmans endowed chairs at Rice and at Stanford. Shortly before his death, Ken renamed the Oshman Chair at Stanford to the Stephen E. Harris Chair, in honor of his lifelong friend who had been his PhD mentor and was the first to hold the chair.

The Sunday *New York Times* obituary carried the heading "M. Kenneth Oshman, Who Brought Fun to Silicon Valley." It stated that ROLM "embodied the informal management style that came to set the Valley apart from corporate America . . . In the 1970s and '80s, ROLM was the best example of an emerging Silicon Valley management style that effectively broke down the barrier between work and play."[138]

# The L in ROLM

Walter Loewenstern grew up in Houston, Texas. He married Karen Langton in 1972. They have three children and three grandchildren who bring them much joy.

Walter has enjoyed retirement, saying, "I worked hard, succeeded, and didn't have to prove I could do it again." He has been active on the board of the Hoover Institution for more than twenty years and is on the board of Junior Achievement Worldwide, with particular interest in its program to help Russian

2004 photo courtesy of the Computer History Museum.

youth understand capitalism. He has served as president of Vail Valley Institute, an independent forum for thought and dialog, and as a director of Hope Services and the Sensory Aids Foundation. He's a member of Tau Beta Pi.

Walter and Karen have been generous supporters of Ballet San Jose for twenty years. Karen was a significant factor in bringing professional ballet to Silicon Valley. Walter invests in real estate, the stock market, and high-tech start-ups. They recently relocated from Beaver Creek, Colorado, to West Hollywood. "We wanted to add some excitement to retirement by associating with friends who have connections to the movie business," he said. "Bottom line is, I've had a good life."

# The M in ROLM

Bob Maxfield was raised in Wichita Falls, Texas. He married Melinda "Mo" Harrison after graduating from Rice. They had two daughters during the early years of ROLM and later were divorced. In 1990, he married Kathie Hullmann, the author of this book.

2004 photo courtesy of the Computer History Museum.

After ROLM, Bob never returned full-time to the corporate world, feeling he was very lucky once and that was enough. He has relished the freedom of having the time to pursue his many other interests—family, philanthropy, academics—in addition to advising the next generation of Silicon Valley entrepreneurs.

Bob was a venture partner with Kleiner Perkins venture capital firm for several years and since then has been an angel investor and advisor to numerous start-up companies. He has served on Echelon Corporation's board since 1989, when Ken Oshman became the start-up company's president. He stepped into temporary full-time top management twice at Echelon, first when President Bea Yormark died suddenly and again during Ken's illness. He has also served on the boards of Software Publishing, Saratoga National Bank, Vadis Corp., Knowledge Revolution, and Fogdog Sports.

Bob is president of the nonprofit Maxfield Foundation, which he established in 1986 to support education, science, and other philanthropic interests. Two projects that he has actively supported are making significant contributions to free, online education: Connexions, a web-based platform providing universal access to free education content, and

OpenStax, which develops high-quality textbooks and courses that are freely available and easily customizable.

Bob was a consulting professor in the School of Engineering at Stanford University for twenty years, teaching a graduate course (Business Management for Engineers), participating in research projects, and advising PhD candidates. He was a very active board trustee of Rice University for nineteen years, chairing the finance and investment committees. He received the Distinguished Alumnus Award and the Distinguished Engineer Alumnus Award from Rice University. For more than twenty years he has been active on the board of trustees of the Santa Fe Institute, a research organization that has pioneered the trans-disciplinary study of complex adaptive systems. He has published several academic papers in connection with SFI and Stanford.

Bob is a member of Phi Beta Kappa, Tau Beta Pi, and Sigma Tau. He is an avid jet pilot and enjoys skiing and scuba diving and spending time with his two granddaughters.

# ROLM TELECOM PRODUCTS TIMELINE

....................

The ROLM CBX became increasingly sophisticated and enriched due to new capabilities added over the years. Some changes were software-based only; others also involved hardware, such as phones, PhoneMail, or CBX interface cards. Software releases (known as Rels) upgraded the system to accommodate new major features, add minor ones, enable new hardware products, clean up bugs, and generally increase processing and call-handling efficiency. This timeline presents the new products and capabilities that ROLM offered with its telecommunications systems between 1975 and 1987.

## 1975

**CBX**—The world's first widely distributed, broad-application, digital, computer-based phone system for companies that needed between 80 and 800 telephones. Successfully took market share from AT&T, the world's largest corporation.

## 1976

**Rel 2**—Corrected for memory errors in early dynamic RAMs and brought out additional features that weren't included in the original introduction because of time constraints.

**Rel 3**—Included hunt groups, additional Least Cost Routing features, Call Detail Reporting, and Direct Inward Dial.

# 1977

**CAS (Centralized Attendant Service)**—For companies with multiple facilities within a single geographic area, such as retailers (Macy's, Bloomingdale's, etc.). Directed all incoming calls to a central location for transfer to appropriate location. Reduced the cost of having underemployed attendants at each store.

**ACD (Automatic Call Distribution)**—Targeted businesses that received a large volume of calls, such as hotel and travel reservations, catalog sales, credit card authorizations, insurance claims, and newspaper classified advertisements. Facilitated handling each call professionally in as short a time as possible.

**Rel 4**—Included Direct Inward System Access (DISA), an alternative to Direct Inward Dial.

# 1978

**ETS 100 (Electronic Telephone Station)**—ROLM's first desktop telephone. One of the world's first phones with a built-in microprocessor and a display that showed information such as the calling number. A multiline telephone and intercom combination targeted at executives and their assistants.

**LCBX**—Connected two CBXs to increase maximum size to 1,500 lines.

**SCBX**—A downsized CBX in a smaller cabinet. Covered between 48 and 144 lines.

**Rel 5**—Focused on increased processing speed; also upgraded Route Optimization, ACD, and CAS. Included Satellite Operations capability,

Common Control Switching Arrangement, and Automatic Network Dialing.

# 1979

**VLCBX**—Expanded product to 4,000 lines through a distributed, 32-bit computer architecture, using a unique token-passing bus local-area network (LAN) that tied multiple CBX computers into a single system. Had a new real-time operating system based on a unique high-level systems programming language, RPL (ROLM Programming Language), and all-new application code, including code that permitted multiple nodes to communicate with one another on a peer-to-peer basis over the CBX LAN.

**VSCBX**—For systems with as few as twenty-four extensions.

**ROLMNet**—A suite of options for companies with multiple, distant offices.

**Data Switching**—ROLM's first Office of the Future product. A small desktop box that compressed the data signals from a terminal or personal computer (Data General, HP, DEC, or IBM) and then transmitted the signals to the CBX to be sent on to the host mini- or mainframe computer. Significantly reduced wiring needs and demonstrated that the CBX could be the hub of voice and data processing.

**REMS (ROLM Electronic Messaging System)**—Provided basic email function before commercial email existed. Was pulled from the market after initial trial due to uncertain accessibility because it ran in the CBX's backup CPU.

**ETS 200**—Adapted the ETS 100 for ACD.

**ETS 300**—Adapted the ETS 100 for CAS.

**RAC (ROLM Analysis Center)**—Processed mailed-in call records and provided facilities management reports for large CBX clients that subscribed to the ROLM-provided service. Facilitated corporate telecom managers' control and understanding of costs.

**CMR (CBX Management Reporter)**—Packaged report formats for telecom managers of smaller CBXs to run reports on-site, to increase understanding of telecom costs and usage.

**Rel 6**—Added Sprint and Execunet to Route Optimization.

**Rel 7 Data Communications**—Allowed the switching of data via telephone wiring.

# 1980

**FlashPhone**—A standard push-button phone with an extra button that facilitated use of a single-line phone as a two-line phone. OEMed from Stromberg-Carlson.

**RAC Remote Polling**—Enabled RAC in Santa Clara to remotely access clients' CBX Call Detail records via long-distance telephone lines, eliminating the need for data records to be mailed in.

# 1981

**Autovon Compatibility**—Certified the CBX for use by the military.

# 1982

**PhoneMail**—Voice message system, permitted retrieval of messages from anywhere in the world at any time. Unique greeting and mailbox based on extension number, an industry first. Used an external operating and storage system connected to the CBX.

**ROLM Gateway**—Gateway to telephone company T1 trunks and private network D3 digital transmission systems, allowing high-volume voice and data traffic.

**AFACTS (Automatic Facilities Test System)**—Monitored the performance of and verified system integrity to external facilities such as direct trunks and private networks.

**User Remote Polling**—Gave customers with multiple CBX installations direct access to call detail records of all their CBX facilities over standard telephone lines.

**X.25 Interface**—Accessed packet switching networks.

**Asynchronous Data Communications**—Enabled customers to switch voice and data simultaneously at speeds up to 19.2 kbps. Used a unique data submultiplexing method, allowing up to forty data connections to use the same system capacity as a single voice connection.

# 1983

**ROLMphones**—World's first family of digital phones, proprietary to the CBX. Digitized the voice at the handset, allowing voice, data, and power transmitted over a single pair of wires to the CBX. Came in models 120, 240, 400, and 400D.

**Cypress**—Possibly the world's first desktop device that provided information retrieval via a smart data terminal integrated with a smart feature telephone. An all-in-one digital phone, calculator, Rolodex, speakerphone, intercom, and computer terminal to access databases and mini- and mainframe computers.

**CBX II**—Permitted high-speed transmission of data, using an updated Data General 16-bit processor. Existing CBXs could be upgraded with board swaps.

**ROLMLink**—Transmitted voice, data, and power over one twisted-pair of wires, an industry first.

# 1984

**Cedar**—Combined ROLMphone capability and the Cypress terminal, and doubled as an IBM-compatible personal computer. Had 512 KB of memory, two drives for 5¼-inch floppies, a printer port, and a nine-inch graphics monitor.

**Juniper**—Connected a ROLMphone to an IBM personal computer and displayed the telephone information data on the PC. Cypress, Cedar, and Juniper were in the market category known then as IVDTs—integrated voice/data terminals.

# 1985

**9000**—The VLCBX redesigned with a new bus and improved interconnections between the nodes for very-high-speed handling of voice and data. Used the original VLCBX 32-bit processor and supported 8 × 8 digital voice encoding. Encompassed CBXs from 800 to 10,000 lines.

**8000**—New name for CBX II. Encompassed forty to 800 lines.

**7000**—New name for the installed base of original CBXs.

# 1986

**Redwood**—A separate, fully digital system for between two and forty lines. Used only ROLMphones.

# 1987

**IBM 9751**—VLCBX code ported to run on a commercial microprocessor, with new cabinets and attendants console. Obsoleted the 8000 and 9000. Was the most successful product developed during the ROLM-IBM merger.

# ROLM MIL-SPEC PRODUCTS TIMELINE

.....................

ROLM Mil-Spec Computer products continually evolved from inception in 1969 until 1985, when the Justice Department required that IBM sell the division as a condition of the merger with ROLM. This product summary focuses on the various CPU and memory designs that were the core of the products.

**Packaging**: All but two Mil-Spec computers were installed in the standard military Air Transport Rack (ATR); the case was a practically indestructible metal box 7.62 inches wide x 10.12 inches high, with variable length depending on configuration. Printed circuit (PC) cards of 7 x 10 inches were inserted from the top crosswise and clamped in from the sides with wedges. The ICs straddled a copper bar that conducted heat to the case. Each card had an aluminum cover to provide stiffening. Depending on the product, additional memory or I/O capability could be added within the chassis if slots were available, or in additional chassis either connected by cable or bolted on daisy-chain fashion.

The **1650** and the **MSE/800** were the exceptions to this form factor. The **1650** came in a half-size ATR (3.81-inch width) with the cards mounted lengthwise. The **MSE/800** was a rack-mount computer designed to U.S. Navy environmental specs.

All products introduced from 1978 on had an enhanced version of the original packaging, with plug-in power supply (47-400 Hz AC or 28v DC) and top-access clamping wedges.

**Mil-Specs**: All products except one met the military environmental specifications of both Mil-E-5400 Class 2 and Mil-E-16400 Class 3, which include case temperature from –67 degrees F (–55 degrees C) to 203 degrees F (95 degrees C), vibration to 10 Gs at 5 to 2000 Hz, shock to 15 Gs, and humidity to 95 percent. The exception was the **MSE/800**, which met only Mil-E-16400.

# 1969

**RuggedNova 1601**—Introduced at the Fall Joint Computer Conference 1969; first shipped in March 1970. Military designation for the product: AN/UYK12(V).

CPU was the Data General (DG) Nova design, adapted for mil-spec environments; used latest MSI TTL from Fairchild; 16-bit instruction set and memory busses, but internal processing was in four 4-bit nibbles. Had external control panel.

Full ATR chassis with fourteen slots: five for CPU, two for optional Extended Arithmetic Unit (EAU) module (HW multiply/divide), two for optional 2K MOS read-only memory modules, five for I/O modules. Used 400 Hz power supply.

Core memory of 4K x 16 words at 2.4 microseconds cycle time, came in bolt-on chassis. Up to eight chassis could be added.

Biggest production program was Dalmo Victor's ALR-46 and 46A, used on F-4 and F-111 aircraft.

# 1972

**RuggedNova 1602** AN/UYK19(V)—ROLM-designed microprogrammed computer with extended instruction set, including hardware multiply/

divide, vectored and nested interrupt processing, file search, stack processing. Had twice the memory and 64K 16-bit words. Used same external control panel as **1601**. Full ATR chassis with twenty slots: nine for CPU, two for optional semiconductor memory modules (ROM or CMOS static RAM), four for one 8K x 16 core memory module, five for I/O modules.

New 8K x 16 words core memory, 1 microsecond cycle time, more than twice as fast as the **1601**. Memory expansion chassis: up to three additional 8K x 16 core memory modules could be bolted on, and up to four additional modules of 32K x 16 core memory in an external chassis could be connected by cable.

Major production program for this and all **1602** successors was for the Army Security Agency.

# 1974

**RuggedNova 1603** AN/UYK27(V)—New CPU compatible with **1601**, but up to six times faster, depending on instruction mix. Had parallel 16-bit internal architecture. Had an integrated control panel. Used same 8K x 16 core memory as **1602**, at 1.2 microseconds cycle time.

Full ATR chassis with four slots for CPU, five for option I/O modules, one for optional Extended Arithmetic Unit (EAU) module, one for optional semiconductor memory module, and slots for up to two 8K x 16 core memory modules, at 1.2 microseconds cycle time. Used 47-440 Hz power supply.

# 1975

**1664** AN/UYK28(V)—Used an enhanced **1602** CPU plus three-board hardware floating-point unit (FPU). Had new microcode to support Executive Mode security and enhanced interrupt processing. Had bank switching for up to four 64K-word blocks. Full ATR chassis with twelve slots for CPU; no I/O or memory slots. Had optional wrap-around external heat exchanger.

8K x 16 core memory, 1 microsecond cycle time, packaged in bolt-on chassis, with up to four 8K modules installed. Additional memory could be installed in cable-connected external chassis.

# 1976

**1603A**—Upgraded **1603** with two semiconductor memory option slots plus six slots for I/O plus slots for up to two 16K x 16 core memory modules, 1.2 microseconds cycle time.

**5605 CPU**—Single-module CPU with microprogrammed instruction set identical to **1602**, but reduced from nine PC boards to a single two-board folded module. Was used in the **1650** and later the **1602B**.

**1650** AN/UYL34—Compact half-ATR chassis with the single-module **5605 CPU**. Weighed less than 30 pounds and had up to two 16K x 16 core memory modules, 1 microsecond cycle time; 28v DC power supply and no I/O slots.

# 1977

**1666** AN/UYK64(V)—CPU was same as **1664**, but had two-module Memory Management Unit (MMU) for directly addressing up to 1024K words of memory with page switching (2K bytes) to map to 64K address space. Had up to four 16K x 16 memory modules and no I/O slots.

**1606**—Same as **1666** but without the three-module floating-point unit (FPU). Used in the Raytheon SLQ-32 program (radar warning and chaff deployment for surface ships).

**1602A**—Upgraded **1602** to include 16K x 16 word core memory modules, 1 microsecond cycle time, and additional I/O slots.

# 1978

**1602B**—Used **5605** CPU module. Had 16K x 16 core memory modules, 1 microsecond cycle time, and more I/O slots than the **1602A**. Was ROLM's first product using the enhanced ATR chassis.

# 1979

**MSE/30**—Announced as "the first of ROLM Mil-Spec's Eclipse product line," compatible with DG's Eclipse computers. Had a new CPU design implementing the Eclipse instruction set. Had same memory and packaging as **1602B**.

# 1981

**1666B** and **MSE/14**—Functional replacements for the **1666** and **MSE/30**. New microprogrammed eight-card processor (four cards for CPU, three for FPU, one for MMU); compared to fourteen cards for **1666**. Had two versions of microcode, one for the **1666** instruction set and one for DG Eclipse instruction set. Could be field-upgraded from **1666B** to **MSE/14** by swapping out two boards.

Used new 32K x 16 core memory module. Packaged in enhanced ATR chassis. Had 8 I/O slots and up to two 32K x 16 core memory modules. Could expand up to four 64K x 16 memory modules. A later version had dynamic error-correcting semiconductor memory.

**MSE/800**—Used DG's powerful 32-bit, Eclipse MV/8000 computer re-laid out and packaged for rugged shipboard rack-mount chassis (not ATR). Had dynamic semiconductor memory. Was the first mil-spec machine to run an Ada compiler, in 1982.

**Model 4050 Disk Subsystem**—Provided for an eight-inch Winchester recording disk that had 35.6 megabytes of mass-storage capacity. The 3.2-cubic-foot chassis weighing 110 pounds met military specifications. Was ROLM's first stand-alone mil-spec peripheral device.

# 1982

**Model 4150 Disk Subsystem**—Upgrade to **4050**, designed to operate in severe environments such as up to 30,000-feet altitude.

# 1983

**Ada Work Centers**—A complete family of Ada software development systems, including computer system hardware, compiler, and the ROLM Ada Development Environment software—productivity tools to improve the efficiency of the design, development, and maintenance of customer application programs written in the Ada language.

# 1984

**Hawk/32**—Airborne mil-spec version of DG's MV/8000. Had new, high-performance processor based on LSI Logic Gate Arrays. Full ATR package contained processor and semiconductor memory, no I/O slots.

**MAGNUM 4200 Disk Subsystem** for Hawk/32.

**MSE/14 Micro** New processor design on a single board using Eclipse instruction set.

# NOTES

....................

## PREFACE

1   James M. Poterba, "Capital Gains Tax Policy Toward Entrepreneurship," *National Tax Journal* XLII (1988).

2   "The Top 100 New Issues," *Forbes* (December 2, 1985), p. 164.

## CHAPTER 1: THE ROADS TO ROLM

3   Claudia Cruz, "56 Years Ago, a Plane Crashed in Old Mountain View," MountainViewPatch.com (February 1, 2013), accessed October 1, 2013.

4   Ken Oshman, audio interview by John McLaughlin, "Conversation with Ken Oshman," Silicon Valley Historical Association, July 19, 1995 [SVHA].

5   SVHA.

6   Computer History Museum, *Competing with Giants*, Speaker Series (video), moderated by Leo Chamberlain, May 19, 2004 [CHM].

7   Mary Wadden, *Silicon Valley: The History in Pictures* (Menlo Park, CA: Silicon Valley Historical Association, 2013), p. 74.

8   Stephan Wilkinson, "Born in a Garage," *Technology* (February 1982), p. 2.

## CHAPTER 2: TARGETING THE MILITARY

9   Chris Warren, "Connecting the Dot.Coms," *Rice Sallyport* (Spring 2005), p. 20.

10  Millie Bobroff, "Robert Maxfield: The 'M' in ROLM," *Saratoga News* (September 30, 1981), p. 1.

11  SVHA.

12  Gregory Boyce, "1971 vs. 2011: High Unemployment, War, Broken Government & Social Unrest," *Economy in Crisis: America's Economic Report* (December 26, 2011).

13    "Computer Optimizes Use of Flight Test Time," *Aviation Week & Space Technology* (August 19, 1974), p. 45.

14    SVHA.

15    SVHA.

16    SVHA.


## CHAPTER 3: SEEKING A BIGGER MARKET

17    SVHA.

18    "Silicon Valley Tech Chronicles: Happy 40th Birthday Silicon Valley!," *Examiner. com* (January 8, 2011), accessed October 10, 2013.

19    Benjamin M. Elson, "Firm Keys Growth to Low-Cost Computers," *Aviation Week & Space Technology* (August 19, 1974), p. 43.


## CHAPTER 4: BATTLING A GIANT

20    "Tyson Selects ROLM CBX," *Poultry Times* (January 15, 1979).

21    "Conversation with Ken Oshman," audio interview, Silicon Valley Historical Association (July 19, 1995).

22    "Ma Bell Fights Off Invasion of Her Domain," *U.S. News & World Report* (August 14, 1978), p. 55.

23    Ibid.

24    Ibid.

25    "Compaq, ROLM, NCR Ads Win High-Water Marks," *Computer & Electronics Marketing* (November 1985), p. 1.

26    "Over-the-Counter Markets," *Wall Street Journal* (November 5, 1976), p. 26.

27    CHM.

28    John Markoff, *What the Dormouse Said: How the Sixties Counterculture Shaped the Personal Computer Industry* (New York: Viking Penguin, 2005), pp. 275–278.

29    "Sir John Clark," *The Telegraph* (December 6, 2001).


## CHAPTER 5: BARELY MANAGEABLE GROWTH

30    *ROLM Interconnect Newsletter* (April 17, 1978).

31    "Its Past Success May Haunt Coradian," *New York Times* (August 26, 1981).

32    Ibid.

33    "A Hot New Challenger Takes on Ma Bell," *BusinessWeek* (February 12, 1979), p. 94H.

34    "Silicon Valley Success Story," *New York Times* (June 3, 1979), p. 1D.

35  R. Grossman, "Betting on Risky Markets Paid Off for ROLM," *Electronic News* (April 1979), p. 44.

36  Thomas J. Murray, "The Hot New Computer Companies," *Dun's Review* (January 1979), p. 52.

37  Charles J. Elia, "Nifty-Fifty, Swollen with Technology Issues, Showed a Median Price Gain of 16.5 Percent in July," *Wall Street Journal* (August 1980).

38  Bradford W. Ketchum, "The Inc. 100," *Inc.* (May 1981).

## CHAPTER 6: A GREAT PLACE TO WORK

39  David Packard, *The HP Way: How Bill Hewlett and I Built Our Company* (New York: HarperBusiness, 1995), pp. 80–81.

40  ROLM Corporate Human Resources, ROLM Philosophy Monograph (1984).

41  Ibid.

42  Ibid.

43  Goodwin Steinberg with Susan Wolfe, *From the Ground Up: Building Silicon Valley* (Stanford, CA: Stanford University Press, 2002).

44  Ibid.

45  Letter from Leo Chamberlain to Gibson Anderson (June 30, 1983).

46  "Striking It Rich: A New Breed of Risk Takers is Betting on the High-Technology Future," *Time* (February 15, 1982).

47  SVHA.

48  SVHA

49  Roger Skrentny, "Spotlight on Silicon Valley's 'Laid Back' Style of Management," *Management Review* (December 1984), p. 10.

50  Steinberg, *From the Ground Up.*

51  SVHA.

52  Robert Levering, Milton Moskowitz, and Michael Katz, *The 100 Best Companies to Work for in America* (Menlo Park, CA: Addison-Wesley, 1984), p. 309.

53  *Time,* "Striking It Rich."

54  Steve Kaufman, "ROLM Scores Points with Employees and in the Marketplace as Amenities for its Staff Bring Handsome Dividends," *San Jose Mercury News* (September 28, 1981), p. D1 (Business Monday).

55  Joan Tharp, "M. Kenneth Oshman Tackles Telecommunications Goliaths," *The Executive SF* (March 1982), p. 8.

56  Levering, Moskowitz, and Katz, *The 100 Best Companies to Work for in America,* p. 309.

57  "Behind the Scenes at the Fall of ROLM," *BusinessWeek* (July 10, 1989), p. 82.

58  Ibid.

59    SVHA.

60    "ROLM's Leap into Office Automation," *BusinessWeek* (February 16, 1981), p. 78.

61    Everett M. Rogers and Judith K. Larsen, *Silicon Valley Fever: Growth of High-Tech Culture* (New York: Basic Books, 1984), p. 146.

62    CHM.

63    SVHA.

64    Steinberg, *From the Ground Up.*


## CHAPTER 7: TELECOM'S PARADE OF PRODUCTS

65    *BusinessWeek*, "ROLM's Leap into Office Automation," p. 78.

66    Jessica Copen, "Data Communications Added to Phone Switch," *ABA Banking Journal* (August 1981).

67    *BusinessWeek*, "ROLM's Leap into Office Automation," p. 78.

68    "New Glamour for the Office PBX," *BusinessWeek* (April 13, 1981), p. 122.

69    "Voice Mail Improves its Delivery," *BusinessWeek* (December 13, 1982), p. 84A.

70    Ibid.

71    Cited with permission from WBEZ Chicago's *This American Life,* http://www.thisamericanlife.org/radio-archives/episode/203/transcript.

72    "Why ROLM's Star Isn't Burning as Bright, "*BusinessWeek* (August 2, 1982), p. 54A.

73    Ibid.

74    "What's News," *Wall Street Journal* (November 18, 1983), p. 1.

75    "An Advanced PBX Shows Why IBM Bought ROLM," *BusinessWeek* (November 28, 1983), p. 102.

76    Jonathan Chevreau, "ROLM Takes the Lead with Digital Desk," *Globe and Mail* (May 27, 1983), p. B18.

77    Robert Violino, "State-of-the-art PBX Awaited from ROLM," *Information Systems News* (November 14, 1983).

78    "How Do You Spell Connectivity? ROLM," *Think* (January/February 1984), p. 30.

79    Jonathan Greer, "ROLM's New Switchboard Wows Analysts," *San Jose Mercury News*, (November 18, 1983), p. 16E.

80    Tracy Kidder, *The Soul of a New Machine* (Boston: Little, Brown and Company, 1981), p. 239.

81    Glenn E. Bugos and Albert J. Henry, "Sydis and the Voice/Data Terminal Craze of 1984," *IEEE Annals of the History of Computing* (2004).

82    Ibid.

83  Eric Berg, "The Phone-Computer Fusion," *New York Times* (September 18, 1984).

84  Ibid.

85  Mark Hall, "Not Deadwood Technology," *Micro Communications* (December 1984), p. 14.

86  Bugos and Henry, "Sydis and the Voice/Data Terminal Craze of 1984."

87  John Eckhouse, "ROLM's Phones Tie with IBM PCs," *San Francisco Chronicle* (November 2, 1984), p. 37.

## CHAPTER 8: MIL-SPEC MARCHES FORWARD

88  *ROLM Printout* employee newsletter (November 1977).

## CHAPTER 9: DRINKING FROM A FIRE HOSE

89  *BusinessWeek*, "ROLM's Leap into Office Automation," p. 78.

90  Ibid.

91  Ibid.

92  Letter to Bob Maxfield from Burt McMurtry (November 22, 1981).

93  "Firms that Prosper Even in Recession," *U.S. News & World Report* (November 8, 1982).

94  Carrie Dolan, "ROLM's Merger Could Fulfill Its Dream of Fighting AT&T on Equal Footing," *Wall Street Journal* (September 27, 1984), p. 3.

95  "Linking Up to Boost the Electronic Office," *BusinessWeek* (March 21, 1983), p. 144.

## CHAPTER 10: A PIVOTAL YEAR

96  Frederick Rose, "Mitel and IBM End Accord for Joint Work to Design Voice, Computer Equipment," *Wall Street Journal* (June 14, 1983).

97  "IBM Buys Another Key to the Automated Office," *BusinessWeek* (June 27, 1983), p. 27.

98  James A. White, "IBM Plans to Buy 15% ROLM Stake for $228 Million," *Wall Street Journal* (June 13, 1983).

99  "IBM Makes a Deal with ROLM," *Fortune* (July 11, 1983), p. 6.

100  *Think*, "How Do You Spell Connectivity? ROLM," p. 30.

101  Dolan, "ROLM's Merger Could Fulfill its Dream of Fighting AT&T on Equal Footing."

102  "Japan PBX Market Cracked by ROLM," *New York Times* (January 16, 1984).

103  "California-based ROLM Beats Out Giants to Win Right to Sell PBXs in Japan," *Globe and Mail* (Wednesday, March 31, 1984).

## CHAPTER 11: THINKING THE UNTHINKABLE

104  David E. Sanger, "IBM to Purchase Company on Coast for $1.25 Billion," *New York Times* (September 27, 1984), p. 1.

105  "What's News," *Wall Street Journal* (September 27, 1984), p. 1.

106  Everett M. Rogers and Judith K. Larson, "Silicon Valley Fever: Growth of High-Tech Culture," *U.S. News & World Report* (October 22, 1984).

107  David E. Sanger, "ROLM Chief Said He Sought IBM Link," *New York Times* (October 10, 1984).

108  Dolan, "ROLM's Merger Could Fulfill its Dream of Fighting AT&T on Equal Footing."

109  Adam Lashinsky, "Portraits of Power," *Fortune* (November 27, 2006).

110  Videotape of ROLM Shareholders Meeting (November 21, 1984).

111  Ibid.

112  Ibid.

113  Ibid.

114  *Forbes,* "The Top 100 New Issues."

115  Videotape of ROLM Shareholders Meeting (November 21, 1984).

116  Thomas C. Hayes, "At ROLM, an Independent Style," *New York Times* (September 26, 1984), p. 29.

117  John Hillkirk and Lorrie Lynch, "Are Suits and Saunas Compatible?" *USA Today* (October 2, 1984).

118  "IBM and ROLM Cope with Prenuptial Jitters," *BusinessWeek* (November 19, 1984), p. 166.

119  David Sanger, "A Driving Force Leaves ROLM," *New York Times* (January 15, 1986).

120  SVHA.

121  *BusinessWeek,* "Behind the Scenes at the Fall of ROLM."

## CHAPTER 12: DANCING WITH THE GORILLA

122  *BusinessWeek,* "Behind the Scenes at the Fall of ROLM."

123  Miller Freeman, "Subtle Changes at ROLM Since IBM Took Over Could See the End of the Company Identity," *Electronic Times* (September 24, 1987).

124  Bugos and Henry, "Sydis and the Voice/Data Terminal Craze of 1984."

125  John Dix, "Siemens' Saturn I Bows," *Network World* (September 22, 1986).

126  *BusinessWeek,* "Behind the Scenes at the Fall of ROLM."

127  Ibid.

## CHAPTER 13: BLINDSIDED

128  John Markoff, "IBM to Sell ROLM to Siemens," *New York Times* (December 14, 1988).

129  Ibid.

130  Copy of letter from Ken Oshman to Jack Kuehler (December 18, 1988), in Bob Maxfield's files.

131  James Mitchell, "ROLM Name Fades from Landscape," *San Jose Mercury News* (September 26, 1996), p. E3.

132  Ron Wolf, "ROLM Deal Done," *San Jose Mercury News* (December 13, 1988).

133  Mary Anne Ostrom and Tom Schmitz, "ROLM Workers Get Few Answers," *San Jose Mercury News* (December 14, 1988).

134  "For PBX Makers, the Future Is Later," *BusinessWeek* (February 25, 1991), p. 88.

135  James Mitchell, "ROLM Name Fades from Landscape," *San Jose Mercury News* (September 29, 1996), p. E1.


## EPILOGUE: ROLM'S LEGACY

136  "The Valley of Hearts Delight," *Stanford Magazine* (Centennial Issue, 1991), pp. 182–183.

137  CHM.


## APPENDIX A: UPDATES ON THE FOUNDERS

138  "M. Kenneth Oshman, Who Brought Fun to Silicon Valley," *New York Times* (August 14, 2011).

# BIBLIOGRAPHY

....................

Berlin, Leslie. *The Man Behind the Microchip: Robert Noyce and the Invention of Silicon Valley*. New York: Oxford University Press, 2005.

Caddes, Carolyn. *Portraits of Success: Impressions of Silicon Valley Pioneers*. Palo Alto, CA: Tioga Publishing Company, 1986.

Chapman, Robin. *California Apricots: The Lost Orchards of Silicon Valley*. Charleston, SC: American Palate, a Division of The History Press, 2013.

Dear, Terrence E., and Allan A. Kennedy. *Corporate Cultures: The Rites and Rituals of Corporate Life*. Menlo Park, CA: Addison-Wesley Publishing Company, 1982.

Kidder, Tracy. *The Soul of a New Machine*. Boston: Little, Brown and Company, 1981.

Leavitt, Harold J., and Homa Bahrami. *Managerial Psychology: Managing Behavior in Organizations*. Chicago: The University of Chicago Press, 1988.

Levering, Robert, Milton Moskowitz, and Michael Katz. *The 100 Best Companies to Work for in America*. Menlo Park, CA: Addison-Wesley Publishing Company, 1984.

Malone, Michael. *The Big Score: The Billion Dollar Story of Silicon Valley*. New York: Doubleday and Company, 1985.

Markoff, John. *What the Dormouse Said: How the Sixties Counterculture Shaped the Personal Computer Industry*. New York: Viking Penguin, 2005.

Packard, David. *The HP Way: How Bill Hewlett and I Built Our Company*. New York: HarperBusiness 1995.

Rogers, Everett M., and Judith K. Larsen. *Silicon Valley Fever: Growth of High-Technology Culture*. New York: Basic Books, 1984.

Steinberg, Goodwin, with Susan Wolfe. *From the Ground Up: Building Silicon Valley*. Stanford, California: Stanford University Press, 2002.

Wadden, Mary. *Silicon Valley: The History in Pictures*. Menlo Park, CA: Silicon Valley Historical Association, 2013.

# ABOUT THE AUTHOR

....................

Katherine Maxfield distributed phone books one summer during high school in Ohio. That did not lead to her twenty-five years of work as an employee and consultant for technology companies in Silicon Valley. An MBA did, coupled with her innate (as in, who knew?!) ability to translate technology into features and capabilities that customers needed and could relate to—marketing. After retiring from the corporate world, she turned from writing marketing and business plans to writing fiction, with the help of an MFA in creative writing. Her short fiction has appeared in numerous literary journals, and her personal perspective pieces have appeared in the *San Francisco Chronicle*. She lives in Saratoga, California, with her husband.

# INDEX

..................

*Page numbers in italics refer to photos, illustrations, and boxed segments.*

ROLM Gateway, 314

ROLM GmbH (Germany), 206

ROLMLink, 183, 187, *188–189*, 191, 230–232, 266, 315

ROLMNet, 313

ROLM Philosophy, 129, *130*, 150, 156, 263, 295, 302

ROLMphones, 185–198, *192*, 245, 291, 315

    legacy of, 293, *294*, 297–298, 300, *300*

ROLM Resale, 297–298

RPL (ROLM Programming Language), 170, 172–173

RS-464, 113

RuggedNova 1601, *30*, 318

    at 1969 FJCC, 30–32

    capacity of, 33

    Maxfield and design of, 28–30

    sales of, 41

    testing of, 32–33

RuggedNova 1602/1602A/1602B, 41–44, *44*, 318–321

    Army Security Agency and, 77

    upgrades on, 206

RuggedNova 1603/1603A, 76–77, 206, 319, 320

RuggedNova 1606, 320

RuggedNova 1650, 104–105, *105*, 317, 320

RuggedNova 1664, 104, 319–320

RuggedNova 1666/1666B, 320, 321

Ryans, Adrian, 126

## S

sabbaticals, 136–137, 260

sales

    all-time high increase in, 236

    under IBM and Siemens, 232–233, 289, 291

    offices, direct, 118–200, 126, 156, 219–221

    and service, international, 221–222

    training for, 69–70, 298–299

    *See also* distribution; marketing; profits/net income; revenue

sales targets

    for 1971, 36, 38–39

    for mil-spec products, 207–208

    for ROLMphones, 193–194

*San Francisco Chronicle*, 201

San Jose campus, 210–212, *212*

*San Jose Mercury News*, 185, 283–285, 291–292

Sant, Dave, 70, 111, 295

Santa Clara campus, 132–135, *135*, 138–141, *139*, *141*, 202–203, *203*, 292

Santa Fe Institute, 310

Saturn, 289

SBC, 225–226

SCBX, 113, 312

Schmeir, Larry, 74–75

Schoolcraft, Heidi, 142

Schultz, Gaymond, 176, 295

Schwartz, Bernard, 256–257

Schwartz, Wolfgang, 169, 235

Scientific Data Systems (SDS), 20–21

Sederquist, Dave, 75

Seidel, Tony, 258

semiconductors

    in 1950s, 7

    in CABX/CBX, 61, 87

    in Nova mini-computer, 19

Shea, Dan, 219

Shell Oil, 86, 210

Sheppard, Bob, 191

shock, testing RuggedNova for, 32–33

Siemens, 277–292

Siemens ROLM Communications, 291

signs, ROLM, *43, 158, 255*

Silicon Valley, arrival of, 66

Skillings, Bruce, 72–73, 79, 93, 147–148

skunkworks, 174–178

SL-1 PBX, 114, 174, 270

Slosberg, Pete, 295

Smith, Dan, 219, 296

Smith, Don, 134

Social Security Administration (SSA), *221*

software codes/development

    CBX and, 57, 61, 63, 80, 108, 116, 299

    CBX II and, 266–267

    IBM and, 247

    phones and, 82

    Plessey and, 218

    RuggedNova computers and, 41–42, 77, 104–105

    upgrades, bugs and, 86–89

    VLCBX and, 170–174

solid-state memory, 67

Sonsini, Larry

    IBM merger and, 247–248, 251

    IPO and, 97–98, *99*

    Plessey and, 218

    on ROLM legacy, ix–x, 302

Spacewar game, 32

spares program, 69–70

Speas, Dirk, 125, 193–194

Sperry Univac, 16, 46

Sporkin, Stanley, 98–99

sports, 138–139

Sprint, 225

Standbro Drummond advertising agency, 72–73

Stanfield, Chris, 232, 248, 256

Stanford Industrial Park, 24

*Stanford Magazine*, 301

Stanford University, 1

    work-study program of, 3–4, 6–8, 56

Steinberg, Goodwin (Goody), 134, 158, 210

Stensrud, Bill, 176, 295

Stevens, Ann, 295

stock

    buy back of, 236

    hot, 120–123

    IBM partnership and, 232

    on NYSE, 112

    public offerings of, 97–100, 213, 227–228

    splits, 78, 96, 121

stock options, 99, 143–144, 260, 264

stock purchase plan, 144

Stone, Doug, 198

Stratacom, 295

Stromberg-Carlson, 115

"Studies of Optical Frequency Parametric Oscillation" (Oshman), 7

success, attributes of, *131, 132–133*, 302

switch boards, 52, *52*

switch hooks, 193

switching, digital, data and voice, 57–58, 161–163, 186

SX2000, 226

Sydis, 178, 200, 295

Sylvania, 2, 8

    work-study program and, 3–4

system configuration, *172–173*

Tyson Foods, 86

## U

UBS, 110
United States vs. AT&T, 75, 90, 223–226
United Telephone Company, 111
UNIVAC, 16, 39, 46
Universal Oil Products, 174
UNIX, 170, 172, 224
upgradeability, 175–178
    CBX II and, 181–185
Upshot, 296
U.S. Army
    ILS (integrated logistics support) of, 209
    Security Agency, 77
*USA Today*, 257–258
USCBX, 176–178
    ROLMphones and, 190–191
U.S. Department of Defense, 37, 205, 209, *211*, 212
User Remote Polling, 315
U.S. Justice Department
    AT&T and, 75, 90–91, 223–226
    IBM and, 242
    IBM/ROLM merger and, 250
U.S. military-industrial complex, 37, 205
*U.S. News & World Report*, 217, 249
UTC (United Telecommunications), 110, 112, 120

## V

Vallco Park (Cupertino), 24–25, 34, 42–43, *43*, 45
Valley of Heart's Delight, ix, 25, 301
van Bronkhorst, Ed, 97
Varian, 174
Venture 100, 122

venture capitalists
    mil-spec products and, 33–34
    second round with, 96–97
    start up and, 14, 20–24
    telecom products and, 60
VLCBX, 169–174, 219, 313, 316
    expanded capacity of, 181–182
    installation of, 238
    PhoneMail and, 180
VMX, 295
voice/data integration. *See* integrated voice and data
voice digitization technology, 173–176, 181
voice messaging systems, 165–166, 178–181
voice switching, 162–163
VoIP (Voice over Internet Protocol), 270, 301
VSCBX, 183, 219, 313

## W

*Wall Street Journal*
    annual Nifty Fifty list of, 121
    CBX II and, 184–185
    on IBM partnership and merger, 233, 249
Wang, 200, 214
Wang, Emil, 179, 259, 296
Watkins, Laura, 179
Watson, Mitchell, 262, 265, 278
Welch, Peter, 70
Wells Fargo Small Business Investment Company (SBIC), 34, 60, 97, 99
Western Electric, 50, 89, 223–224, 229
Wetherell, Merle, 29, 41–42
Wheelwright, Steven, 125–126
White House, 116, 221